# 1 OUT OF 10

Peter Hyman was a key strategist to Tony Blair from 1994 to 2003, working at Number 10 for more than six of those years. He was Head of the Prime Minister's Strategic Communications Unit between 2001 and 2003. Prior to that he was an adviser to Gordon Brown and the late Donald Dewar. He left Downing Street at the end of 2003 to work at Islington Green School. He is married with two daughters and lives in London.

Peter Hyman

# 1 OUT OF 10

From Downing Street Vision
to Classroom Reality

VINTAGE

Published by Vintage 2005

2 4 6 8 10 9 7 5 3 1

Copyright © Peter Hyman 2005

Grateful acknowledgement is made to the following for permission to reprint previously published material:

Extract from *FLOW* by Mihaly Csikszentmihaly published by Rider. Used by permission of The Random House Group Limited.

Extract from *School Improvement Reports: From Failure to Excellence* (Secondary School edition) by Tony Attwood, used by permission of First and Best in Education (www.firstandbest.co.uk).

While every effort has been made to obtain permission from owners of copyright material reproduced herein, the publishers would like to apologise for any omissions and will be pleased to incorporate missing acknowledgements in any future editions.

The names and identities of all the children herein and, where necessary, some of the adults at the school have been changed in order to protect them.

First published in Great Britain in 2005 by Vintage

Vintage
Random House, 20 Vauxhall Bridge Road, London SW1V 2SA

Random House Australia (Pty) Limited, 20 Alfred Street, Milsons Point, Sydney, New South Wales 2061, Australia

Random House New Zealand Limited, 18 Poland Road, Glenfield, Auckland 10, New Zealand

Random House South Africa (Pty) Limited
Endulini, 5A Jubilee Road, Parktown 2193, South Africa

Random House UK Limited Reg. No. 954009

A CIP catalogue record for this book is available from the British Library


ISBN 0 09 947747 5

Typeset by SX Composing DTP, Rayleigh, Essex
Printed and bound in Great Britain by
Bookmarque Ltd, Croydon, Surrey

For Corinna, Lilah, Hannah,
Inge and Robin

# CONTENTS

# FOREWORD

I feel immensely fortunate to have had ten exhilarating years in politics, including more than six working for the Prime Minister at 10 Downing Street. I was convinced that anything I did next would seem less exciting or fulfilling. I was wrong. I hadn't accounted for the extraordinary vibrancy of Islington Green School or the thrill of working in an inner-city comprehensive.

I wanted to write about the contrast between these two worlds: between Westminster and the frontline, theory and practice; between a world of power, of the establishment, of meetings, speeches and policy-making, and the world of one thousand inner-city teenagers, with all the challenges of literacy, expectations, poverty, behaviour, all the exuberance, fun and humour of children finding their own particular path from childhood to adulthood.

So this is my personal journey from the corridors of power to the corridors of an inner-city school. It isn't a blow-by-blow account of the events of the government or the ups and downs of the Number 10 personalities. Nor is it a detailed or academic analysis of education policy. There are plenty of people far better qualified to write that book.

Instead, the journey has allowed me to explore the relationship between the big picture and the small picture; to explore too the different leadership challenges faced by a Prime Minister trying to change the country, and a headteacher trying to transform a school.

In the last year I have looked at politics through fresh eyes. I have found that the jolt of reality has made me rethink some of my strongly held views and has made clearer some of the urgent challenges that the government and education face in the future.

Most of all I hope I have captured just some of the flavour of two very different worlds – politics and teaching – each of which, ultimately, has the same goal – making the next generation more successful than the last.

Peter Hyman
January 2005

# ACKNOWLEDGEMENTS

Thanks are due to Julie Hall for getting me into politics. Gordon Brown, the late Donald Dewar, and Tony Blair for putting up with me as an adviser.

To Tony Blair I owe special thanks, for giving me the chance to play a part in the exciting events of the last ten years and for the privilege of working at Number 10. He was a great person to work for.

Around Tony Blair and the government have been a team of hugely talented and hard-working people – political advisers and civil servants – who became good friends and inspiring colleagues. Alastair Campbell, who I worked next door to for the last seven years, I must thank for his friendship, humour, support for the school, and for ensuring there was never a dull moment. Philip Gould for being a good friend, an infectiously optimistic colleague and for teaching me most about the craft of political strategy. A special thanks to my colleagues in the Strategic Communications Unit who were a professional, decent, and funny group of people to work alongside.

All made the political journey enjoyable and rewarding.

This book would not have been possible without headteacher

Trevor Averre-Beeson. I have enjoyed working with him immensely and have learned a huge amount from him. I owe him a big debt of gratitude.

He and the other members of the senior management team at Islington Green School – Angela Gartland, Emma Catt, Paul Blum and Eileen Griffin – made me very welcome, gave me huge support and were willing to give much of their busy time helping me find my feet. I owe a big debt to all of them.

Many thanks to governors, ex members of staff, current members of staff and students who have given me words of wisdom, helped me learn a little of the craft of teaching, and at the same time been good, lively, funny, challenging company: Cec Darker, Jane Fielding, Pete Hillman, Ted Reilly, Chloe Parker, Jess Ward, Mike Harpham, Kenny Wellington, Marek Ostoja-Ostaszewski, Nick Hampton, Sherry Davis, Denis Dineen, Tonya Mascoll, Keith Murzello, Jill Howson, Paula Dunkley, Dee Irving, Dioan Whyte, Declan Hambling, Rachel Anderson, Tracey Wilson, Alan Parker, Karen Becker, Ken Muller, Ann Neal, Lou Baron, Esti Dan-Gur, Gill Young, Debbie Smith, Mandy Seeburn, John Challinor, Margaret Maden, Pam Fajkus and the rest of the staff and students at Islington Green School.

Thanks to Gail Rebuck for her faith in me, and to Jason Arthur and the team at Vintage for their editing, design, and publishing skills.

For their help on the book I would like to thank Adam Lury, for his challenging thinking at the beginning; Michael Barber for his wisdom, encouragement and friendship.

To David Miliband I owe a large debt for his advice and support. Over the last few years he has not just been a close friend but a colleague who, more than anyone else, has stimulated me with political ideas.

To Sanjay Singhal a special thanks for his help and friendship from beginning to end; for his brilliant eye for narrative, and his willingness to take my phone calls at any time of day or night.

I would like to thank Budge and Roger Little for their support and their wise comments on drafts.

Thanks to Inge and Robin Hyman for everything: their love, support, pep talks, the use of their house, their blunt comments. To my father a special thanks for reading every draft, often more than once, and for improving everything from grammar to the ideas.

Finally, and most importantly, I would like to thank Corinna for her love, her patience, her encouragement when it was most needed and her detailed and perceptive comments on the text. Her instincts are second to none. She, above everyone, has made the last year possible.

# POWERS OF PERSUASION

I'm at Number 10 and I'm late. It's the last Saturday in September 2003. All is quiet at the centre of power. I'm at my desk frantically looking for the relevant notes, cuttings, books, sheets of facts, lists of government achievements and all the drafts of Tony's Labour Party conference speech. My filing system is in its usual chaos. Philip Gould, Tony Blair's political consultant, is in a car outside on a double yellow line, phoning me every two minutes and telling me to get a move on. I put all I can into my briefcase and carry the rest. I open the famous, heavy, black, front door without dropping anything and yank it shut behind me.

I stagger out into the street, through the iron gates at its entrance, and get into the back of the car beside Philip. 'Let's go,' I shout at the top of my voice. We set off for Bournemouth for what is likely to be my final Labour party conference as a member of Tony Blair's inner circle.

Philip has worked for the party now for eighteen years, through bad times and good. He never stops moving or doing except when he power-naps. Shoulder-length hair billowing, baggy suit swaying, he's either on his mobile having intense conversations, working out, taking vitamin pills or writing memos. Today it's four things at once – speaking to his daughter on the phone, talking to me about the speech, flicking through papers and, every now and then, leaning back, closing his eyes and vaguely sleeping.

Both of us are obsessed with New Labour and what we call 'the project' – the ongoing struggle, first to change the Labour party and now to change the country. We both believe this is the time to renew it, move it on – but we are fretting over the state of Tony's conference speech. Every year we do the same – only this year we are convinced it is in worse shape than ever before at a similar point in time.

I have worked on all of Tony Blair's conference speeches since he became leader in 1994. My job is political strategy, a mix of policy, communications and politics. I run Number 10's Strategic Communications Unit, an outfit of about ten people whose job it is to step back from the day-to-day and help to plan the Prime Minister's positioning, message, communications and his speeches for the months ahead.

Each year Tony has managed to use the conference speech to gain momentum. Modern politics is all about momentum. Stagnate, drift, wobble, and the media or, if strong enough, the Opposition, will pounce. From the first conference speech in 1994 announcing the end of the sacred Clause 4 of the Labour party constitution, to my personal favourite, the 'forces of conservatism' speech of 1999, we have succeeded in seizing the agenda.

This year's speech, however, is going to be the hardest. Not just because the decision to invade Iraq has divided the party and the country. Or because two Cabinet ministers have resigned over the issue and are daily upping their rhetoric of denunciation. Or because Lord Hutton's enquiry into the death of the scientist Dr David Kelly has not yet reported. But because the party is having one of its periodic existential moments when it is flirting with the purity of opposition, rather than the compromise of government. There is something else going on too. The polls and the newspapers keep saying that trust in Tony Blair as Prime Minister is collapsing; that we are no longer believed; that many think we are not keeping our promises. Yet at the same time our opponents are nowhere. A view is gaining credibility: that the next election is now in the bag, so why not replace Tony Blair with a Labour leader more loved by the party?

Philip and I look through the newspapers in the car. All predict a terrible week for Tony and the government, with the unions making mischief and difficult conference votes on foundation hospitals, tuition fees, and Iraq, but it's the front page of the *Financial Times* that grabs our attention: it says Labour's lead would go up by six points if Chancellor Gordon Brown were leader. This is the perfect ammunition to fuel more press speculation. If, as the paper suggests, Gordon is both more in tune with the party and potentially better electorally, then what is the point of Tony Blair? For the first time Tony is seriously vulnerable. This will have to be a speech where he goes back to first principles and tells the party why it is worth keeping faith with him for the next few years.

This conference speech is also more of a challenge for me personally. In previous years I have worked closely with Alastair Campbell on it. Many afternoons have been spent on the top floor of his home in Gospel Oak, drinking tea – me irritating him by playing pool against myself on his miniature pool table – egging each other on into writing even purpler passages, either about the 'evil' Tories or about the 'Age of Achievement' New Labour would be ushering in. But Alastair has just resigned as Director of Communications and is not coming to conference. Having worked with him since 1994 it is a sad time for me and I am already missing his energy, fun and sheer force of personality. I will have to do more of the preparation and co-ordination myself.

I had provided Tony with a file ten days before conference to help him prepare for the speech. It contained essays and articles on the key themes; it had thoughts from MPs and ministers such as Alan Milburn and John Denham, and from David Miliband, former head of the Number 10 Policy Unit and then Schools Minister. I had also got a number of contributions from the frontline, including from some of the best headteachers.

Philip and I are chatting eagerly and nervously in the back of the car; both with that 'we're going on an outing' buzz about us. We are an hour from Bournemouth. There is always a sense of anticipation about conference and a lively but tense team spirit. Party conferences matter because they put the parties and the party leaders head-to-head with opponents. At the end of the three party conferences, the political world has a strong sense of who has momentum and which leader is in the best shape.

There are really four Labour Party conferences rolled together: one that takes place on the conference floor with constituency delegates taking part in debates; another that is played out through the media which consists of the main Cabinet speeches and the debates around them; another that involves endless receptions, dinners, late-night drinking; and finally the conference which is the gruelling hell of the Leader's office trying to get the speech ready for Tuesday afternoon. Each year some bright spark suggests moving the Prime Minister's speech to the last day of conference to bring it in line with the other political parties. Each year Tony and the rest of us writing the speech reject the suggestion because it would mean three more days of agony – we are always delighted to get it out of the way by Tuesday.

Philip nods off. Another power-nap. I start focusing on the speech. Tony spends a week at Chequers before conference, honing his thoughts. Then there are three days of round-the-clock refinement down at the conference venue. The speech is a crystallisation of ideas and political strategy – the culmination of months of thinking. It is Tony's best take on the government, his own vision, the point in the political journey we have reached. It gives journalists, the party and wider opinion formers a moment of clarity. Yet, the paradox is that, despite all the effort, a week later the speech is often forgotten.

Tony had produced a first draft in the form of a note to Philip and myself two weeks before. It is two thousand words long – a third of the final length – and, common to these first drafts, it gives a real insight into Tony's state of mind, the stuff he wants to get off his chest. Frustration is the word that sums it up. Tony and I both know there are passages in it that will not make the final speech. One stands out: 'Former members of the Cabinet or Government who find inordinate courage, once they leave, to speak their mind'. There is also a risky passage of self-examination: 'Six and a half years have taught us a lot. When we announced the first boost to public spending, we thought it would quickly transform. When we announced an intention, we thought it became a reality of its own accord. When we thought we could see the path ahead clear . . . the unanticipated blocked our path, diverted us down alleyways unknown to us, confused our direction.'

Some of this critique will remain in the final speech but in softer form. The draft builds from these two thousand words by gaining personal stories, chunks of policy, and government achievements.

Politics, to an extraordinary extent, is about words. What is reported are the speeches of politicians, the articles they write, the interviews they give, the statements they make in the House of Commons. Prime Ministerial speeches are made to big gatherings like party conference and small gatherings like the opening of a crèche in a constituency, to a banquet at the City of London, at the start of a religious festival or the retirement of a colleague. Politicians are always looking for jokes or one-liners to open these events. Gordon Brown famously demands, 'Got any jokes?' when he meets someone he knows in the street.

The power to persuade is what makes a successful leader. That was the conclusion of Richard Neustadt in his famous book, *Presidential Power*. It is even truer today. Leaders must not just do the right thing but must persuade people they are doing the right thing. Passing a law doesn't make something happen if those implementing it – the police, the teachers, the medics – aren't convinced of its merits. Legislation is, in many ways, less important than winning support.

Tony has deep self-belief in his own powers of persuasion. He believes he can convince the party of anything given enough time with them. He believes he can persuade euro sceptics to love the pound, though that battle will have to wait. He believes the country can be changed fundamentally by persuasion and cajoling, not bludgeoning.

That's why he likes writing most of his speeches himself. In this he has much in common with Harold Wilson, who believed that using speechwriters was a transatlantic custom to be deplored: 'To anyone who has issued an invitation that you have accepted, they do not want to know whether you can read – that is assumed – they want to know what you have to say in your own words, even if it rates only B-plus, B-minus or lower.'

Tony hates the niceties of speeches. He does very little of what most politicians believe to be essential: thanking lots of people, praising others for their efforts. He likes to get on with the speech. To him that means getting the argument right. As a trained barrister he believes that his duty is to make an argument with a beginning, middle and end, and one that holds up to scrutiny. Many of the other techniques of speechwriting, such as the repeated beginning to sentences ('We shall fight on the beaches, we shall fight on the landing grounds, we shall fight in the fields . . .'), he can do without, though will occasionally accept them. As for anecdotes or stories about real people – Tony finds they hold up the argument and will generally only use them in a conference speech where he accepts that you have to break up an hour-long argument. However much I have tried to make the case for stories being more memorable than statistics, he will always prefer to use a fact rather than a case study.

There are a number of people who get involved in writing speeches, particularly those on policy, but it is known for being a thankless job. It has become harder as the years go on to satisfy Tony with the drafts he is given. It is a running joke at Number 10 that any civil servant who becomes Tony's speech co-ordinator – which means the compiler of material and occasionally first draft writer – falls out with Tony because they just can't provide what he wants. It is very hard to write in someone else's voice, particularly if they increasingly know what they want to say and would rather write it themselves.

As Philip wakes up from his nap, I'm in a reverie of my own, remembering, with chilling clarity, one of my most dispiriting speechwriting episodes. It was soon after we got elected. Tony was speaking to sixth-formers at the Methodist Central Hall. All party leaders were speaking at this packed annual event, and I had produced and polished what I thought was a stylish, flowing draft, that would connect with the audience. Tony had accepted it. We went together to the hall. I sat at the side, waiting excitedly for my words to cascade from the Prime Minister's mouth. Tony was called to speak. He marched up to the lectern, looked out at a thousand students, held up my speech, and in front of their eyes and mine ripped it into quarters. 'Let's do away with the prepared speech,' he said, 'and let me tell you what I really think.' Afterwards he told me, in a matter of fact rather than reassuring way, that 'It was not appropriate for me to read out a speech in that setting.' To keep my sanity in the years that followed I justified the many occasions when drafts were scrapped or altered by saying to myself, and others, that the initial draft had been a catalyst, 'something for him to bounce off, something to crystallise his own thoughts'.

By the second term, Tony was regularly getting up early in the morning on the day of a speech and rewriting it all himself, usually with his favourite black fountain pen. On other occasions, when there was no time, he would read out a policy speech with an obvious lack of enthusiasm and then at the end extemporise his own thoughts and come alive as he did so. Alastair and I would get closest of anyone to Tony's voice, but even then he would be wary that our language was over the top, our attacks too brutal. I am from the school which thinks that an attack on political opponents ought to be a jab to the solar plexus, not a cuff around the ear. Tony would regularly ask me when I handed him a draft: 'Are there any Hymanisms in here?'

I have often pondered what makes a great speech. In the end it's not just about the cleverness of the writing, but the circumstances in which it is delivered. The best speeches capture a moment. They require the drama of war or death, or they struggle to come alive. They tell a truth or galvanise a people: Churchill at the low point of war rallying the country; Earl Spencer, despite being an unpopular figure, with the world mourning the death of Princess Di. Other powerful speeches are ones of protest or defiance: Martin Luther King protesting against segregation and bigotry; or Nelson Mandela at his trial.

For me conference is less enjoyable than it was a few years ago. It's the longest period I am away from my wife and two young daughters, and also I rarely leave the corridor on which my room, Tony's suite and the speechwriting room are housed. When I do it's for a quick walk on the beach or a trip out for fish and chips, but since we got into government, and more recently since September 11th, the security is so tight that leaving the cordon that surrounds the Prime Minister's hotel results in about thirty minutes of walking and queuing to get in again.

On this day, to get into Bournemouth's Marriott Hotel, security is even stricter than the previous year. Philip is stuck in the security cabin. He has brought a box down with him with a computer printer and various contraptions inside and predictably the strict security people not only want to scan the machine several times but demand Philip dismantle his printer piece by piece.

I start thinking about what Tony is going to want from us when we finally get inside the hotel. The great debate of this speech is how to demonstrate that the government has momentum and ideas to carry it forward while also showing that we are standing firm and not bowing to pressure.

Only two Prime Ministers in the twentieth century lasted more than six and a half consecutive years. Asquith was the first, though the Battle of the Somme soon lost him his job. Thatcher was the second. She came back from the Westland controversy, party divisions and bad polls to win a big majority in 1987 – but it required a major feat of renewal.

Tony Blair's success in reshaping politics in Britain is still underestimated. The repositioning of the Labour party, its two landslide victories, the dire state of the Tory party, and the dominance of our agenda should all be credited to Tony's strategy. So those of us around him, who want New Labour to evolve, feel almost impertinent in suggesting we change that winning formula.

My argument is that the world has moved on since 1994

when Tony became leader. We no longer need to reassure people we can be trusted with government. We have proved that. I believe passionately that you cannot create a modern social democratic country by stealth. You have to argue for higher taxes to pay for education and health, argue for greater tolerance for minorities, argue for greater opportunity for those denied it. We have to build a grassroots movement that will sustain New Labour in the long term. We have to use our powers of persuasion. I had written Tony a note a few weeks before conference saying that New Labour had to move to a new phase in which we were more confident in our ability to shape the ethos and instincts of the country. Tony acknowledges this, in part, in the speech: 'I know the old top-down approach won't work any more. I know I can't say, "I'm the leader, follow me."' I believe it will be a waste if the only message from the conference speech is no backing down. We have to describe the next phase of New Labour.

We are finally ensconced in the hotel from where we barely move in the next three days. The view of the sea is stunning. I'd forgotten quite how pretty Bournemouth is, the Isle of Wight Needles in one direction, the Dorset hills in the other, and masses of sandy beach in between. Philip is proudly showing me the state of the art computer and printer he has now installed in his room. An hour later he is cursing it for failing to churn out any paper. Philip lives by his memos. They are an art form: succinct, always fresh, insightful. I have spent nearly ten years reading them, reacting to them, arguing about them, but now, at this crucial moment, they look like drying up. New technology is about to triumph where all our opponents have failed – in silencing the Gould memo machine.

Tony is spending most of the conference in angry, frustrated mood. He is not a table-thumper, he doesn't shout at people.

His preferred method is the 'Why don't they understand me' rant. Much of it is aimed at a party that in his view does not understand the realities of today's world. Why does Labour have to go through this ritual of betrayal? Tony's frustration with his own party runs deep – and for much of the party the feeling is mutual. Most politicians are creatures of their formative political years. Margaret Thatcher reacted against what she saw as the failed mushy compromise of the post-war settlement, including the patrician Toryism she inherited. Tony has an allergy to old Labour. It's not just that he finds policies such as nationalisation and high direct taxes barmy. He also hates losers, hates impotence, hates meaningless protest. He breaks out in a rash at the thought of being lumped with the failures of Labour's past. He believes he benefits from not being of the party, that he is above it and beyond it, constantly challenging it to take up positions not within the normal range of its safe compass. Tony's assumption is that he loses his unique appeal if he becomes just another Labour leader who the party are comfortable with. If something is popular with the party there is a part of him that thinks there is probably something wrong with it.

On Sunday morning this frustration is channelled effectively into his best interview since the 2001 election – a barnstorming performance on BBC's *Breakfast with Frost*, in which critics are swatted away majestically. But to some on the Left – and a couple of *Guardian* journalists I bump into – who have opposed the war on Iraq and are still bitter, the tone of 'You numbskulls, can't you admit Iraq is better off without Saddam?' does not go down too well.

Tony returns from Frost to his hotel room where we ask him what he has had for breakfast to have made him quite so fired up. 'I just want to get on with it,' he says. Getting on with it also means getting on with the speech. Conference is always a balance between writing the speech and using Tony's time to meet delegates and go to receptions. Philip's printer is now working and the memos are flowing.

By Sunday lunch more of the speechwriting team arrive: David Bradshaw, who works in the Strategic Communications Unit with me, a talented and prolific writer, ex-*Daily Mirror* journalist; and Bruce Grocott, now Lord Grocott, Tony's former parliamentary private secretary, now Chief Whip in the Lords. Bruce and David are particularly good on the one-liners and the clap lines. Writing sentences that make an audience applaud is a real skill: *Labour has introduced a Minimum Wage* – no applause or sporadic clapping. *We should all be proud that it is this Labour government, this New Labour government, that after one hundred years of campaigning, has introduced Britain's first ever Minimum Wage* – wild foot-stamping applause. Bruce and Tony have always got on well, but Bruce is unashamedly old Labour. His view, oft repeated, is that if you stay in the same place long enough your opinions come back into fashion. Both of us are chastened by the logic of one of Bruce's comments: 'Why is it,' he says, 'that Tony goes to Congress in America and butters them up, he opens a hospital and butters them up, he visits the CBI and says what they want to hear, *but* when he comes to the Labour conference he insists on telling the party what it *doesn't* want to hear?'

We say that this kind of perversity, the desire to constantly challenge the party rather than pander to it, is what makes Tony such a courageous leader. And there is truth in this. So many ministers, so many leaders of all parties, go to their party conference and give them what they want to hear. What has always made Tony different is that he uses his speeches to educate and to cajole into fresh positions. After each conference speech, when we have gathered to do a post-mortem of what worked and what bombed, we have always been surprised at what the New Labour party applauded. Tough on crime passages got rousing applause. Fiscal responsibility was now a source of great pride. Bruce is not convinced. 'This reads like a lecture,' he says. 'There's no chance of applause for page after page.'

Philip, Tony's chief of staff Jonathan Powell and I are in Tony's suite going over the argument again. Tony insists that we can't just bang on about fairness: we need to 'ally fairness to the future, confront people with the tough challenges ahead'. Leo, Tony's three-year-old son, comes in with a toy car and drives it through bits of fruit and discarded speech drafts on the coffee table. It's seeing Leo that makes me miss my two daughters. Cherie comes out of the bedroom dressed in a glamorous trouser suit. Her light touch always makes us feel that the current crisis is not as bad as it seems. She is ready for a round of receptions. Tony and Cherie kiss Leo goodnight. He is off to bed. We continue our heated discussion about the speech. Conference is always a strange combination of Blair home life, and intense work environment.

On Monday Tony has to be at the National Executive Committee, Labour's ruling body, at 7.30 a.m. where his vote makes the difference between winning and losing on foundation hospitals. David Hill, Alastair's replacement as Director of Communications, finds this all too reminiscent of the 'smoke-filled rooms' of past Labour conferences. Tony then has to go to the funeral of Gareth Williams, the clever and drole Leader of the Lords who had died suddenly the week before at the age of sixty-two. This means that for much of the key writing day Tony is completely out of action. We still don't have a speech and there are barely twenty-four hours to go.

Philip and I go off to talk through the big argument again. Vision is more important to a party of the Left, for the Left trades in hope, in progress and the future. The Right's juices flow when they are railing against an enemy, a threat to their way of life: foreigners, high taxes, socialism, communism, asylum seekers, lone parents, gays, loony councils, young people, Europe, television, permissiveness. The Left dreams of the good society, the end of poverty, full employment, a community of equals, children growing up with life chances, trains that run on time, hospitals that cure people, schools that unleash the potential of all, foreign aid ending world hunger. We have activists who join the party because of their ideals. They want to change the world, they want tunes to march to. And that has been New Labour's big problem. We committed two sins. The first was to tell the party that some of the old hymns would no longer do – higher taxes, nationalisation of industry, socialism. The second was to win power. With power comes responsibility and, worse, compromise. Idealism has to be tempered by realism. So where Labour once had a giant but often unelectable heart, New Labour has a hard-nosed but successful head – and by the second term it was clear that some were looking forward, or back, to the unfettered days of Opposition.

While Tony is at the funeral, Gordon is making a powerful speech on the conference floor. But the last line, which in speechwriting terms is brilliant, appears to be a direct challenge to Tony: 'At our best when at our boldest, at our best when united, at our best when Labour.' The clear implication is that Tony is not Labour and his reforms will divide the party. Gordon refers to Labour more than forty times in the speech but not once to New Labour. When one of Gordon's aides is asked what happened to the New in New Labour, the answer is: 'It was a long speech, something had to give.'

Tony returns from the funeral, and is told about Gordon's speech. He is relaxed about it. He says repeatedly to those in the office that it's not an ignoble ambition to want to be Prime Minister, but Gordon's speech has upped the stakes. We all know Tony's will have to be even better than usual. He closets himself in his hotel room, and does not emerge for several hours. We pace up and down the corridor waiting for something to emerge. We keep muttering to each other. 'It's Monday and we don't have a speech.'

At about 9 p.m. a number of us go in to see Tony. He is in a white bath robe, his hair dishevelled, surrounded by a dozen different drafts of the speech. This is familiar Monday night territory. 'It just doesn't work yet,' he says repeatedly under his breath. 'The argument is not right. The second half doesn't work. The policy section is hopeless. Why do we have this problem every year? How do we do policy?' The panic over policy in the speech does recur each year: too much policy on too many subjects and it is boring to listen to; put in too little and the speech feels lightweight. But what's the best way of grouping policy? How do we make the most of the vast number of policies the government has implemented? Each year we plump for one of two solutions. Either we fall back on headings such as economic, social, political, international – which we all think is a bit tired – or we run through the main areas in sequence: economy, jobs, health, education, crime. One year we used value-based headings – 'opportunity, responsibility, community, trust' – which in my view had the most power. The other issue is how much the speech should rely on a big argument to carry it and how much new policy is needed. New policy, if it is too bitty, can get in the way. On the other hand, we don't want journalists saying they have heard it all before. Increasingly Tony is relaxed about adding new policy, realising the conference speech is an occasion for the big picture and not lots of detail. I am feeling that I have been through this debate too many times.

Matthew Taylor, who has just joined Number 10 from

running the think-tank, the Institute for Public Policy Research, or IPPR, is witty and irreverent. This is the first time he has been involved in one of these iterative and painful speech marathons. He attempts to ease the tension with examples he has collected of humorous Labour quotations. His favourite is: a GMB union delegate to the party conference, 'And I tell this conference: genocide is not just morally repugnant but politically unacceptable.' Tony laughs.

Room service appears with a cooked evening meal on a trolley under a giant silver dome, which the waiter removes with a flourish. 'Just leave it there, please,' Tony says politely. Cherie enters the room having just returned from some receptions, and urges Tony to eat. He reluctantly moves towards the table where Cherie has laid out the meal. We all walk to the door to leave them in peace.

'Peter can you stay a second?'

I turn back into the room.

'Can you find me a quote? There's this beautiful saying from the bible, Proverbs, I think, twenty-something, that says exactly what we want to say in this speech. I want to use it at the end. It's something like – if we faint in the day of struggle we have little strength.'

'I'll get it,' I say. Feeling that he needs reassurance I add, 'You know this will be a great speech. You know it has great depth, and a powerful argument. It will really work on the day.'

He looks thoughtful. However strong they may look in public, politicians, like all of us, need reassurance from those they trust. The danger is that they end up with a court around them of people who only say, 'You're great.' Tony has never had that problem. I was one of several who thought the only point of being an adviser was to give blunt advice.

I leave the room and go back to my bedroom to look for the

obligatory hotel bible. I open the bedside drawers. No bible. I look in the cupboard under the television. It's a mini-bar. Is this the only hotel room in Britain without a bible? Is this yet another symbol of the decline in values? Found it. It's in a clothes drawer. I look for the quote and find Tony is almost spot on. It's Proverbs 24: 10. I return to his room. The security man on the door lets me in with a key. I tell Tony the good news. 'If we faint when there's trouble then we have little strength.' Tony says: 'That's the right quote, but there are more poetic versions. Have you looked at the King James bible?' Where will I get a King James bible at 10 p.m. on a Monday night? I phone the only person I know will be working at this hour, the Number 10 Duty Clerk, the heroic person on duty through the night to take messages and sort out logistics for the Prime Minister at Number 10. He calls me back within the hour. 'If we faint in the day of adversity, our strength is small.' That's more poetic. Tony will like it. I leave the quote on a piece of paper for him and return to the speechwriting room to improve other parts of the speech.

The room has sofas, armchairs and a table with two computers on it, but the place is wrecked: strewn with early drafts of the speech, random notes, bits of food, empty drink cans. We are charged with improving the policy section, making the middle flow better, and working on the personal stories. I get started on the education section. I have been determined for weeks to have a passionate passage that makes our drive for opportunity and education come alive. This is the core of the New Labour project.

I'm in mid-flow. It's now about one in the morning, and I know I'm finding it harder than previous years. After ten years of writing for Tony, I crave the chance to express my own ideas. I feel I have written about education, responsibility, New Labour on so many occasions, it's time for me not just to write about it, but experience the reality of it.

Neil Kinnock enters the room and starts telling us stories. He reads bits of the speech, suggests a few lines, generally keeps us going. He reassures us with tales of last-minute conference speeches he wrote in the Eighties. We all feel great loyalty and affection for Neil. We get to bed at about 3.30 in the morning having put a new version of the second half of the speech under Tony's door. We know he will only use bits of it, but we have given him something to react to. I sleep very badly with lines going through my head, thinking about what has been missed, what needs to be done.

Tuesday is speech day. I am driven by nervous energy. The speech has to be completed. The facts need to be checked. Any real people mentioned in the speech need to be checked out so that they don't turn out to be hostile to the government and undermine our case. In most cases we use caution and remove the name altogether, using instead 'a young boy on Merseyside' and 'an elderly woman in the North West'. From 7.30 onwards Tony hands over his handwritten changes piece by piece and I rush to get them typed up. Chunks are shifted around. Tony is brilliant at bringing order and flow to a speech that only a few hours before has seemed disjointed and patchy. It's 11 a.m. and the speech is at 2.15. Now's the time for last minute judgements. These are crucial decisions. Does the joke at the top work? Will people laugh when Tony says: 'Someone said I should come on and do a rendition of "Always look on the bright side of life".' We are divided. I don't like it much. Others do. Most importantly, Tony wrote it himself. He leaves it in. The other joke is about there being no natural Tory territory, 'Not in Scotland. Not in Wales. Not in the cities. Where on earth is natural Tory territory?' The punchline is: 'Ascot, Debretts, the Carlton Club'. David, Bruce and I like this line but we know it is unlikely Tony will use it. Class war is not his natural habitat, and I have already succeeded in getting in a resounding denunciation of hereditary peers. Ascot is soon removed on the grounds that ordinary punters go to the races and so it would backfire. Debretts and the Carlton Club then follow. The joke no longer has a punchline, but later it goes down perfectly well in the hall – partly because of the late addition: 'We knew the Tories didn't have a heart, now we know they don't have a heartland.'

More seriously, this is our last time to judge the Iraq section. Is it robust, yet conciliatory to those who opposed the war? Some think Tony has a chance of being heckled, particularly in the passage that says: 'I would make the same decision on Iraq again today.' Tony says nonsense. He is proved right later when, to everyone's surprise, he gets big applause for the Iraq passage.

It's midday. I go off to sit in peace in my hotel room and read the speech one more time from beginning to end, trying to spot glaring mistakes. I come back to Tony with four or five small but possibly important changes.

At 12.30 we all gather in a tiny room where the autocue has been set up and Tony can go through the speech as if he is delivering it. This helps him iron out any passages that are hard to say, and it immediately becomes clear what works and what doesn't. Tony whispers the speech, with us straining to hear him, in order to protect his voice for the big performance.

It's about 1.25 and I've made the classic match day mistake of not getting dressed in suit and tie early enough. Time is running out and I am still in my jeans and T-shirt. While Tony is making final changes to the speech I dash to my room and start shaving. I am the worst shaver in the world. My neck is the scene of yet another carve-up and I have again failed to grasp the basic principle that blood drips – and it always drips on white shirts more than any other colour. Within minutes my best shirt has blood on the collar. I take it off, dab some tissue on my neck, put on another shirt and race back to the autocue room. I press my neck hard with the tissue and hope for the best.

Tony is getting annoyed that the end of the speech is still not working. 'It's all in the wrong order,' he shouts. He tears out a page of the speech, rips off paragraphs and reorders them. The woman doing the autocue has eight half-written scraps of pages in front of her and has to piece them together. Tony then leaves for his room. It's 1.40. I'm handed these torn offerings to make sense of whilst he is gone. We manage it, somehow.

David Bradshaw and I start proof reading the speech. It's 2 o'clock. We print out a big typed copy for Tony. If the autocue breaks down he needs a hard copy to read from. Ninety-seven pages take forever to come out of the machine. We hand-write the page numbers. It's 2.12. We assume Tony is waiting in his room for the speech before walking down to the conference centre. He isn't. He's gone. I run down the hall of the hotel clutching the speech, rush into the street and see Tony and the rest of the party a hundred yards ahead. I catch them up.

In the conference hall waiting room I pace nervously. It's gone 2.15 but the hall is still filling. I suddenly have the urge to check whether one of the last-minute changes is in the final version or not. I try to find it in Tony's speech which is lying on a table in front of him. 'Too late to change it now,' he says. 'No, everything's fine, it's a great speech,' I say, thinking I have unnerved him.

Tony is anxious about how it is going to be received. The hype has prepared us for a bad reception, and he always takes a few minutes to warm up on the really big occasions. There is an agonising few minutes more as the hall continues to fill.

Tony is called. I wish him good luck. He leaves for his grand entrance as I make my way quickly into the hall. There are no seats left so I stand by the side, watching. I prefer standing anyway. I like pacing and fiddling during Tony's speeches. He gets a warm welcome from the outset, a long, standing ovation that quite takes him aback. I am relieved.

You know within minutes whether the speech will work in the hall: the jokes go down well, the audience is clapping, Tony starts getting the timing spot on. Tony's conversational style, combining passion and explanation, is far more effective than the old fashioned bludgeoning rhetoric that can get the party faithful going but leaves much of the public cold. The speech works. The middle section, the policy, the ending all come together. It is only when you hear them properly delivered that it all makes sense. The section that I know will stand out for the media is 'I can only go one way. I've not got a reverse gear.' The lack of sleep, the relief that it is working, the thought that this is the last conference speech I will work on, unexpectedly bring tears to my eyes. However, the speech, as I feared, only does one job. It shows Tony's resolve but does not launch 'renewal' as a concept. The first draft had talked explicitly about a new phase of New Labour. The final draft doesn't.

As the standing ovation begins and Tony leaves the podium, I make my way back to the waiting room to congratulate him. He is watching the TV, seeing the audience still applauding. He is taking his shirt and tie off as he has been sweating so much in the hall. 'Shall I go back out there?' he asks as the applause continues. He puts the shirt and tie back on and goes out for more applause. The speech has been a triumph. Anyone who thought Tony didn't have the appetite left has been proved wrong. He's still only fifty. Tony Blair is back. But for how long?

One thing still nags away at me – our current buzzword: 'renewal'. Good as the speech was, I am not sure we have resolved the key issues.

Where is New Labour heading? Are we making a big enough

difference on the ground? And I am not sure I can be part of another speech, writing yet more words. I am not sure I can spend any more time in the claustrophobic political bubble of Number 10, however exhilarating it has been. I started out ten years earlier an idealist. For all the compromises of government, I remain an idealist. I believe in the power of politics to change people's lives. I believe in doing rather than standing on the sidelines carping. But is politics working? Or is a life in politics missing the passions and concerns of 'real people' who are getting on with their lives and tuning out?

I decide that renewal has to apply to myself and not just New Labour.

I want to do something more hands on, more in the real world.

It's time to stop writing and stop talking and start doing.

It's time to leave Number 10.

# THE COLOUR PURPLE

The first time I meet him he is standing like a new father next to his pride and joy – his Fender Stratocaster guitar. There is a Beatles calendar on the wall. He is over six feet tall and broad shouldered; mid-forties, in a blue suit, a pale blue shirt and a purple tie. He is middle-class yet has a classless feel to him. He radiates dynamism and impatience. This guy wants to get things done. His name? Trevor Averre-Beeson. His job? Headteacher of Islington Green School.

'Welcome,' he says. 'Water or coffee?' I later discover that anyone who asks for tea intensely annoys Trevor. He has coffee on the boil permanently and water is easy. He doesn't want to waste his or anyone else's time making tea.

'Water, thank you.'

He takes me on a quick tour of the school. Standing in the playground and looking up at a monstrous tower block, he says: 'They thought it was cool in the Sixties, clever design, all that, but of course it's hopeless to teach in. The corridors are too long and narrow. They invite people to charge down them.'

In the fifteen months since Trevor arrived, the school has passed its Ofsted, having failed the one before, and has seen its

GCSE results steadily improve – though even now only 28 per cent get five good GCSEs, well below the national average. Money is coming into the school and he proudly shows me the newly opened dance and music studios that have taken over the top floor of one of the other decrepit buildings.

Behaviour and attendance are getting better, Trevor says. The year before he arrived 349 children out of a school then of 1,150 had been excluded from lessons; an extraordinary statistic. Now it's only five.

Behaviour may be better but cheekiness is not yet banned as one of my classroom visits shows. 'Is this the new headteacher?' says an impish twelve-year-old, looking up from a maths lesson and pointing at me. 'Taking over from you is he?'

'No, you're stuck with me,' Trevor says with more amusement than irritation. We walk on through lilac corridors. Trevor has spruced up the insides of the old buildings. 'I decided to feminise the place a bit,' he says, 'to calm down the teenage boys.' I've seen no evidence yet whether pastel shades have hobbled the raging hormones, but as if to prove his point, Trevor leads me into a classroom with twenty-five children glued to computer screens. The teacher, dishevelled and bearded, beams at his headteacher: 'See – they're all wearing their new school uniform and all working away quietly.'

Trevor likes school uniforms. 'The teachers told me introducing school uniforms would be a disaster, no one would wear them, but we decided to have a go. I wanted them purple, the school colours. Again the teachers said no one would wear purple, but I decided to give them away to those already at the school, and I tell you, they went like hot cakes. Children were queuing at break time to get their new blazers, and parents insisted their children wore them properly because they had got them free.' Trevor, I soon realise, is deeply committed to purple. It is his clearest signal that the school is changing. He's even bought a purple car.

I have paid many visits 'to the frontline' – schools, hospitals, police forces – to get a feel for what is happening on the ground. I usually come away refreshed and optimistic. It is always remarkable what an inspiring leader and dedicated staff can achieve. This visit is the same, but I am here for a different purpose. I am looking for a school to work in for six months.

I want to find a comprehensive in London, not too far from where I live. Education is, after all, the government's Number One priority. It is where my heart lies. Education, education, education. I'd written the words so many times in Tony's speeches: 'Education, the route out of poverty', 'The fulfilling of potential, vital for the knowledge economy.' I can't think of anything more challenging or different than working in a school. After ten years at Westminster I crave the jolt of reality. I had asked the Department of Education to recommend a school that might be willing to take me on. I had asked for a 'bog-standard school with a good head'. I want to go somewhere typical of inner London, but improving.

That morning, a dingy autumn day, I had driven down Upper Street, the pulse of trendy Islington, with its rows and rows of restaurants. I passed the most famous of them, Granita – the place where Tony Blair and Gordon Brown had supposedly brokered a deal – and headed down to Essex Road before I turned into Packington Street towards the school. I felt apprehensive. I had told no one at Number 10 I was thinking of leaving and it felt furtive and slightly naughty. I also felt guilty about leaving Tony, particularly when he has been so vulnerable after the Iraq war and when others in the office had also left. However, I comforted myself with the thought that Tony needed new blood and that this was the time, well before an election, to be doing something new. Even so, it's deeply disconcerting.

High, terraced houses flanked the streets, each of them million-pound properties owned by London's editors, advertisers, lawyers, and bankers, but within a couple of hundred yards, the change was noticeable. Graffiti on the walls, litter on the pavements. Louise Casey, New Labour's tenacious anti-social-behaviour czar, would have announced a 'crackdown' on the spot. In the near distance the good housing gave way to bad.

To the right I had noticed two things simultaneously: a dirty seven-storey tower block and a sign – purple on white – saying Islington Green School. Why had they built a school in a tower block? I turned into Prebend Street. Withered flowers in cellophane wrappers were attached to a lamp-post next to a zebra crossing. A death, possibly a murder? A car accident? The pub opposite the school was called 'As Good As It Gets'. The electric doors of the car park swung open and I drove in. Skips filled with debris were strewn about. This felt every bit the grim inner-city comprehensive of my expectations. I headed for the entrance. The reception area was bright and very purple, with big colour photos of children matched by glossy school prospectuses on the tables. This could be the lobby of a bank – well, almost – but it all brought to mind American political strategist James Carville's insult at a particularly ineffective make-over by one of his opponents: 'It's like putting lipstick on a pig.'

As we sit down to talk after our tour I ask Trevor if he is willing to take me on. He thinks I am a bit odd, giving up the glamour of Number 10. He also, I suspect, worries about whether I am going to be of any use. But as he ponders the prospect he thinks I might be given a roving role – part classroom assistant, part strategist. 'A kind of Minister Without Portfolio,' he says with a grin. 'But you do realise the irony don't you? This is the school Tony Blair should have sent his children to.' I had visited Tony's house nearby many times, but I had not realised that Islington Green School was the actual school involved. I wasn't sure I should be going to the very school that had sparked such a painful controversy in 1994 and 1995. That dreadful experience came flooding back to me: the *Daily Mail* breaking the story that Tony's eldest son was not going to an Islington school but travelling miles across London to a grant-maintained school, one that had opted out of local authority control. I remember our panic at the time. Tony had just become leader of the Labour party; we were desperate to get off to a good start; we wanted nothing to stand in the way of election victory. This was one of the first of many occasions when Tony came under immense personal as well as political pressure. However much we said that he would be the only Prime Minister to send all his children entirely through the state sector, the nastier personal attacks from the press and political opponents succeeded in convincing much of the public that Tony had sent his child to a private school.

For months Tony was accused of hypocrisy. There were fifty schools, people said, between his house and the London Oratory where his son was to go. Even if he wanted to send his son to a Catholic school there were other Catholic schools, they said, including some in Islington, that were far nearer. There were accusations of rows between Tony and Education Secretary David Blunkett, that Labour party policy was being altered to bring it in line with the Blairs' decision. The truth was that, even before his own decision, Tony had been reluctant to attack grant-maintained schools head on because a lot of them had good heads doing positive things. Tony won some support from anxious middle-class parents wrestling with the same dilemmas when he said: 'I am not going to make a choice for my child on the basis of what is the politically correct thing to do', but for others 'the sake of my child' explanation was the same justification as for sending a child private. Blair, they said, was now endorsing private education. The other effect was a trawl by all the newspapers to see what further 'embarrassments' they could find among the decisions of other ministers. I had no children of my own at the time; I had no real appreciation of the agonies of 'liberal' parents, desperate not to be accused of hypocrisy whilst trying to do the best for their children. At regular intervals in the next ten years Labour ministers and advisers would come under attack for decisions about their own children, and it remained one of the hottest controversies within the party. One person told me that their decision to send their child to a private school was the most painful, traumatic, divisive, decision his family had ever made. Yet, he said, once you have taken the mental leap and started considering private schools, there is no looking back – what is on offer is quite simply better.

The year the Blairs 'snubbed' Islington's schools was the year that GCSE results in Islington went down to below 18 per cent of children getting five or more A to C grades, bottom in the country. Middle-class parents were doing in their hundreds, what the Blairs were rationally doing themselves: looking for another school with better results.

Islington Green School, the nearest school to the Blairs' Islington home, failed its Ofsted inspection in 1997 and went into 'special measures', the education equivalent of intensive care. The Ofsted report, despite an attempt to use diplomatic language, was damning.

> Islington Green has several strengths. But it has weaknesses such that my judgement is that in accord with Section 13 (7) of the School Inspections Act 1996 special measures are required in relation to the school. Her Majesty's Chief Inspector has come to the same judgement. The weaknesses are outlined in these main findings and are detailed in the full report.

Standards are variable throughout the school and vary greatly from subject to subject. Standards of attendance are poor, as also are those of punctuality, both to school and to lessons. They are consistently below what is nationally expected or educationally acceptable.

The quality of teaching throughout the school is highly variable. An unacceptably high proportion of teaching is unsatisfactory or poor. A major cause of the poorer teaching is the teachers' inability to control ill-disciplined pupils.

Other characteristics of the weaker teaching include lack of adequate planning and preparation, poor use of time within lessons, expecting and demanding too little of pupils, and a failure to enthuse or motivate pupils because of a slow teaching pace and poor choice of teaching methods.

The quality of education is lowered by the state of the buildings. The main building is, in many areas, in disrepair. Many rooms, corridors and public areas are shabby, dirty and not conducive to good learning.

Far too many pupils are noisy, rude, and occasionally aggressive, both in and out of classrooms. The school has a policy on behaviour but that policy is not being consistently implemented by all teachers. Pupils are not consistently being taught the principles and practice of civilised behaviour.

When, under Trevor, the school passed its inspection in February 2003, the Ofsted report was a lot better. 'The headteacher is a visionary and transformational leader who is working strategically to move the school forward; he is ably supported by senior managers and by a number of other staff in key posts of responsibility.'

This is clearly a challenging school, but one beginning to turn itself around. In many ways it should be a good place, and Islington the ideal borough, to get some frontline experience. But as I spend a few days reflecting on my visit I feel pulled in different directions, so I go to see Tim Brighouse in the Department of Education. He is sturdily built, with dishevelled hair, and has just been appointed London Commissioner, having run Birmingham LEA, with the remit of turning round London schools. He is a great figure in the education world, popular amongst teachers for his supportive and inspirational style, passionate about the ability of state schools to make a difference.

Islington Green turns out to be one of the fifty-seven schools being targeted for special attention in London because it has under 30 per cent good GCSEs. I discover that it has a lot of built-in problems. It has twice as many boys as girls, because there are several girls' schools in the borough that many parents choose first. It has no sixth form, which can make it hard to attract teachers and means there are no post-sixteen role models for the students to follow. I had been a strong advocate of giving London different treatment because the problems seemed to be worse than the rest of the country and politically the damage done by the performance of a few inner-London boroughs had the potential to drag down the reputation of all secondary schools.

'It's all about an achievement culture,' Tim says. 'These schools are at one of three stages. They either have an achievement culture established, or have one that is shaky, or are just getting a toe hold. Our job is to show we can make a difference, to show that those from the poorest backgrounds can succeed.'

I look at some of the analysis on London schools that he has given me: Only 59 per cent of pupils get their first choice school in London compared with 85 per cent in the rest of England; the flight to the independent sector is 13 per cent in London and 7 per cent in the rest of England; yet we already spend 21 per cent more per pupil in London than in the rest of the country. Islington Green itself has 49 per cent free school meals compared with a national average of 17 per cent; 34 per cent of pupils have English as an additional language compared with 8 per cent in the rest of England; 10 per cent change schools mid-term compared with 6 per cent, plus there is a larger than average teacher turnover, and there are larger numbers of asylum seekers. The school is remembered in the area as having a 'golden' period under Margaret Maden, who took over as head at the age of thirty-four in 1974 and attracted more middle-class students to the school, including the children of some famous academics and journalists. The school had a reputation for being left-wing, hippy even, with no school uniform – in contrast to Highbury Grove, a former grammar school up the road, run at one point by Rhodes Boyson who went on to be a Tory minister. Pink Floyd included some students from Islington Green on their album, *The Wall*, creating a controversy amongst those who felt 'we don't need no education' were inappropriate lyrics.

The scale of challenge does not seem daunting for Tim Brighouse. 'We've got to show in the next few years that we can break the cycle of deprivation. For these children our job is to fill their pockets with confidence.'

He may not have been daunted but I was.

However much you try to leave the prejudices behind, an image forms of this type of inner-city school: knives and guns, violence and abuse; teachers being attacked and having nervous breakdowns; children out of control, corridors taken over by gangs; drugs being peddled in the playground. One such story, that was dragged up in every newspaper article about Islington Green School, involved what turned out to be a false allegation of a student attacking a pregnant teacher; just another dent in the reputation of a school described throughout its history as a 'sink school'.

Working in a school like this would be a million miles from my current life. What skills do I have? Do I have the patience? Do I have the authority? Will I be listened to or ignored? And that's just by the teachers. What will the students make of this middle-class guy descending from government?

I phone up Trevor to discuss it with him and he adds to my worries. The head of Cambridge Education Associates, the company that has run the LEA since its privatisation in 2000 (the first LEA to be contracted out) has been on to him, demanding to know why I am coming. Also, the Lib Dem council is uneasy, and the NUT rep stood up at a staff meeting and complained that a New Labour person was coming to the school. A heated fifteen-minute discussion ensued in which there was agreement, grudgingly, that I should be allowed in.

Trevor says to me: 'I want you to come in and meet some of the deputy heads and governors,' so I turn up two weeks later, at 8 a.m. on the way to Number 10. Trevor's room is crowded. His black leather sofa is occupied by three well-dressed women, and there is a fifty-year-old man looking serious on another chair. The whole thing is a little overwhelming.

Trevor introduces me to the senior management team and the governors. The serious-looking man is a Lib Dem councillor. He's obviously suspicious.

Trevor says: 'Well Peter, why don't you kick off with a few words on why you want to come. Then we'll let people ask questions.'

'I have been working for Tony Blair for nearly ten years. I am now keen to change and do something different. I have always been interested in education. The DfES recommended this school. So here I am.'

I hadn't expected a room full of Jeremy Paxmans but I was soon in for a breakfast grilling.

'May I put it to you,' says the Lib Dem councillor, leaning forward, 'that you want to use this for your own political ends.'

'What would those be?' I ask.

'Your own New Labour . . . ends.' He sneers.

'I'm here for no political reason,' I say. 'I just want to get a feel for the challenges of the frontline. In national media terms Islington is still seen, however unfairly, as a bad-news story, so I am hardly here to jump on a bandwagon.'

'Have you ever worked with teenagers?' asks a small middle-aged woman in a smart suit with funky blonde hair, who I discover is Angela, the senior deputy head.

'Not exactly,' I say.

'Do you know what teenagers are like?' she tries again.

'Well, I've got a nephew who's fourteen and a niece who's twelve.'

'No, do you *really* know what teenagers are like?' Angela titters, a knowing titter. 'Is there anything you wouldn't do?' she continues.

I don't know what she means.

'Like what?'

'She's got a duty rota to fill,' Trevor says. 'You'll be on play-ground duty before you know it.'

'I'll do anything you want,' I say enthusiastically.

'Well, I think it's a great opportunity for us,' says Trevor in what I am later to discover is his usual relentlessly optimistic manner.

I'm more daunted now than a few weeks ago. There is a disconcerting sense that I am letting myself in for a nasty shock. It's a risk, but one I'm not going to back out of now. As I get up to leave the room, the ordeal over, Angela shouts after me: 'Have you got your Valium yet?'

# A POLITICAL EDUCATION

'That seems very noble,' says the Prime Minister.

He has his jacket slung over his shoulder, held by two fingers, one of his characteristic poses. He is about to go upstairs to the flat after a hard day's work at Number 10.

He pauses.

'Yes it *is* very noble.'

I have just told him I am going to work in a school. He knows I want to leave and has tried to talk me out of it. This is a relief of course because everyone dreads telling their boss they're off and hearing the response: 'Well, goodbye then.'

The only way to convince him I really mean it is to make clear I have somewhere else to go. 'Let's discuss it further,' he says, going upstairs. That's his way of saying this seems inevitable but I might have one more go at changing your mind.

Loyalty is the single most prized attribute in a political adviser. Ministers in general, the Prime Minister in particular, need people they can trust, people they can be frank with, people who know their mind, can speak for them, interpret them to others, help them through the bad times. The longer you are there, the more you are valued, the harder it is to leave. Most advisers last three or four years. I had been with Tony for nearly ten. Much as Tony talked about change – 'Everywhere is change' – much as he urged the Labour Party, the country, the professions, the unions to change, he didn't like change around him, in his own office. He believed in and trusted his small group of political advisers.

In the few weeks that remain until I depart at Christmas I have a lot of tidying up to do, a lot of goodbyes to say. I've accumulated assorted bits and pieces and now try to box it all up. For the first time I drive through the gates of Number 10, and park my car in the street to load up. I think back and ponder, perhaps excessively, whether I have made any difference to anything. I reflect on my luck at having got involved in such an exciting period of Labour politics.

Until the age of about fourteen I was obsessed with cricket and football. Obsession is the right word. I used to memorise cricketers' middle names and on occasions whole scorecards from games – the runs, the wickets, the extras – and could recite them to any unsuspecting person who asked. Then, almost overnight, cricket was replaced by politics. Ian Botham and Viv Richards gave way to Margaret Thatcher and Neil Kinnock. The Falklands War was the event that symbolised the transition. It gripped our household. My parents loved politics and were both Labour. I was glued with the family to the TV every day. Thatcher became a hate figure. My grandparents, who had fled Vienna with my mother and uncle when the Nazis arrived in 1938, were both staunch Labour supporters too. My grandfather often repeated his view like a mantra: 'They will have to drag that woman kicking and screaming from Number 10.'

The second event that galvanised me was the 1992 General Election. It was a strange, lonely, painful time for me. I was in Iowa, a small American state known for its cattle and not much else. I had been sent there on a work placement from City University where I was training to be a journalist. For a month I was to be a reporter on the *Daily Iowan*, a thin newspaper that catered for the mostly student population of Iowa City. On election night, I listened alone to Brian Redhead on a crackling radio, as he delivered the bad news. It was particularly bad and surprising news because the university library's most recent British newspaper was *The Times* from the Saturday before polling day which had the front page headline 'Labour 7 points clear'. I was certain Labour would win. As the results came in, I got sadder and sadder, and I scuttled round the campus looking for someone British to commiserate with. Someone who cared about the result one way or another would have been a start, but there was not a single person that evening, or on subsequent days, who raised an eyebrow at the devastating news that the Tories were still in power in Britain. This lack of interest did not however stop me persuading the editor of the *Daily Iowan* that I should write a comment piece on the result. This is the one and only political column I have ever written, and it was to an audience 99.9 per cent of whom I am sure to this day don't know who Neil Kinnock or John Major are.

Under the brilliant headline pun: 'Major disaster for Great Britain', Peter Hyman from London, England, wrote:

Great Britain effectively became a one-party state last Friday. The Conservative Party won an historic fourth term. For large proportions of the population the result is a disaster. It is a vote for stagnation, for growing inequalities between rich and poor, and the run-down of public services at the expense of the few who can afford private health and education. It means a half-hearted attitude to European integration and no interest in the environment. Britain will be rudderless with a nonentity

36

at its head, and a Cabinet of sickly accountants lecturing the poor for not being rich, mocking the unemployed for not having jobs, ignoring the old and sick and keeping quiet when the chairmen of large companies give themselves 35% pay rises.

For the Labour Party a fourth successive defeat is a catastrophe and could spell the end of the party in its present form. It won't be enough to think that things will be better next time with a new popular leader. The party no longer represents its old constituency of the working class. Yet it has failed to broaden its appeal to the greater numbers who now consider themselves middle class.

I got one piece of feedback, one letter to the editor from the other Brit, who must have been lying low. He told me not to panic, the Tories were great for the country.

The third preparation for my life in politics was working on the BBC programme *Behind the Headlines*, a show in which Tony Banks for Labour and Jeffrey Archer for the Conservatives cross-questioned guests on relevant topics from road pricing to capital punishment. I remember Jeffrey Archer being friendly and earnest but humourless. What I remember most about Tony Banks was the row I had with him about animals. He is a fanatical animal lover and made the case that if there was a choice between saving one of his relatives or the last of any species, then auntie would always be first for the chop. I argued that it was immoral to put any animal before a human life.

It was at this time that I channelled the obsessive side of my personality into consuming political speeches and interviews. Two people gripped me. One was Brian Walden, the former Labour MP and political interviewer, because I loved the theatre of political interviews and was hooked, in particular, by the ones Walden had done during Thatcher's most shaky period, just after losing Nigel Lawson. I had these interviews on tape and watched them repeatedly: 'Prime Minister, you mean you don't know if you could have kept your Chancellor if you had got rid of Alan Walters?' The other was Mario Cuomo, the then Democrat governor of New York. He was the most moving and brilliant orator I ever heard, speaking in stories, weaving moral fervour and political belief together seamlessly. Watching and reading his speeches convinced me of the romance of politics: that you could rouse people by your words to believe in better things, to lift your sights beyond your daily life, to come together in a common cause.

It was during my time at the BBC that I met Julie Hall who had just left as Kinnock's press secretary following Labour's 1992 General Election defeat and was herself working there. She introduced me to Gordon Brown who needed an additional researcher, and I went for an interview. It was brief and to the point. We talked about both doing history at university, and Gordon then asked me if I was committed to the Labour Party. I said Yes. He said, 'I want you to find some tax loopholes for me.' I assumed I had the job.

For the next ten years I got the kind of political education it would be hard to replicate. I became a special adviser at a time when there was a group of politicians and advisers in the Labour party with the determination and talents to transform British politics, and I was on their course taking their subjects:

Tony Blair – Principal and Director of Political Strategy. Specialist subject 'Winning big majorities from the centre ground'. Controversial second year course: 'The forces of conservatism in Britain 1900–2000'. One-to-one tutorials offered on 'Old Labour's post-war failings'.

Gordon Brown – Director of Long-term Goals. Specialist subjects: 'Twenty-two Tory tax rises, 1992–1997'; 'Tax credits: 1997 onwards'. Annual lectures on 'Prudence for a purpose'.

Peter Mandelson – Dean of the School of Political Positioning. Wide-ranging courses offered include: 'Intimidating political editors'; 'Off-the-record briefings without leaving finger-prints'; and 'Ignoring irritating backbenchers'. Two-hour lecture specials include: 'Why the Freedom and Fairness campaign of 1986 was Labour's best ever' and 'The Dome was going well while I was in charge of it.'

Alastair Campbell – Doctor of Spin. Seminar courses include: 'The bovine media 1992–2004'; 'The lying BBC 2001–3'. Publications include: *Daily Mail: The Most Evil Newspaper in Britain*; *Burnley and Labour: Twin Givers of Joy*; *Running Whilst Shouting: How to Stamp on a Story While doing the Marathon*; *Funeral of HM Queen Mother: A Line by Line Rebuttal of the Charge that the PM or Anyone Else Muscled In.'

Philip Gould – Professor of Focus Group studies. Doctoral thesis on: 'The living rooms of middle-class homes in Edgware and Watford, and the political views of those who inhabit them.' Seminar group to visit key homes to re-enact famous focus group moments. (Additional trips to Milton Keynes and Putney living rooms optional.)

David Miliband – Head of the Faculty of Third Way Studies. Courses on 'Social Democratic Hegemony in Europe'. Regular seminars include: 'Is another crack-down on crime entirely necessary?' and 'Debating the

Left's three legged stool – ethical market, civic society, democratic politics'.

Anji Hunter – Professor of Power Politics. Specialist subject: 'Making things happen'. Practical (vocational) courses include: 'How to get 300 cheering school children on Dudley High Street in thirty minutes', and 'Getting the Tory establishment to love a Labour Leader'. Special evening 'soiree seminars' – '3 winning ways of shmoozing Labour backbenchers'. Drinks provided.

These were my professors. I was a keen and willing student. I joined them as a young, naïve, idealist, passionate about wanting to make a difference. I believed in one thing above all else, perhaps the influence of my Jewish upbringing, that discrimination of any kind was abhorrent, that people from all backgrounds should be given an equal chance to succeed. Also, again perhaps influenced by my father, a publisher, growing up surrounded by books, I believed the route to success was through education and learning. I was ambitious too. I wanted Labour to win again, and I wanted to be part of it.

In the coming years I studied a political craft – policy formation, media relations, strategy, communications, campaigning, political organisation – and ten years on, when I looked back, I realised I had learnt some key lessons, lessons I would be able to take with me on the journey that was about to begin: lessons about leadership and lessons about what made for successful change.

One Parliament Street is the name of a building opposite the Treasury on Whitehall. It is a modern office for MPs, full of hotel-style carpets, gold banisters and wooden panels. On the walls are portraits of former leaders and Prime Ministers; each a hideous distortion of a great Parliamentarian. On the second floor of this building, from 1992 to 1994, was most of the Shadow Cabinet. Robin Cook, Frank Dobson, Donald Dewar, Jack Straw, Neil Kinnock, George Robertson, Tony Blair and Gordon Brown were all in narrow rooms close to each other. Each had one or possibly two special advisers. Gordon had three, and I was very much the junior to Ed Richards and Neal Lawson.

At One Parliament Street all the parties were represented though they were allocated different floors, and three types of conversation were going on in the bar on the first floor after work. Tories met, gin and tonics in hand, to tear each other apart over Europe. Lib Dems met, white wine spritzers in hand, to prove to each other why Proportional Representation would change British politics. Labour advisers met, Perriers in hand, to discuss power. Europe, PR, power: the three main parties between '92 and '97.

Gordon Brown had told me to go and see Nick Brown who was in the Treasury team and who could tell me all about tax, so I met with him in the House of Commons tea room. Surrounded by Tory ministers and well-groomed waiters, it was an exciting, if bizarre, way to do business. Nick told me that we had the help of a tax expert and the aim was to save money through closing tax loopholes, so in the run up to the election we could show how to invest in public services without having to raise taxes.

'But I know absolutely nothing about tax,' I said, concerned I would fail my first assignment for Gordon.

So, I beavered away for several weeks with a tax accountant from a city firm and I started to understand tax havens, off-shore trusts, share schemes. I could see immediately why accountants and lawyers make so much money in this area; it was baffling. I couldn't see how we were going to achieve the big savings Gordon wanted, and Gordon was getting impatient.

He arranged to meet the tax expert with me to thrash it out.

It was the first time I saw Gordon devour policy detail and spew it up in perfectly formed political strategy. He had just come off a plane from the States and was clearly exhausted. He sat down in his room and looked at the bits of paper on tax before him. Each included areas of complicated tax law that I had been struggling with for weeks. Within ten minutes he said to the tax expert, 'Can't we save two billion on this one, one billion on this one and then close that one?' The tax expert provided some caveats but Gordon had cut through the detail and he was up and running. I was in awe.

The tax loopholes were part of a bigger picture that Gordon had worked out meticulously. In April 1993 Gordon wrote to his staff on a scrap of paper, in his characteristic capital letters – which he finds easier to read having lost the sight in one eye when playing rugby – about what was holding Britain back. On some of the examples Gordon had handwritten the difference between the old Labour approach and the New Labour approach. Even under John Smith's leadership, as early as 1993, Gordon was writing about New Labour: 'Old Lab nationalisation, New Lab competition. Old Labour government spending, New Labour employer spending.'

'This is what we must deal with:

A  IRRESPONSIBLE EMPLOYERS WHO REFUSE TO TRAIN (Old Lab govt spend, New Lab employers spend)
B  CITY INSTITUTIONS THAT WORK FOR THE SHORT TERM ONLY
C  BANKS THAT OVERCHARGE AND UNDER PROVIDE (Old Labour regulation, New Labour = competition)

D A SCHOOL SYSTEM THAT FAILS TO MEET THE STANDARDS WE NEED

E SOCIAL SECURITY SYSTEM THAT DOES NOT ENCOURAGE OPPORTUNITY

F A TAX SYSTEM THAT FAILS TO DISTINGUISH BETWEEN SPECULATION AND INVESTMENT FOR MODERNISATION

G A CONSERVATIVE FINANCIAL ESTABLISHMENT, UNACCOUNTABLE, USELESS FOR THE PROBLEMS OF THE MODERN WORLD (Old Lab: nat, New Lab: compet)

H COMPANIES THAT THINK LITTLE OF THE LONG TERM WHETHER IT BE THE ENVIRONMENT AND DO NOT OPERATE IN THE PUBLIC INTEREST. NOT ALL COMPANIES NOT EVEN THE MAJORITY OF COMPANIES BUT POLLUTERS AND PROFITEERS AT THE EXPENSE OF THE PUBLIC INTEREST

In repositioning Labour on tax and spend, the economy, and the role of state, Gordon was every bit as much the creator of New Labour as Tony. What Gordon was to do as Chancellor was set out in those years. His great strengths as a politician are focus and consistency.

Later, he wrote a note for those in the office called the 'The Economic tasks before us':

When Labour has won, in 1945 and 1964/65 in particular, it has been seen by the majority of people as:

The Party of economic competence – trusted as managers of the economy.

The Party of economic opportunity – the party that will make people better off by giving them new chances at work.

The Party of economic change – the party that will improve and transform our society for the better.

He outlined our problems in stark terms. Following what was widely seen as the disastrous Shadow Budget put forward at the 1992 election which had led to the Tories' devastating Tax Bombshell assault on our plans, Gordon set about transforming Labour's image on tax and spend:

Despite the advance made between 1987 and 1992 and despite the Tories' taxing and borrowing and devaluing, Labour is still seen as:

A party that taxes irresponsibly
A party that spends money inefficiently
A party that will always take the easy option
A party whose full employment aspirations are not realisable
A party whose economic policy may well be run by the unions
Generally a party that will hold people back rather than help people move on, in other words that we are a threat to people's aspirations

Gordon went on to explain that we should enter the election as the party of economic opportunity for all, not unfair privileges for a few. 'What does equal chances mean for the 1990s?' he wrote:

It means opportunity . . .

- In education before 5 – dividing line – the Tories no longer believe in nursery education for all; Labour does
- in school-time education – dividing line – upgrading our teaching
- in help to stay on after the school leaving age
- in access to college and university
- in in-work training
- in time off for developing skills
- in removing barriers to women working e.g. childcare
- in right in the workplace itself
- in employment opportunity
- in the chance to start a business or become self-employed
- in social security where responsibilities are matched by rights
- in help to avoid poverty
- in access to affordable housing
- in access to preventative and curative health.

Opportunity was Gordon's great theme then and is his great theme now. It is what drives his politics and his actions and his unswerving pursuit of it has made him Labour's most successful Chancellor.

For Gordon and Tony there were no illusions about the scale of the changes needed, and they were single-minded enough to make it happen. There was a real sense of hunger, discipline and dynamism at that time in the second floor corridor of One Parliament Street – but there was a nervousness too. Would it once more, as on the last four occasions, all be in vain? Was Britain simply never going to vote for Labour again?

Gordon was constantly putting you on the spot. You wanted

to deliver for him. He was powering forward and had no time to stop and dither. While other Shadow Cabinet ministers on the corridor were pacing themselves, Gordon was a whirlwind of frenetic activity. You either produced the goods or he would use someone else. He demanded rigour, and he had a laser-like ability to focus on the flaws in your argument or see how an opponent would attack it. He was the master of the political dividing line. On any issue he worked out where the Tories would come from and how Labour must distinguish itself from them.

The most important lesson Gordon taught me was that if you focus on an objective relentlessly enough you achieve it. This has been borne out every day he has been Chancellor with the relentless pursuit of the goals he set out in Opposition. Gordon's tactic is that if he bats for something 110 per cent and everyone else goes at it about 90 per cent, his persistence pays off. He wins many battles in government on that basis. He gives 110 per cent and he expects 110 per cent loyalty in return. It is impossible to give any less and have a meaningful relationship with him. I regretted that, when I ended up working with Tony, it became more difficult to engage with Gordon, but I understood that it was inevitable.

While John Smith was playing the long game, and Tony Blair was shaping the Home Office brief, Gordon was redefining the Labour party on the economy. But I was soon to get a very different experience of political life.

Donald Dewar, Shadow Social Security Secretary, a tall, gangling man, former lawyer, art and book collector, who was in the room next door to Gordon, was looking for a sole researcher. I would do press and policy on my own. This was my big chance.

If Gordon was trying to get on the *Today* programme every day, Donald was trying to do the reverse. He had been told by

John Smith to shut down Social Security until the Social Justice Commission, run by the Institute for Public Policy Research, had reported. Donald relished the task. For a young researcher eager to prove himself, the objective of *not* being in the newspapers was a challenge I hadn't expected. Here was a politician who didn't want publicity.

I started badly. Donald was making a speech to pension fund managers and I thought what he was saying on the future of pensions was worth reporting, so I took the unilateral step of making copies of the speech and distributing them around the press gallery. I arrived at work the following day brandishing a copy of the *Financial Times* with Donald's speech positively reported on page 5. I was swelling with pride at my handiwork and showed it to Donald. He was underwhelmed. He knew it might start a trend. 'Let's keep a low profile,' he said.

From then on we had a constant but friendly battle over his press releases. I would complain to him that the main story was buried on page 3, or that to start with the key point would help journalists – a title even would point them in the right direction: 'Dewar slams Tories on pensions', for instance. Donald would invariably take it out. Donald didn't do slamming. He did gentlemanly dissection and it was all the more credible for being that way.

Donald taught me the value of authenticity in politics. He was a trusted figure in Westminster and hugely respected by the media who saw him for what he was – a man of integrity. He didn't pander to the common denominator. At a time when Labour's presentation was becoming slicker, Donald was heading in the opposite direction. It seemed as if he hadn't bought a new tie or suit in decades. He used big words. He read widely. His idea of a holiday was to spend time in Glasgow writing book reviews. One of his famous sayings was 'Travel narrows the mind.' I asked him what he meant. He said: 'Have you seen our backbenchers?'

If you passed Donald's office early in the morning or late at night he would be there speaking into his dictaphone, his characteristic 'um-er' between each word. He never stopped replying in person to every constituent who wrote to him. No standard letters, no fob-off answers; he would try to get to the bottom of each one.

At that time the leader and the Leader's office seemed a distant and mysterious world somewhere in the House of Commons. I had met John Smith once or twice since working with Gordon, and I shared the respect for him amongst the Party and the Shadow Cabinet. I had also sat in the House of Commons gallery to watch one of his finest Commons performances where he had branded John Major 'the man with the "non-Midas" touch.' I have not heard a wittier speech in the Commons since. However, I could sense too, and share, the exasperation that some had for the 'one more heave' strategy that John Smith employed, the assumption that if Labour held tight it would win next time round. I think he was right, we would have won, but to sustain us in power and lock out the Tories, possibly for a generation, required far more brutal changes. Incremental change versus shock treatment? This was my first taste of one of the great dilemmas of those trying to change organisations.

I got into work on 12 May 1994 to the news that John Smith had been taken to hospital with a suspected heart attack, and Donald Dewar, his closest friend, was at his desk looking agitated. A few minutes later, there was a call from a tabloid newspaper, the ultimate intrusion, no pleasantries, just the blunt question: 'Can you comment on John Smith's death?' At that point we didn't know he was dead. Donald put the phone down and checked with the Leader's office. Indeed he had just died, aged fifty-five. Donald left to make his lonely way to the hospital.

On that second floor there was a numb, disbelieving, hush. I felt the enormity of what was happening and was deeply sad for

John's family and for Donald who I knew it would hit hard. I met Anji Hunter, Tony's key member of staff, as she came out of the lift on the second floor. She saw me in tears and thought something had happened to Tony. 'Have you heard,' I said, 'John Smith is dead.' She was momentarily relieved that Tony was fine, then she too reacted with shock and sadness at the news.

Donald went to Scotland to help arrange the funeral which I went up for. His speech was beautiful and captured John Smith. 'He could start a party in an empty room and often did,' was a great line and summed up both John's warmth and Donald's wit. I became very fond of Donald. I was delighted when he became First Minister of Scotland; he was born to do the job. When he died at sixty-three in 2000, I felt I had lost a wise teacher, who in my early days in politics had shown me the value of being yourself, the value of public service.

I watched the comings and goings on the second floor in the days that followed John's death: the plotting, the deal-making. It was clear to me then, and is even clearer now, that both Tony and Gordon should have stood. The party would then have made up its mind. I don't believe a head to head campaign would have let in another candidate, nor would it have been acrimonious. The Tony Blair, John Prescott, Margaret Beckett campaign that went ahead was carried out in a fraternal spirit.

When Tony's campaign was up and running he needed extra help. I was keen to be part of our big push for power and saw in Tony someone with the ideas, vision and, most of all, the courage to make it happen. Working with David Miliband I wrote a speech on social security which had the line, which now seems blindingly obvious, but at the time was cutting edge: 'High welfare bills are not a sign of socialist success but of economic failure.' It was an article of faith that Labour wanted to spend more on benefits, so for Tony to say we want

49

welfare bills down because we want people in work not on benefits was radical. I remember sitting on the floor of his cramped office in June 1994, discussing the speech with him, and being struck by his energy and determination to transform the Labour party. He was a huge dynamic force willing the Labour party forwards.

On the strength of that New Labour speech and my help on others, as well as some press office duties, Tony offered me a job. On a trip to his Sedgefield constituency he turned to me and said he would like me to work for him permanently. I was sorry to leave Donald but delighted with this new opportunity. I knew it was going to be an exhilarating run-up to the election.

The first sign of the new world I was entering was the office pager. It was to be attached to my waist for the next ten years (except at night when it went on my bedside table). Whenever its high-pitched beeping went off I would have an initial shudder, fearing the worst. Would it be an impending scandal, a speech that had backfired, a politician in trouble? That pager was a constant and unwavering source of anxiety. When I finally handed it in as I left Number 10, it was with a euphoric sense of relief. A mobile phone does not, for some inexplicable reason, have quite the same ability to terrorise.

I started as a member of the Office of the Leader of the Opposition, but like any novice I had a few teething troubles. In Bristol on a regional tour we were visiting the workshop of Nick Park, the creator of Wallace and Gromit. Good imagery we thought. Very popular, very middle England. I was on the look-out for photo opportunities. We also wanted a picture that could be used by the national, not just the regional, papers. There was a model of Wallace and Gromit's living room. It had a large window on one side. I suggested to Tony that he poked his head through the window so that he was effectively on the set. I got Anji to agree to the idea and we managed to persuade Tony, who was normally very cautious about these things, to go along with it. Sure enough, the picture was a sensation. It filled page 3 of the *Mail*: Tony grinning from ear to ear on the Wallace and Gromit set. I went up to Peter Mandelson, the following day, expecting straight 'A's from the professor of presentation He looked at me with one of his sarcastic snarls and said: 'Tony Blair is attempting to become Prime Minister; he is not auditioning to be a game show host.'

No photo opportunity ever quite matched that one for cheesiness, though I did get Tony to wear a jelly hat going round a Kit-Kat factory and have 1,000 tennis balls rain down on him for the *Western Mail*. Later I learnt that pictures should also carry a message. Novelty is not necessarily a good thing in its own right.

On another trip I was taught a second lesson. On the way out to Cornwall one day I was in what can only be described as like a sofa in the sky. It was a tiny aircraft – some kind of RAF machine. I hate flying, and Tony was feeling a little shaky too. It was Anji who came to the rescue, sitting between us, comforting us both. I held her hand most of the way, I recall. In the middle of the flight the RAF man left his cockpit and came towards us, rummaged in a cupboard at the back and handed us a Mars bar and some peanuts: in-flight hospitality. He then, to our relief, sat back down again, at the controls. On the return flight, we went on a small commercial airline but by this time I was hugely apprehensive and, when the plane prepared to make a landing on the way home, nerves got the better of me and I protested loudly, saying that this was pointless as probably nobody was going to get off.

The one person who did get off was sitting behind us and heard the conversation. He wrote to Tony Blair:

Dear Mr Blair,

I was returning from a business trip of the Middle East on the 16/2/96 when you and your group joined the BA flight from Plymouth.

It was extremely disturbing to hear the comments of the gentleman with you regarding the fact that the aircraft was routed to Newquay – its normal pattern. To state 'probably only one person will get off here' was extremely naïve, the impression given was one of failing to recognise the importance of Cornwall – unfortunately all too familiar. I trust you appreciate the importance of Cornwall. I believe that our country needs a change of Government. My concern is that even if a change takes place Cornwall will remain isolated. Are you able to offer me any words of comfort?

Tony replied with many words of comfort and I learnt the need for discretion – you are always on show – and I carried that forward into government.

No one should underestimate the will to win at that time, nor the fear of losing again. Common to all the modernisers in the Labour party were the scars caused by battles with the Left – including Militant – in the Eighties. For this generation, Labour was a party that lost elections spectacularly, that disregarded the views of the electorate, that had a series of unpalatable, extreme, often suicidal policies and that was crucified by the newspapers, fairly in the past but unfairly in the case of Neil Kinnock. For this generation – and particularly those who stuck with Labour rather than joining the newly formed SDP – their political life was consumed with the painful process begun by Neil Kinnock to haul Labour back from oblivion.

Today, with Labour dominating British politics and in power already for several years, that world is beginning to fade in the memory, but understanding the psychological imprint on the minds of Tony and Gordon is crucial to understanding their actions in government. In the eyes of this generation the Labour party had been like a restaurant that had poisoned its guests. The effect of the Winter of Discontent, the piles of rubbish, the dead not buried, the economic incompetence, the high taxes, the unilateral disarmament policy, was to poison the electoral bloodstream.

Think of that restaurant. If you had come home after what you thought was a good meal and been violently ill for a week, what would make you return? It wouldn't be enough to change the menu; you might be a little convinced by a health certificate in the window, but not very; you might be curious if they started cooking different food, Italian maybe instead of French; but would you believe the conversion to be genuine? A new chef might do the trick, but would he just be a new front-man producing the same dangerous food? In the end a combination of new chef, new menu, redesigned restaurant, opened under a new name would be needed, and even then you would only consider it at the point when you were getting bored or had been turned off the other restaurants on the high street. But what about the few loyal regulars who stuck by the restaurant through thick and thin, would they still come to eat at the revamped one? Or would they see the restaurant as being too different? They would need some reassurance that the same homely values and family atmosphere remained, despite all the changes. As for the restaurant itself, despite its picking up customers and becoming more successful, the self-confidence might not return. The lurking fear would remain, that one of the oysters would be off, that an out-of-date prawn or contaminated burger could at any point start a new bout of poisoning.

This is how Tony saw the Labour party. That others saw, instead of poisoning, merely a case of mild indigestion, a one-off error, baffled him. Others were softer on Labour's failings because they came from Labour families, they were instinctively Labour, they gave Labour the benefit of the doubt. Tony didn't. He combined real respect and affection for the Labour party that he saw in Trimdon, in his Sedgefield constituency, with a complete lack of sentimentality about the party in general. That allowed him to do whatever was needed to make it electable once more. As long as Tony was leader, the Labour Party would be sensible and cautious. We would never again have penal tax rates, never again take risks with the economy, never again be weak on defence, never again pander to the unions, never again be anti-business or anti-market or anti-entrepreneurship. These were acts of faith: Blair beliefs that were non-negotiable. They were the tramlines on which a future Blair government would operate. Tony would never again let the Tories be the party of ambition. He would not let Labour represent a rainbow coalition of the poor and dispossessed, minorities and factions, whilst having nothing to say to the vast swathes of Britain who saw themselves as middle class or well on the way to becoming so.

The goal was clear at this time and it was a goal that was shared amongst all the key players. Unlike in government where there are competing objectives, there was only one objective: get into power. Without power, we could put none of our principles into practice.

The way to do it, we believed, was to move Labour ruthlessly to the centre ground and steal back the clothes we had lost to the Tories. No raid was too audacious. The family, why was that a Tory issue? Three days after becoming Leader, Tony did an interview with Brian Walden in which he said: 'Do I believe that it is best, it is easiest, that kids are brought up in a normal stable family? The answer is yes, I do believe that.' He went on to say: 'Can I tell you what is extraordinary is the degree to which people have ended up associating the Left with certain thoughts that are a million miles away from ordinary people.' I had gone with him to the interview and had agreed with what he had said, but was very worried by his use of the word 'normal' which I thought was inflammatory and would create headlines which he might not have wanted. In the car on the way back he was momentarily worried before saying: 'I said what I believed.'

The actions we took – the wooing of the newspapers, the crafting of policy, the people Tony met, the relationship with business – were all about us moving to the centre ground. I remember the excitement of placing tough crime or welfare stories in our target newspapers – the *Sun* or the *Mail* or the *Sunday Times*. I helped to organise a business tour of the country, where Tony spoke to every regional Chamber of Commerce and CBI at business breakfasts. The message was the same in every place. Labour has changed; you don't need to fear us any more; we can do business together.

Tony was the master at stealing Tory clothes and Tory territory, but he needed a big symbol that the party had changed for good. He found two. The first was to get rid of Clause 4 of the Labour Party constitution. The second was to change the Party's name.

History was made in Tony's bedroom on a Sunday in June 1994. After weeks of putting it off, he got down to rewriting Clause 4 of the Labour party constitution himself. Kathryn, Tony's daughter, was having a party downstairs, so we were banished upstairs. I had worked with David Miliband on potential words. Alastair Campbell and Derry Irvine had suggested other alternatives, the former's populist, the latter's legalistic. Tony was determined to do two things: write a successful ethical statement for the main clause and produce sufficiently pro-market sentences for the subsequent paragraphs to demonstrate New Labour's conversion from nationalisation to a sensible economic policy. Tony's clause ended up being eighty-three words. I attempted to do one in roughly the same number as the existing wording – 50-odd – but he felt his was more personal and what he wanted to say: 'By our common endeavour we achieve more together than we can alone.' My contribution to the paragraph was 'power, wealth and opportunity in the hands of the many not the few'. I remember Barbara Castle saying that she could live with the new Clause 4 because of this phrase, because she said it was truly radical and what the party stood for. I'm not sure Tony saw this as the kind of endorsement he was expecting.

On the Clause 4 tour that followed, I spent hours on the road with Tony in working men's clubs and halls, where he was trying to win over the party to this symbolic but dramatic change. We would stop his chauffeur-driven car on the way home, at about 10.30 at night at a fish and chip shop, and completely startle the owner who wasn't quite sure if it really was Tony Blair. Then we would stink the car out with a pungent fish and vinegar smell as we talked about whether the party was coming round to the new Clause 4. Tony would always begin by saying: 'They're turning, they're turning. I've always said they just need to hear a decent argument and they will be convinced.' Tony believed that if he was out round the country working hard, giving his explanation, he could convince the party of anything. The party members were persuadable because they too knew this was our last hope of getting back to power. These were happy times, before the pressures of office, the huge army of civil servants and the machinery of government – just a small band of believers trying to make things happen.

Those meetings also made me realise that those who oppose

change use all kinds of excuses rather than just saying they don't agree. On the Clause 4 tour, I was amazed by the number of members who didn't debate the issue but attacked the process. 'It's being rushed through.' 'You're not allowing us the chance to amend it.' 'It's unconstitutional to do it in this way.' 'You're by-passing party conference.'

At the Clause 4 conference at the Methodist Central Hall in Westminster, I had my first major speech panic. I had got the speech on disk and had given it to the woman who did the autocue – but the autocue wasn't working. I started shouting at anyone I could see that we had to get it mended immediately. The problem was sorted, but my outburst had not made me many friends. This was the speech where for the one and only time I experienced the meaning of the phrase 'go weak at the knees'. I was so nervous about it, so nervous that the bits I had done would be wrong or not work, that as I was listening to Tony speak to a packed hall, my knees buckled. They crumpled and I thought I would fall over. I saw Alastair give me a stare as if I was going slightly mad. I improved as the speech went on and eventually became used to watching Tony speak.

The new Clause 4 was a clear statement of one of Tony's two big ideas: community; the other being modernisation. Tony believed that the problems of society were at least in part down to 'too much taking and not enough giving'; too many rights, but few obligations in return. He believed in this passionately as the way to rebuild social solidarity which was core to both his Christian beliefs and what the country needed. He also believed that the Labour party needed to return to its ethical roots. Ends mattered more than means. The added benefit was that it allowed us to reconnect with centrist opinion formers for whom 'values, standards, knowing right from wrong' mattered.

In the wake of the death of the small boy Jamie Bulger, caused by two other children, Tony had written a speech in which he expressed passionately his view of community. 'Self-respect is in part derived from respect for others, the notion that we are not just buyers and sellers in some market place, or individuals set in isolation, but that we are members of a community that owes obligations to others as well as ourselves and that depend on others to succeed and prosper.' He saw common endeavour, community, as the best way of fulfilling individual aspiration. I remember having a lengthy debate with him in which I argued that solidarity or community was not just a means to an end but an end in itself. Meaning in life comes from family, friends, social interaction, doing good to others. The age-old debate between political philosophies comes down to this. Are humans instinctively individualistic as the Right would have it, looking after their own? Or are they intrinsically social beings, acting together, to survive? Whilst community as an idea often appeared vague, in government it resulted in a fundamental change in approach – a new contract between citizen and state – something for something. So the New Deal, for example, gave the unemployed five options and the individual had to choose one of them or lose their benefits.

Tony's most powerful idea, though, is modernisation. This is what really animates him. Modernisation is to Blair what privatisation was to Thatcher. Privatisation was her way of resolving what she saw as the great problem facing Britain in 1979, the over-powerful intrusive state in hock to the unions and outdated ideology. 'State versus market' was her battle. What Tony saw, eighteen years on, despite her revolution in the private sector, were a series of unmodernised and outdated institutions: the constitution, the Criminal Justice System, the NHS, comprehensives. For him 'old versus new' was the great divide. For the Labour party this meant transformation from old to new Labour. For the country it meant moving from an old to a new Britain.

Tony hates sentimentality. He does not believe that tradition is a good enough reason to defend anything. It has to be justified today on its own terms. Whether it's Clause 4 of Labour's constitution or trial by jury he does not believe that tradition should be preserved if it gets in the way of results. However, it was hard for us to be too explicit about this goal, because 'old Britain' had more supporters than 'the state' had when Thatcher launched her assault, for most of us want to blend the old with the new. We want to celebrate our great history and traditions whilst carving out a new role for the country. In other words old Britain was not nearly as unpopular as old Labour.

The other problem with modernisation, as many of us kept telling Tony, was that it lacked values. Modernisation was a word that Left or Right could be equally comfortable with. Tony's response was that we were modernising 'for all the people', whilst our opponents favoured the 'few'.

So, going into the election we had a surfeit of themes: community and modernisation from Tony; Gordon was driving forward on his opportunity agenda; the new Clause 4 included our aim 'to put power, wealth and opportunity into the hands of the many and not the few'. Each was powerful, and none inconsistent, but it was a challenge to weave them into a coherent whole, and in government a greater challenge when the same messages had to make sense of hundreds of government initiatives.

What we were creating, though we didn't realise it at the time, was a party with strong appeal in the country, but few supporters amongst opinion formers. For the Left we were abandoning some deeply held attachments. For the Right we were stealing their clothes. But in the country a party that attempted to combine enterprise and fairness was the party the public had craved for generations. Tony didn't tire of quoting Maurice Saatchi's comment that the choice historically was between the Conservatives who were cruel but efficient and

Labour which was caring but incompetent. Tony thought that it was not beyond a party to be both responsible with your money and compassionate to those most in need.

This New Labour position, even eight years later, caused Tony much vexation. What he saw as a commonsense new position was still being carped at from all sides. He was to write a private note in 2002 which he then turned into a speech that showed his anger and frustration. Some of us felt it was a bit defensive, but it came from the heart and defined his politics:

> There is still a sense that New Labour confuses people, even those in our own ranks. Even now a large part of the political discourse in Britain assumes that the true Labour party is one that puts trade unions before business, is indifferent to financial discipline, addicted to tax and spend, is liberal on issues of crime, generous in state benefits for the unemployed or socially excluded, backs the producer interest in public services and is, give or take the odd exception, pacifist in defence and foreign policy. Since this government is plainly none of these things, ergo, we are not real Labour and are 'unprincipled'.
>
> This of course suits the right-wing in politics. They love the true Labour party. Its positions made it unelect-able. But it also suits many on the Left. It is the Labour party as pressure group. We campaign against those with the power. We fight for these positions, rejoice in our principles, are given the odd crumb from the governing table and avoid the harsh realities of sitting at the table and taking decisions. We changed all these positions after eighteen years of Conservative government. I am not so naïve as to deny many changed them to win. Banging your head on a brick wall hurts. At some point if you want to stop hurting you devise the brilliant solution of

ceasing to bang your head on the wall. But changing these positions to win was never the right reason for changing them, nor can it sustain us over the long term. The right reason for change was a principled one.Those positions, hallowed by the party over many years, were a tangled and mistaken view of the party's raison d'être and values.

I shared much of Tony's frustration, but I had fewer hang-ups about old Labour. That was the advantage of being younger. My generation had not fought Militant. I had none of the scars from the internal Labour battles of the Eighties. My political antennae were less obsessed with the iniquities of old Labour, though I was as determined to make Labour electable. I was not in awe of the Tories as some clearly still were. The Tory party I saw was one that went out of control under Thatcher, and was now disintegrating under Major. Given what was stacked against the Labour party – including some hugely effective Tory news-papers – I believed we had to get rid of any inferiority complex that New Labour had not yet swept away. As the election approached I focused my attention on two things: our offer to the people, and a sustained attack on what a Tory fifth term might do to the country.

It struck me that New Labour needed something tangible to offer the British people. Vague promises wouldn't do. We were always up against simple and powerful messages from the Tories that had real emotional pull: tax cuts, tough on crime, anti-Europe. What was Labour offering? The far-away promise of better public services? Stronger communities? The public needed measurable symbolic policies. What was striking, when you talked to the public in focus groups, was that what seemed small to the com-mentators and opinion formers seemed substantial and relevant to the public. So I devised the pledge card with its five costed pledges: cutting class sizes, cutting waiting lists, punishing young offenders, getting 250,000 unemployed back to work, and economic stability – each of them showing a key priority, then explaining how we would pay for them. This was our offer to the people.

I was equally aggressive at wanting us to land blows on the Tories. The big decision when attacking your opponents in politics is whether to go for their past record or their future threat. It was always tempting to talk about the past, because that had happened and was provable. In the case of the Tories: the poll tax, three million unemployed, boom and bust, negative equity. What *might* happen was based on quotes and policy documents and open to more doubt. Yet people voted prospectively, so we decided the key was to make the past record into a future threat.

Gordon, with Harriet Harman, had been attacking the Tories relentlessly on their 'twenty-two tax rises' and in particular the imposition of VAT on fuel – 'The elderly having to choose between being hungry or cold'. We had made our promises not to raise the standard or top rate of tax. I now wanted people to understand the risk that came from a fifth Tory term. The Tories had attacked us with their Demon Eyes poster, a picture of evil eyes surrounded by red velvet proclaiming 'New Labour, New Danger'. They were playing heavily on people's fears that after eighteen years that Labour was still a risk. Yet because the Tories were doing badly, no one in the media was giving a thought to what might happen if the Tories got back. I wanted an attack that brought this to light. After all, if the Tories got back after the ERM disaster and all the sleaze they would assume they could never lose. 'They would stop at nothing,' in the words of our campaign.

Given the quotes the Attack Unit had dug up at Millbank, we believed we could make the charge stick that the Tories, and in particular Ken Clarke, would put VAT on food if they got back in. Working with our advertising agency we devised a poster of two hands crushing an egg – I thought it looked more like someone dripping with oil but I lost that battle – with the caption 'Last time VAT on fuel, next time VAT on food'. Gordon didn't like it. He thought that when he had to defend the poster in the media there would not be enough evidence to stand up for the attack. He didn't want to have to withdraw it. In the end we agreed on a question mark after 'VAT on food' to show we weren't certain. The poster caused hurried meetings between Clarke and Major to decide whether to rule out all future VAT increases, which they failed to do. The fifth term attack continued during the campaign itself, and was vital to us gaining a bigger majority.

There have been few more successful transformations of any organisation than the change from old to new Labour. Why was it so successful? Because, to use the jargon, the 'burning plat-form' was in place. The party knew that the old ways wouldn't do. There was also a single, united goal that linked everyone and created a will to win. Tony was good at Opposition. He worked out immediately that it was not about opposing, but being a government in waiting. For the first time in its history a Labour leader was not trying to balance factions as Attlee, Wilson, Callaghan and John Smith had done. Instead Tony was saying, 'Modernise or die.' People knew and believed there was no alternative.

It's easy to forget now that, despite all the reassurance, despite our bee-line to the centre ground, despite the change of name, large numbers of people were still wary of the Labour party before 1997. It's easy too to forget how many of our new supporters were voting Blair in 1997 rather than Labour. Newspaper columnists, editors and business leaders, mainstream opinion in general, all made the same point: 'We're voting for Tony Blair and not the Labour party. We trust Tony, but we're not sure of the rest.' What people now see as the deliberate attempt to make Tony into a presidential figure or to carve out other members of the Shadow Cabinet was not the intention. What we all knew, and were being told, was that Tony was the great asset; Tony had the star quality. It was as if, after eighteen years of the Tories and the grey years of Major's government, people were desperate for a young dynamic leader to make politics colourful again, and make people believe again.

These exciting years came to a head at the Festival Hall on 1 May as all those who had helped on this campaign and past campaigns, our new supporters and old, gathered for an extraordinary celebration. There was huge relief that we had done it. I and so many others had never quite believed it was possible. Just five years ago I was in Iowa, not taking any part in an election campaign, knowing none of the players, having no political training or skills. Just five years ago the political world was asking whether Labour would ever win again. Now I was working for a man who an hour earlier had been phoned up by John Major and congratulated for winning the biggest political prize.

I had no idea then quite how much those focused, tense, often draining Opposition years, creating New Labour, getting elected, were just the easy bit. Far harder, we were to discover, was creating a New Britain.

# THE BIG TIME

I never expected to work at Number 10. At the back of my mind I was convinced that when the time came, when we finally won the election, Tony would have a different set of people, older and wiser, ready to take over. I couldn't believe that I would one day be walking through the most famous front door in the country and working at the centre of power.

Like thousands of tourists, shut out by the iron gates of Downing Street, I had only ever seen Number 10 briefly in the distance. I could never quite see the house and assumed it was on the left-hand side. The first shock on 2 May 1997, as I joined the throng of party workers lining the street, was that it was in fact on the right. The second surprise was that there were no numbers 1 to 9, just Number 10, Number 11 for the Chancellor and Number 12 for the Chief Whip. I stood there drained and disorientated, having left the Festival Hall celebrations only three hours earlier. I was bewildered by the size of the victory, a swing of 10 per cent to Labour, a 179 majority – the biggest ever, with the Tories getting their lowest share of the vote since 1832.

I remembered phoning Alastair Campbell in Tony's Sedgefield

constituency at 11 o'clock the night before, after the exit polls had suggested a landslide, crowing at the size of the victory. Alastair seemed to be in a deep gloom and told me in no uncertain terms that there were strict orders from Tony not to be complacent.

As Tony and Cherie made their way up Downing Street to the acclaim of hundreds of party workers – Cherie gave me a big hug when she saw me – the change in the Labour party, the upheaval that had created New Labour and ditched Old Labour seemed vindicated. Now I saw first-hand the extraordinary continuity of the British constitution. In Number 10 the civil servants who had served John Major for six years had to welcome Tony Blair as their new leader. There were many in the building quite understandably in tears as they watched their former boss depart. As I was to discover, Number 10 is an intensely intimate place where everyone pulls together in good times and bad. For someone like Alison Blackshaw in the press office, who had admired and personally liked John Major, it was an extraordinarily emotional change. To become within a few hours Alastair Campbell's personal assistant even though he had done more than almost anybody to bring down John Major, was heroic on her part.

I was not formally offered a job at Number 10. As polling day got closer, I started to think about the future, but like others in the office never dared raise the issue with Tony in case it looked presumptuous. Now I assumed I had a job because I was told there would be an introduction to Number 10 first thing in the morning.

When I first entered the Cabinet room, with its huge coffin-shaped table, specially designed so that ministers at each end can see each other when they speak, I suddenly realised how much my life had changed. The only chair with arms is the Prime Minister's in the centre, facing towards the garden, under a portrait of Sir Robert Walpole. Tony was on his own and stood up. I thought it would be the chance to congratulate him properly on his astonishing victory, to reminisce about the campaign. Tony was having none of it. He doesn't dwell. He moves on. That was behind him. It was as if a huge chore had been completed and the real business was now at hand. He started talking about the first actions he would take, the first speeches he would give, the proposed changes to Prime Minister's Questions in the Commons. As he had said on the steps of Number 10: 'Enough of talking. It is time now to do.'

For me, doing meant getting security clearance, getting to know the building, carving out a job for myself. There were lots of rules to learn, such as how to classify documents: top secret, secret, confidential, restricted or nothing and what those levels all meant. Number 10 was split up into distinct units. The private office sat closest to the Prime Minister and was where the private secretaries, the key civil servants, co-ordinated government business. The duty clerks were in charge of the flow of papers coming in and out of the private office. The parliamentary section answered parliamentary questions from backbenchers and helped the PM prepare for Prime Minister's Questions. The correspondence section dealt with the mail, which tripled when Tony became PM. The political office, paid for by the party, liaised with Millbank, backbenchers and the unions. The policy unit on the second floor devised policy and liaised with departments. The press office dealt with the media in general and the political lobby in particular.

The secretaries working in two basement rooms overlooking the Number 10 garden were known as the 'garden room girls', ever since Lloyd George introduced the typing pool eighty years earlier, and this was a term that most of us found patronising and sexist. We were determined to get rid of it, but in true democratic style asked them to decide and put it to the vote. Almost unanimously they voted to retain the name. The tradition counted for more than the actual words – perhaps a lesson for us. Despite the vote, in the years I was at Number 10 I could not bring myself to call highly professional secretaries 'girls'.

I had spent the last few months in the war-room of Millbank Tower, an open plan office where, around the central war-room table – along with Peter Mandelson, Philip Gould, Alastair Campbell and Margaret McDonagh, then the General Secretary of the Labour Party – we had plotted the election. Then, we could all communicate with each other rapidly, but now many of us were being despatched to different corners of Number 10. Some remained at Millbank. Others were going into different departments. The winning team was being broken up. That team spirit would never be recreated in government, though we fleetingly came back together at the next election.

My world was changing. I was not yet thirty but this was the big time. Everything we did made news. Any stray comment could cause trouble. When we left Number 10 for lunch we would be walking on to millions of TV screens around the world as reporters did their pieces to camera in front of the door. (For those who wonder how the Number 10 door remains permanently shiny I discovered that there are in fact three Number 10 doors, which are rotated every six months or so: the door you can see, a second door that is being cleaned, repaired or painted and a third door that is 'available for tours'. Though what kind of audience a black door attracts in theatres round Britain is hard to guess.)

I read through the pamphlet we were given about Number 10:

Number 10 is much larger than it looks from the outside. It is in fact two buildings – an 18th century town house, the original 10 Downing Street, on the street front and at the back a former grace and favour residence facing

Horseguards. The two were joined in 1735 when George II gave the royal residence to Robert Walpole as First Lord of the Treasury. Over the years the original design has been added to, not always logically with the result that the house can be a confusing place for newcomers. 10 Downing Street serves as the office of the Prime Minister and his residence during the week, as well as being a public building used for a variety of state functions hosted by the Prime Minister. Most of the furniture in the public rooms belongs to the house and much of it is extremely valuable. Many of the pictures are on loan from national museums and galleries and from the Government Art Collection.

This was the official description. The unofficial one came from Number 10's previous occupants many of whom seemed to loathe the building. Margot, wife of H.H. Asquith, Prime Minister from 1908 to 1916, described it as: 'an inconvenient house with three poor staircases . . . liver-coloured and squalid.'

The staircase that led to the state rooms, lined with black and white photographs of former Prime Ministers – donated when they leave office – gave me a privileged glimpse of Britain's extraordinary history. Those pictures never lost their excitement and power, however many times I was to ascend those stairs in the coming years. However, I also came to feel another emotion, an unease at the formal hierarchical world of the British establishment. There was an otherworldly quality in a lot of what we heard and saw, in stark contrast to the informality of Opposition. Robin Butler, the Cabinet Secretary, amused David Miliband on day one with his proud comment that 'The Cabinet Room is now fitted with all the latest mod cons,' as he gestured to a telephone on a side table.

Number 10 is a bizarre place to work. It has a hundred rooms and is a listed building – a country house masquerading as the centre of power, genteel state rooms side by side with functional office spaces. At any one time a state room could be occupied by the Prime Minister going global in a press conference on Iraq, while in the next room a routine meeting on transport policy was being carried out. Many meetings are, rather surreally, disturbed by the tunes of regimental bands practising on Horseguards Parade, just behind Number 10. There is something very English, almost amateurish about the idea that the country – and at one time of course the Empire – can be run from an eighteenth-century terraced house, on a cul de sac in Westmintser. One American visitor, who was familiar with the White House, remarked cuttingly, 'There is not exactly a buzz about this place.' Indeed, with people working away in the small offices around the building, there is quite often an eerie calm, cut off from the rest of government, cut off from the country, cut off from the people.

I was soon sitting in one of the grand state rooms having my security interview, perched on a gold-leafed chair with a green silk cushion, a Persian rug on the floor, portraits of distinguished looking men on the walls, a hefty chandelier sparkling from the ceiling. Opposite me was a slightly scruffy security services man, or so I thought, but I later found out he was a retired policeman – I imagine because he was cheaper. The interview seemed to be going well. My relatives had cleared the first hurdle. None were blackballed as terrorists; those that were foreign had been allowed through. And in response to a searching question about any drink problems I might have, I convinced him that I would spend little time in Westminster pubs blurting out state secrets for kicks. Then he looked up with a knowing curl on his lip.

'Ah ha,' he said, as if he was Hercule Poirot piecing together an Agatha Christie mystery. 'Jewish,' he said – followed by a pause long enough for me to take in the seriousness of the charge. 'Have you ever visited Israel?'

'No, actually I haven't,' I said.

He ploughed on regardless. 'Well you know,' he said in a menacing voice, 'You can't serve two masters at once.'

With this kind of attitude it's no wonder the civil service is not noted for its diverse intake.

Others were in for similarly probing questions, but he met his match with Alastair. 'Would you ever hand over government information to the press?' the security man asked.

'Yes,' Alastair replied. 'Tony pays me to do so.'

The security check out of the way, it was time to work out where to sit. The advice from previous occupants of Number 10 was always to be on the ground floor. That way you were close to the action. I straddled communications, policy and political strategy. I started sharing a room with Head of Policy David Miliband, but later I moved to the room next to Alastair's.

The government began with a string of bold announcements, the Bank of England was given independence, in the first Budget VAT on fuel was cut as promised. Devolution was underway, the minimum wage would soon be in place, assisted places in schools were being scrapped so that class sizes could be cut. I was proud to be at Number 10 enacting policies I believed would help millions of people.

Meanwhile, however, special advisers were coming under sustained attack. There are good and bad special advisers. Occasionally one does something stupid or thinks he has a view that is worth expressing even though it does not correspond to the ministers he works for. This always leads to disaster, but the vast majority know they are there to serve the minister who employs them. For all the charges of being unelected, and unaccountable, advisers are there to carry out the democratic wishes of the people. From the Left's point of view, indeed from any point of view, it seems daft not to want political advisers to implement the agenda the public has voted for. There are seventy or eighty of them compared with hundreds of thousands of civil servants. That's not many. And bizarrely Ministers of State are not even allowed political advisers. In America there are thousands of political appointments, in France and Germany hundreds. The point is that you need political people to interpret and help deliver the manifesto on which you were elected. That seems to me commonsense.

However, the two cultures – political advisers and civil servants – clashed at first. This was not, as some have seen it, a battle between the political and the non-political. In that battle the civil service almost always won. The story, contrary to popular myth, of the government has been the depoliticisation of ministers and advisers (who become administrators and managers rather than political advocates), more than the politicisation of the civil service. No, instead what we saw was a clash between the modern and the outdated, between the fast-moving, flexible working conditions we had developed in Opposition and what we saw as the often reactive methods of the civil service.

I had grown up respecting the civil service as a great British institution, the people who made British government run smoothly and worked professionally whatever the circumstances. This view had been dented only slightly when I became a civil servant briefly myself in my gap year between school and university. I joined the Department for Education and Science as it then was, based in Elizabeth House in Waterloo, under the leadership of a dynamic Secretary of State, Kenneth Baker. I was on the bottom rung of the ladder, an 'AA', administrative assistant. My job was to collate, and then reply to, comments from teachers and educationalists on the consultation on the national curriculum, a new initiative from the Conservative Government – comments like 'Why is Latin not a core subject?', 'Why is history being crowded out?', 'Why is the curriculum so prescriptive?' Headteachers were, I assume, unaware that an eighteen-year-old was replying to their heartfelt concerns. In my first week in the job, I was bustling down a corridor, delivering a memo to another office, when I was stopped by one of my superiors, taken to one side and told: 'You'll learn soon enough we don't rush around here, you'll show up the rest of us.'

Number 10 has the pick of high flying civil servants who are seconded from departments across Whitehall. So those at Number 10 are some of the best, those like Jeremy Heywood, Godric Smith, Stephen Wall, Sharon White and many others who were creative, highly professional and hardworking. The civil service as a whole, however, was stuck firmly in the approaches of the past. What we discovered in 1997 was not the Rolls-Royce service of popular myth but an organisation ill-equipped to deal with the demands of a fast changing world. Civil servants were still being recruited with far too narrow a set of skills. There were few project managers which meant that many government IT projects ran into the ground and wasted vast amounts of tax payers' money. There were few civil servants skilled at drawing up contracts with the private sector which meant that in public finance initiative and other deals government often got a raw deal. Few departments had modern communication departments able to understand the views of the public or communicate adequately with frontline staff. Most surprisingly, some departments had no writers who could draft parliamentary statements, ministerial speeches or articles.

The best civil servants had to wait their turn, and go through excessive, hierarchical hoops, before being allowed senior jobs. Most civil servants moved jobs so frequently within departments they were never held accountable for delivering anything. Success was measured by any criteria other than the one that mattered: delivery. There was huge resistance to outsiders coming into the civil service, yet some of our best successes proved to be when outsiders and existing civil servants worked together in teams. One glaring anomaly was the division of the civil service into two separate bodies, the diplomatic service and the home civil service. Why on earth shouldn't a good Treasury civil servant be able to apply to be a Foreign Office official? The answer from the diplomatic service was that being a diplomat required special skills that only Foreign Office officials could perform. This was plainly nonsense.

Civil servants seemed to have equal reservations about us. We were informal. We had all worked together for many years. We knew what Tony wanted. We hated process and bureaucracy, which at times counted against us. They would play the long game, knowing that we would need their help navigating the system. They would point out, discreetly of course, that not since Ramsay Macdonald in 1924 had a Prime Minister entered Number 10 without several years' ministerial experience.

There was tension at first. The policy unit advisers knew the ministers well. They could phone them up and deal directly with them. That put them in a strong position. Private secretaries found this difficult as they liked to know everything and do things with greater formality. They tended to write their own little notes on the top of papers the policy unit sent to the Prime Minister. This caused a lot of irritation, but it settled down after a while. In the end both advisers and civil servants needed each other. Civil servants wanted the political insight of special advisers. Special advisers, new to Whitehall, needed to know how to get things done. There was rarely an occasion at Number 10 when the relationship broke down.

There is a healthy debate amongst political scientists and historians about the strength of Number 10, the desirability of creating a Prime Minister's department, and whether the British Prime Minister has become presidential. On one level I side with those who, like Asquith, say that the job of Prime Minister, because there are very few formal powers, is what you make of it. There have been weak Prime Ministers and strong ones. Some, like Attlee, have acted as chairman of a talented cabinet. Others, like Thatcher, always lead from the front. For the ten or so people closest to Tony, the debate was about whether we were more effective as a tightly-knit unit or whether we really gained by building up the capacity of Number 10. What I am in no doubt about is that the federal structure of British government with departments acting as independent fiefdoms, but where the PM's head is on the line for every failure, is unsustainable. Like any chief executive, the PM needs to be in control.

The first big meeting we started to prepare for was a policy unit away day at Chequers to thrash out the policy direction of the government. There was excitement that this was going to be our first trip to the Prime Minister's country residence. A note went round from the garden rooms to say:

## CHEQUERS: FRIDAY 11 JULY 1997

The Prime Minister has requested if everyone could please bring a pair of trainers (no boots) with them to have a game of football tomorrow.

The twelve or so members of the policy unit, led by David Miliband, who combined intellectual rigour with principle and boundless energy, travelled down in a convoy of government cars. It takes about an hour to get to Chequers, forty miles north west of London in Buckinghamshire. A house has stood on the same land since Roman times, but the present redbrick building dates from 1565. It is a beautiful setting for a country retreat, rolling hills and canopies of trees. As we approached the gravel drive entrance armed guards approached the car and asked for all our names. We were welcomed at the door by the housekeeper and shown in to an extraordinary high-ceilinged living room. The walls were adorned with gloomy portraits. There was a grand piano. Along one side ran a balcony where the bedrooms were. Winston Churchill described the place as 'a panelled museum full of history, full of treasures . . . but insufficiently warmed'. A naval officer in blue uniform with blue and white striped neckpiece offered us tea and coffee. A few minutes later Tony arrived looking relaxed in jeans and a shirt. 'Let's get going,' he said, and we traipsed upstairs to the main meeting room which overlooked the grounds. Tony loves Chequers and it's easy to see why. If Number 10 sometimes appears cut off from reality, Chequers is a different world. Sitting in the rose garden at the back, the sun shining, the swimming pool – added by Ted Heath in the Seventies – it is easy to see how a Prime Minister under siege might never want to return to Westminster.

Geoff Mulgan – ex-head of the think-tank Demos and then policy unit member in charge of social exclusion – and I were to kick off the session on the instincts of the government, to try to tease out some of the inconsistencies and see whether there could be a logical synthesis. Tony was always up for blunt presentations. He came back strongly when he thought the attacks were unfair. Throughout my time at Number 10 we were always self-critical. We were always working out how we could do things better.

Now, just two months into the government and with the Budget behind us, we all needed to be clear about where policy was heading. At the heart of our presentation was an argument that ran through my entire time at Number 10: 'big tent' on the one hand, 'enemies' on the other. Everyone bought into the big tent strategy in Opposition. Big tent meant trying to hoover up as much support as possible from all sections of society – but would this approach end up pleasing nobody? More than that, wasn't it essential that people knew who you were against, not just who you were for?

In our presentation we asked:

> In the coming months events or our own choices will mean we move one way or the other – pleasing some people, disappointing others. Should we make some of these choices clearer now, so that those speaking for Labour, or civil servants helping us form policy, know with greater certainty which way to jump? More to the point, do we need greater clarity – in order that some of those who put their faith in us now do not feel they have been betrayed later?

We identified four tensions that had already emerged:

> Tension One: Competition versus regulation.
> Where do our instincts lie? In greater competition opening up markets and deregulation, or in regulation that is in the public interest?

> Tension Two: Greater equality versus defending Middle Britain.
> Are we trying to reduce inequalities and target money at those who have the fewest opportunities, the worst schools and the worst hospitals? Or are we defending those in Middle England who supported us for the first time? e.g. What is our attitude to middle-class tax reliefs like Miras?

> Tension Three: Tolerance versus the moral majority.
> Do we believe that people should be free to get on with

their lives or should we uphold traditional values? e.g. Should we support gay marriages? Should we cut benefits to lone parents? If a majority of chief constables supported legalising drugs what would our attitude be? What is our attitude to immigration? How far do we support censorship on the internet?

Tension Four: New settlement versus pragmatic incremental change.

Has Britain had its revolution in the Eighties, so that it now needs a period of incremental change? Or does Britain enter the next century needing a big shake-up?

On each of these tensions we knew Tony would want a way through. He would not want to choose at this stage. He believed that there was a sensible position that could reconcile the two sides. We tried to accommodate this desire for a Third Way.

On competition we said it was possible to be instinctively free market but willing to regulate business when it imposed costs on society as a whole, for example through what it does in relation to skills, the environment or the family.

On equality we were willing to take action on equality but by active measures to create jobs and an approach defined by rights and responsibilities, not by passive redistribution.

On tolerance, Tony had a well-worked-out position: tolerance of personal behaviour but not of anti-social behaviour. What people do in their bedrooms is up to them, but what they do on the street to others, if anti-social, will be dealt with harshly.

On the speed of change we would combine big bold strokes on the constitution with serious long-term incremental change on public services.

These tensions were to remain but Tony had no intention of positioning himself at odds with our newly-won support.

We broke for lunch, again served in the dining room by naval staff in uniforms. Then the next session was a debate of hard strategic choices. What are the options for getting money to health and education? Are we serious about the environment? Do we have the policies to deliver on education reform? By mid-afternoon we were looking forward to the really important matter, the football.

Playing any game against your boss is fraught with danger. Playing football maybe more so. Would tackling the Prime Minister go down badly? We soon realised that Tony was as competitive at football as he was at politics, and befitting someone who had reached the great office of Prime Minister he was a bit of a lone striker. Passing was not his strength. His fast and furious activity left us all standing.

Every leader plays many roles. Getting these roles in balance, realising that people rely on you to be each one of them at different times, is the essence of good leadership. I once tried to categorise the different sides to Tony's premiership:

*The family man*: who is on the side of hardworking families. This is what attracted millions to Tony between 1994 and 1997. He didn't sound like a normal politician. He is a family man with young kids who knows what it is like to live with teenagers, have your house burgled, lead a pretty normal family life. Of all our different pitches to the electorate, 'working hard for hard-working families' was the one that resonated most, but in turn it was the one that was easiest to forget or become distanced from in government.

*The moral reformer*: Tony's modernising zeal was underpinned by strong Christian values. People know that Tony is a Christian but don't know how much it means to him. The reading he loves most is theological texts. I once offered to get him some recent novels for his holiday reading. 'Cherie loves those,' he said. 'I rarely get into them.' Instead he was on to the Number 10 librarian to track down a book that he had been recommended on twelfth-century Christianity. However, as Tony remarked frequently, he doesn't like politicians wearing their religion on their sleeve.

I, on the other hand, believed it was wrong for Tony to be coy about his Christian beliefs. It was important to Tony, and people – Christian or not – would respect that side of him as authentic. Of all the attacks on Tony in the last ten years the one that struck me as least damaging was the 'St Albion vicar preaching to his flock' in *Private Eye*. What this said to me, even if it was being twisted – was here was a man with honest convictions.

Given Tony's post-modern view of politics – what works is what's best – the ethical grounding was essential. To use a phrase he deployed in one of his conference speeches, it gave him his 'irreducible' core, the bottom line of non-negotiable beliefs. My view was harder to sustain in the second term, when George Bush's deployment of religion to justify his world view, and the Republicans' use of the church to 'get out the vote' in the Presidential election, rightly left many in this country even more sceptical about mixing politics and religion too overtly.

*The patriotic statesman*: The British public like having a world statesman as a leader. The cliché is that when a Prime Minister is gallivanting round the world, the public feel he is not concentrating on the issues of most concern to them. There is some truth in that, but the innate patriotism of the British people also comes through when we are intervening for good in the world. In Kosovo, Sierra Leone and Afghanistan, this was definitely the case. The war on Iraq in the second term, and our support for an American president who the British people intensely disliked, was a different story.

*The pragmatic barrister.* Tony is the best political strategist of his generation. He is the master chess player – a logical, rational thinker rather than an emotional one, trying to position each piece in exactly the right place on the board. He would think about business needing a little reassurance about red tape or tax, about backbenchers needing more face to face time, about columnists needing to better understand his reforms, and about making sure the Tories don't get back into the game. Tony has superb antennae for issues that will flare up: he successfully predicted when asylum or crime would take off, and then got frustrated that the warnings he had given to departments were not heeded.

So these are the four sides to Tony Blair as Prime Minister, and what became clear to me as the years passed is that these four sides needed to be in balance. When the first two were downplayed or got lost we were in trouble. When the public thought by our words or actions that we were no longer batting for them, or when the moral zeal of the PM was not shining through, in short when pragmatic barrister Blair took over, we looked unduly cynical and out of touch.

Crucial to strategy was use of the Prime Minister's time, the most vital commodity at Number 10. How that time was divided up consumed a lot of our energies. It was fascinating to learn how former Prime Ministers had spent their day. Gladstone, who in his first administration had just three staff, spent his day on some very familiar items such as meeting Cabinet colleagues and chairing committees. Other duties are less familiar. One was to write a letter to the Queen after

Cabinet meetings. Another was dealing personally with his postbag which was his first task each day. His private secretary Algernon West summed up the role of the Prime Minister as: 'The Prime Minister has everything to do. The Prime Minister has nothing to do.' By his last administration, and in his eighties, Gladstone was spending seven or eight hours a day sitting in the House of Commons chamber listening to and responding to debates.

For Tony Blair each week had a rhythm that despite the unpredictability of events, became familiar and in some senses reassuring. It began on Monday with a 9 a.m. meeting with his closest advisers. Jonathan Powell, Alastair Campbell, Anji Hunter, Pat McFadden, Sally Morgan, David Miliband, Jeremy Heywood the principal private secretary and myself would meet in Tony's den and sit in the armchairs and on the sofas, with Tony in a swivel chair behind his desk on which were photos of the family. On the window sill was a great photo of himself and Nelson Mandela laughing.

The agenda would be based around Tony's weekend notes that he usually wrote at Chequers and were a list of priorities, issues he wanted sorted, or a strong view of what our message should be. The notes were e-mailed or faxed to us on Sunday night so that we were ready for the morning. This meeting at best drove the week's activities. At worst, several years down the line, it would become a bit too familiar – what we all referred to as 'groundhog day'. All of us had different takes or different responsibilities that in theory gave Tony a picture of what was needed. Sally Morgan and Pat McFadden spoke for party concerns. Alastair advocated a more aggressive approach to the media. Chief of Staff Jonathan Powell's job was to bring it all together, which he did with great skill and a flippant, fast-talking manner. Jeremy gave a pragmatic Whitehall perspective, while having strong policy views of his own. David gave the policy implications of what Tony wanted. Anji gave the view of Middle England plus the concerns of some key opinion formers. I attempted to reflect the public's view through polls and focus groups plus a sense of longer-term strategy.

These meetings were sometimes businesslike, getting through Tony's note quickly. On other occasions there were big discussions, for instance on how to tackle the fuel crisis that had brought Britain to a stand-still, or about why we were not given the credit for delivery on the ground. Tony would show his irritation when departments were not on the case on policy despite many times of asking.

At ten o'clock Tony would meet with the Cabinet Secretary. For a brief period it was Robin Butler, then it was Richard Wilson, then more recently Andrew Turnbull. They would discuss key Whitehall blockages, and the necessary changes.

In the second term I would come out of the 9 a.m. meeting and go straight into my own meeting of the Strategic Communications Unit where I filled them in on the PM's view of the current issues so that they were in the picture. We debated how to handle coming events and I got an update on the communication strategies we were deploying in public services, and on Europe in particular.

At eleven there was a party meeting with the Chief Whip, the General Secretary of the Labour party and a few political advisers. At these meetings it was discussed, for instance, whether Ken Livingstone should be expelled from the party (or later reinstated), what the mood was amongst backbenchers, how the party was being organised.

Then for the rest of Monday Tony tended to have back to back meetings, mostly on the key policy areas.

On Tuesday there was usually a focus on public services reform, with, in the first term, bilateral meetings with ministers. In the second term this was formalised into ministerial stocktakes in the four key areas: health, education, crime and transport. In the afternoon there was usually a foreign visitor, a business person to see or meetings with ministers and backbenchers.

Wednesday morning was taken up with preparations for Prime Minister's Questions, which were cut from twice a week to once a week in 1997. In the first term PMQs were at 3 p.m. and so, because Tony didn't like meetings to distract him, almost an entire Prime Ministerial day was taken up in preparation. In the second term PMQs was brought forward to midday which meant that Tony could have meetings in the Commons with backbenchers afterwards. Diary meetings were also on a Wednesday, sometimes chaired by Alastair Campbell, sometimes by Jonathan Powell. These were vital meetings because they allocated Tony's time. I usually produced a strategy so that we weren't responding randomly to requests. We had a lot of bids and a lot of people in the building competing for his time. Every member of the policy unit would want a bit of the action: 'We need a meeting to sort asylum', 'It's time Tony met the CBI because he hasn't for several months', 'Tony needs to keep the green lobby on board; can he pop into a seminar they are holding?', 'We need to get out of London more. When was the last time he was in Manchester?'

There would also be a series of speech bids. I was always of the view that we should decide what we wanted to say and then find a suitable audience. Invariably though we felt we had to agree to some of the bids, such as speaking to the police federation, or a headteachers' conference or the health service managers' annual conference. We would then argue over the balance between private meetings and public appearances. Tony often complained that visits were a waste of time unless they either got big media coverage or he had enough private time to learn something worthwhile.

The bids we were always amused by and that became a

running joke were those from the Foreign Office private secretary. There would be a long list of foreign potentates and in the typical charming Foreign Office way there was always a reason for seeing them. 'The foreign minister of Mozambique is passing through, he's a vital ally in the war on terror.' 'The deputy foreign minister of Peru is stopping off in London; it will only be a fifteen-minute pop in for TB and will save him having to visit Peru in the next two years.' Alastair started off opposed to all these visits, mocking them mercilessly, but the private secretaries knew that they had an ally in ex-Foreign Office mandarin Jonathan Powell and usually got their way. At least those of us keen on Tony maintaining a domestic profile could be reassured that, unlike leaders of the past such as Harold Macmillan who spent six weeks touring Africa in 1960, Tony's foreign trips were usually mercifully brief.

On either Wednesday afternoon or Thursday morning would be the main political strategy meetings which included a few of us from Number 10 plus Philip Gould, and Peter Mandelson, John Prescott, the party chairman and Gordon Brown – all in different combinations. At their best those meetings powered the government. Gordon would provide his extraordinary political skills for skewering the Tories and keeping them on the backfoot. Tony would provide the strategy for positioning the government.

Often, however, the same circular and unresolved arguments came up. What was the balance between an opportunity message on education and jobs and a responsibility message on crime? Gordon was adamant that by raising the issue of crime we were both fighting on the Tories' agenda and raising expectations that we couldn't ever fulfil. Tony believed with equal passion that unless you empathise and acknowledge the real issues on the street and the real lives people lead, then you seem out of touch and lose people's confidence. These meetings were often a lively conversation between Gordon and Tony with everyone else as spectators.

Thursday morning was Cabinet. For ministers it was the only time in the week they could be certain of seeing their colleagues face to face, and 'in the margins', to use the civil service phrase, a lot of business would be done. For advisers, too, it was the chance to knobble ministers with questions or information. Cabinet itself developed over the seven years I observed it. For the first term, meetings were short and usually pretty dull: the routine of the Leader of the House reporting on business, the Chief Whip reporting on essential votes that week, the Foreign Secretary reporting back on recent visits and future travel plans, and then a few minutes of fairly mundane business. I got the sense that with very few exceptions, Cabinet colleagues liked and got on with each other. Tony had matey relations with most of them, and continued the trend begun by other Prime Ministers of doing serious business outside Cabinet in smaller meetings. By the second term, partly through political necessity, Tony began to use Cabinet more seriously as a forum for discussion, as a way of briefing colleagues on the reform pro-gramme on public services – ministers would take it in turn to present their plans – and on occasions to air controversial issues where the outcome was genuinely in doubt, like whether to introduce identity cards. With hindsight, Cabinet should have been used more effectively earlier. Tony always commanded support around the Cabinet table and it would have strength-ened not weakened him.

On Friday Tony would either work at Chequers or there would be policy away days or he would be tied up with European summits, trips to the constituency or regional visits. The atmosphere of Number 10 was always different on a Friday when Tony was away. You were no longer on edge, thinking you might be summoned at any moment. You could relax a little. Many of us turned up in more casual clothes on a Friday – Alastair invariably in running gear.

If that was the shape of a typical week then a year had a strange flow to it as well. Governed by the parliamentary timetable, the mood of the press, the political landmarks like the Budget, the spending review, party conference, it became clear when we would have good periods and when we would be on the backfoot. Almost whatever we did, this became the pattern. In some ways it was reassuring to know that a good period would probably come along if we stuck in there.

Tony would come back after the summer holidays refreshed, tanned, fizzing with ideas. This momentum carried us through September to party conference where his performance without exception lifted the party, connected with the country and moved us forward. The Queen's Speech would give us some shape in the autumn and things would get a bit more ragged as Christmas approached. Then we tended to have a January that was anywhere between bad and dreadful, either because of a perceived or real winter crisis in the NHS or because of a transport disaster or, in the case of one year, the Mandelson resignation. We often had a torrid three months until Gordon's Budget invariably simmered things down and gave the government shape again. Then there was the tricky period up to the May local or European elections, followed by wild extrapolations about how the results spelled doom for the government, which they never did. Then there was a difficult period as everyone got tired and was desperate for a summer break. August tended to be a silly month with half stories turning into major crises but no one paying attention. Then Tony returned in September and the cycle continued. That is how the political seasons looked to us in government.

The single strangest thing about working at Number 10 between

1997 and 2003 was how the years suddenly crept up on you. One moment I was writing speeches for Tony describing the early years of government – 'We've had two tough years', 'In only three short years we have done such–and–such' – and then years four to six that spanned the 2001 election whizzed by, and we were soon passing Attlee's record for a Labour government and we seemed long lasting, on the down curve. It felt like months rather than years.

The question that occupied us most was what was the mandate for? Everything came back to that question. Had the people been keener on getting rid of the Tories than electing us? Did the size of our majority give us the right to move from reassurance mode to radical reforming mode, or should the first term just be about showing our competence to govern? People knew that the Labour party had to change, but how much did the country feel it needed to change as well? Did people want the New Britain of our slogan, or merely a newish Britain with lots of the old ways kept?

Tony said repeatedly that our opponents would try one of two attacks – that we had reverted to Old Labour or that we were no different from the Tories. Neither would be true, he said, but come what may he did not want to be seen as having betrayed our new supporters by reverting to old Labour. That is why in one of his first speeches he said, 'We were elected as New Labour, we will govern as New Labour.'

For a government of the Left the debate always ends up focusing on one issue. Is it being radical enough? Is it using power to the best effect? Could it be doing more, faster, better? For the Right these are not the considerations. Running the economy well is normally enough, a few tax cuts keep supporters happy, a cultural war against foreigners or Europe gives them emotional connection with a section of the public.

For the Left the bar is set high: utopia. Anything that falls short is seen as betrayal, a missed opportunity. I found, and wrote about in one of Tony Blair's speeches, an extraordinary *New Statesman* profile of Clement Attlee written in 1951, which reflected on what we now see as the great 1945 government. It didn't mention the creation of the NHS once; instead Attlee was berated for failing to use the landslide to create a socialist Britain as a bulwark against the world's capitalist states.

But what is radicalism? Different people had a different test for us. For the right-wing press – some of whom, at least for now, supported us – the test of radicalism was how Thatcherite we would be in rolling back the state, reforming welfare, privatising, tax cutting. For some of the liberal Left radicalism meant constitutional reform. A move from a first past the post voting system to proportional representation was the symbol of radicalism. For others on the Left, it was the amount we raised taxes and redistributed wealth.

Tony was not interested in any of these measures. He knew what Britain needed – a stable economy, reformed public services, stronger communities, a modern constitution, better relations with Europe and the world – and he believed that if he got anywhere close to achieving these goals we would have been truly radical. Of these priorities the one that stood out was public service reform. Tony believed that renewing the public realm was a great progressive cause, as well as a political necessity for the coalition we wanted to support us – that of the middle class and working class.

I was delighted when Tony returned from holiday in 1999 with the theme for his conference speech worked out: the forces of conservatism. That phrase triggered the most radical conference speech of his premiership. His analysis was that Britain had been held back by conservatives who thwarted the forces of progress and that it was time for them to be defeated.

The big debate amongst us was whether this speech was the

end of 'triangulation' or an extension of it. Triangulation was our formula up until then to characterise New Labour: not old left or new right – we were moving beyond both extremes to find a third way. However, the 'forces of conservatism' framework to my mind gave us a welcome opportunity to move on, to return to a bi-polar world in which 'we were right and they, the Tories, were wrong.'

Tony insisted that whilst most of the attacks would be on the Right, there had to be a warning too for the party – that there were strong forces of conservatism on the Left who were resisting change in our public services. Tony, I felt, was right, it was often the unions that resisted change the most, but I also believed that tactically this should be an attack on the Right. Up until the final hours before delivering this speech we were still having the debate. I worked on some of the most emotive passages of the speech with Alastair.

To be the progressive force that defeats the forces of conservatism. The old prejudices, where foreign means bad. Where multi-culturalism is not something to celebrate, but a left-wing conspiracy to destroy their way of life. Where women shouldn't work and those who do are responsible for the breakdown of the family. The old elites, establishments that have run our professions and our country too long. Who have kept women and black and Asian talent out of our top jobs and senior parts of government and the services. Who keep our bright inner-city kids from our best universities. And who still think the House of Lords should be run by hereditary peers in the interests of the Tory party.

The old order, those forces of conservatism, for all their language about promoting the individual, and freedom and liberty, they held people back. They kept people down. They stunted people's potential. Year after year. Decade after decade.

Look at this party's greatest achievement. The forces of conservatism, and the force of the Conservative party, pulled every trick in the book – voting 51 times, yes 51 times, against the creation of the NHS. One leading Tory, Mr Henry Willink, said at the time that the NHS 'will destroy so much in this country that we value', when we knew human potential can never be realised when whether you are well or ill depends on wealth not need. The forces of conservatism allied to racism are why one of the heroes of the twentieth century, Martin Luther King, is dead. It's why another, Nelson Mandela, spent the best years of his life in a cell the size of a bed. And though the fact that Mandela is alive, free and became President, is a sign of the progress we have made: the fact that Stephen Lawrence is dead, for no other reason than he was born black, is a sign of how far we still have to go. And they still keep opposing progress and justice. What did they say about the minimum wage? The same as they said right through this century. They tried the employment argument – it would cost jobs. They tried the business argument – it would make them bankrupt. They then used the economic argument – it would cause inflation. They then resorted to the selfish argument – businesses wouldn't want to pay it. Well, businesses are paying it. Inflation is low. Unemployment is falling. There are one million job vacancies in the country. And two million people have had a pay rise because we believe they are worth more than poverty pay.

These forces of conservatism chain us not only to an outdated view of our people's potential but of our nation's potential. What threatens the nation-state today is not change, but the refusal to change in a world opening up, becoming ever more interdependent.

It was one of those speeches that sounded far more dramatic spoken than it read on the page. This was Tony's first ever attempt to give the Right a serious pounding. It showed real confidence, Tony defining himself on his own terms.

The Right hated it and their columnists got to work picking holes in it, claiming that we were blaming the Tory party for killing Martin Luther King, taunting Tony by saying this was the end of New Labour and the end of his big tent strategy. It was all too much for Peter Mandelson and to a lesser extent Tony. To them this was years of reassurance being put in jeopardy. Those Eighties fears rushed back. We started back-tracking. We tried to explain that we were attacking the Left as much as the Right. I was furious. We had set up a huge debate, written a powerful speech and were now effectively disowning it. We would never again make a head-on assault on the Right. We would return to progressive politics by stealth.

The debate about enemies continued. With the Tories still struggling to make any mark, we struggled to find the definition we needed to make what we believed to be radical reforms come alive. In one of Tony's weekend notes in April 2000, in response to another period when we were trying to hone our message and regain momentum, he wrote:

What is the missing ingredient? One answer is to say: we lack an enemy. Mrs Thatcher had the unions or the public sector. We should find an equivalent. This is the best way, the argument goes, to define who we are for, as well as what we are for.

I would enter a sharp caveat on this and put the argument

a different way. Mrs Thatcher did indeed take on the unions. But the unions at the time, and Scargill, in particular, were grossly unreasonable. They were indefensible in some of their practices. Ditto with parts of the public sector. But, in fact, she proceeded with much more care than historical myth allows. She went out of her way to try to keep NHS workers on board and at least in the first two terms shied away from some of the big struggles.

We don't have that situation. There is no easily identifiable group – saving perhaps the hereditary peers and that is very limited – that can be described as 'holding Britain back'. To invent one, or worse single out some group just to have one, will cause more problems than it solves. It doesn't feel right to me.

I prefer therefore a different way of getting to the same objective. It is to go back to 'many not the few' but in amended form. It is to say: if you're wealthy or privileged, Britain works well for you; but we need to change this country to make it work for the many, for those without the breaks of birth or wealth; for those who can't survive violent swings in the economy, for those who need rising living standards to pay the bills, for those who need good schools and healthcare because they can't afford to buy them, for those who can't afford security guards or live in areas where there is no crime.

In the second term, the debate about enemies lost its meaning. We had found them by the actions we had taken. On Iraq most of the Labour party and half the country were against the government, and the Left opposed many of our plans for public service reform.

New Labour's brand of sensible politics works well at election time when the public re-engage with politics and seek a party committed to sound finances and strong public services – but just being sensible is not why people join parties of the Left. Labour's head, the rational part of every party member, slowly got out of sync with the heart. Tony being a rationalist, a barrister, a persuader, never quite saw this, but it niggled away at me. I wanted us to stir up passion and commitment. I am romantic about politics, an idealist, someone who constantly needs to get turned on by the causes we are fighting for and the wrongs we want to right. I wanted a few more absolutes. So it annoyed me when Tony started appointing Tories to positions to show how broad-minded we were – after eighteen years of Opposition why on earth was ex-Tory minister David Mellor being given a role in sports? Why were we denied the thrill of getting rid of all the hereditary peers, and instead doing a deal to keep ninety-two of them? In all cases it may have been right to let pragmatism rather than gesture politics rule the day, but there is a place for a bit of raw meat in politics. Increasingly, as our opponents and those disappointed by our policies got passionate about their causes, we needed to show more passion in ours. It was easy for me to justify most positions the government took. It was easy to take pride in many of the achievements – whether the minimum wage, peace in Northern Ireland, or the first black Cabinet ministers. Our prudence was indeed for a purpose. But people constantly needed to *feel* that purpose.

For large periods of time in government we believed we were being treated unfairly. Tony expressed this feeling strongly in a note he wrote in October 2000.

There has been a paradox which we've been grappling with, by turns uncertain and a little irritated at it. We feel we have objectively done a good job. Yet even as the evidence of that is increasingly clear, the warmth of the public towards us increasingly has declined.

He believed the feeling began as soon as we were elected in 1997 as a result of:

wholly unrealistic expectations of instant or near instant improvement. We totally underestimated the degree of liberation people felt after the election. The realisation that those expectations cannot be met has punctured not just the euphoria but part of the faith in us. A sense from the outside that we are all-mighty. Because, in fact, we are not arrogant people and don't take our power for granted, we forget that to the outsider, we are indeed in a position of unprece-dented power. People want us taken down a peg. A relentless and well crafted media onslaught, whose principal goal has been to spread cynicism about us and in the Tory press better at setting the agenda than ours, this has been successfully dovetailed with the Tory attack. If the public's expectations were unrealistic, so were ours. We forget: governments aren't liked. They are the recipients of every demand and they can't satisfy them all. They accumulate enemies, groups who feel let down or banned or offended.

His solution was more explanation, but above all:

we need to be in a phase where we patiently govern, explain what we're doing with confidence and a sense of a different calmer style. In the end, we can only do what we believe to be right and tell people about it. A bit like Olivier told Dustin Hoffman to try acting, we should try governing, plain and simple.

From the beginning of 2000 I became obsessed with renewal, and this continued into the second term. Charles Handy once argued that organisations should re-invent themselves while successful, just as they are coming down from their peaks, rather than waiting for a crisis before moving forward. After six years of New Labour and a successful campaign by our opponents to discredit it, New Labour needed to move on and our second mandate needed to take another step forward. So I wrote a note to Tony Blair in spring 2000. It made the case for renewal and he liked it. I put our problems down to a mindset, what I called the 'Eighties time warp'.

> We are too often coloured by the traumas of the Eighties. The public has moved on. We have not. Reassurance was the right strategy. It recognised both the unelectability of old Labour and the hegemony of the Right. And TB I am sure would say that without constant vigilance the party will return to its bad old Labour ways. But the judgement now is whether we are in a different game.

I set out what I believed to be the three key areas where we should be driving forward, showing greater confidence; all three bolstered by my re-reading of George Orwell's brilliant essay on the English people which, sixty years on, seemed to have just as much resonance.

> 1. Education/knowledge economy. '[The English] must get rid of their downright contempt for cleverness. They cannot afford it any longer.' Orwell. If we are to succeed we need to do more than raise standards in the basics. The British anti-intellectualism, 'the too clever by half' swot cut down to size, is a deep cultural trait that we need to overcome. We need to enthuse the whole community,

not just educationalists, in the importance of knowledge and developing creativity and skills throughout life. To make learning something to be proud of, not something to hide for fear of ridicule. But to succeed we may need to take some political risks and lead from the front in finding ways of investing huge extra sums in education.

2. Class. 'England is one of the last remaining countries to cling to the outward forms of feudalism.' Orwell. Britain is still more hierarchical than any other nation on earth. We have customs, honours, snobbery and prejudice that still shuts out too many people from chances in life. State-school students discriminated against by top universities. Only one woman running a FTSE 100 company and she's not British. No black people appointed to the civil service fast stream last year despite hundreds of applicants. We talk about meritocracy. Are we serious about delivering a more classless and open society?

3. Europe. 'English working people as a rule, think it effeminate even to pronounce a foreign word correctly.' Orwell. Our ambivalence to Europe over fifty years has cost us influence and economic strength. Europe is the trickiest of a cluster of issues, from asylum to race, that are about our view of British character where we want to beat off the isolationist Little Englanders. To succeed we may need to take on the press and lead public opinion.

If we got some way down this road Britain would be cleverer, more mobile, more tolerant and outward looking and through all three more prosperous.

The strength of our political position gives us an opportunity for real ambition. To put down deeper roots. To tackle some of the historic problems of Britain. New Labour could become the agent of change that improves the lives of the majority and transforms Britain into a truly modern nation. The time for the second phase of New Labour has arrived.

I took up my obsession with renewal at a meeting of left-of-centre big wigs a while later. The meeting at Hartwell House hotel in Aylesbury brought together the great and the good from the world's Left. It had a guest of honour who mesmerised the audience: Bill Clinton. The last time I had seen him speak in the flesh was at the Chicago Convention in 1996 when he was seeking re-election. Here his talk was primarily on the Middle East. He put forward in a way I had never heard a politician do before the psychological dimension to politics. 'You've got to get inside their heads. On Israel you have to understand the Israeli psychology, the deep sense of insecurity being bordered by hostile countries. You have to win their trust first and foremost then you can try and move forward.' He extended his theme to his political opponents. He said he kept putting himself in the shoes of Republicans. What you have to understand is that they will do anything to get power. Anything. His message was: understand motivation, understand what makes them act the way they do.

Later I talked with Clinton. He gave me his now famous, intense stare as we were talking. I did feel as if he cared about the conversation. I asked him about how you renew yourself in office. Despite the Monica Lewinsky episode he had managed to keep governing successfully. He said that in America the key was to spend the time around the state of the union address in galvanising the government and preparing for the year ahead in a systematic way. Always set yourself new goals. In Britain the equivalent to the state of the union was the party conference speech. September was the time for us to do similar planning.

But it's so tempting for politicians not to move on. They feel most comfortable when surrounded by their most loyal lieutenants, and that is natural in politics when a politician has so many opponents and needs people protection. However, in a fast-changing world, politicians need to replenish their ideas, their themes, their approach so as not to fall behind.

At the point when I left Number 10, almost ten years after Tony became leader, I was proud of all that had been achieved. We had made a real difference but I was worried the attributes that made New Labour so formidable for its first decade, when distinguishing ourselves from Old Labour were the key, were the same attributes that now had the potential to hold New Labour back in the next decade.

# NEW BOY

Trevor had left a message on my mobile phone on Sunday. 'Good luck with it. I know you will be apprehensive, but I'll see you in the morning.' I am surprised and grateful that he has thought about me and bothered to call.

I hate Sunday evenings. I mope about feeling I should be preparing for the week ahead, but not bothering to do so. This Sunday is particularly bad. How should I dress for school? What would the teachers be wearing? Would they be wearing suits and ties? Would I look like some management consultant, or worse an Ofsted inspector, if I pitched up in my usual Number 10 gear? I know that people are divided on how to dress in schools. Do teachers bond with difficult children more if they dress casually and appear more approachable? Or is it better to show respect for the job and dress smartly?

Worrying about what to wear is displacement activity. My real anxiety is whether I will cope. Will I miss politics too much? Will I regret leaving Number 10? Do the teachers hate the government so much that they will take it out on me? Will I have the skills to deal with children whose behaviour, background and problems are, in many cases, a long way from the rarefied Westminster air or my comfortable upbringing? Will I be given enough to do or will I sit bored in a room? Will the NUT rep, who I've been told is a Socialist Workers Party member, give me grief?

I think about two comments made to me before leaving Number 10, both from education experts. Tim Brighouse's inspirational phrase: 'Our job is to fill their pockets with confidence,' still rang in my ears. Then I asked Michael Barber, head of the Prime Minister's Delivery Unit, what I should look out for at the school. He thought for a moment and said: 'The key is do they really have high expectations for their kids?'

Monday 5 January 2004. First day of term. I get up early, put on a suit and tie and leave home for my new life.

It is an early start. Trevor has already dispelled any fantasy I might have that my day might become less hectic. Senior management team meetings – where the Head and the deputies meet – are at 8.20 every morning. Trevor himself gets in at just after 7.30 most mornings, often commuting from Chelmsford. He welcomes me and shows me to my room. 'You're sharing with Grace, the education welfare officer,' he says. 'You'll like her. Someone's fixed you up with a computer.' There is a strong smell of chemicals, either from the photocopier next door, or fresh paint. The room is poky but light. It has two desks, two computers, one telephone between the two of us and a metallic bookshelf. The walls are bare, but white and clean. It is quite a contrast to my office at Number 10, which I had shared with Godric Smith and Tom Kelly, the PM's official spokesmen – a grand high-ceilinged room, with wooden-panelled walls, and views out on to the Number 10 garden, and Leo Blair's trampoline – but given the lack of space at the school, I am grateful just to have a desk.

At 8.20 I enter Trevor's office where three women are already sitting in black leather armchairs. This is the equivalent to my Monday 9 a.m. meetings with Tony in his den. These are the most powerful women at Islington Green School. I had met them briefly before arriving but now they look even more competent and tough. Angela has a bundle of papers and a huge bunch of keys on her lap. Emma, slim, with shoulder length strawberry-blonde hair, is in charge of pastoral support. Eileen, short black hair, smartly dressed, is the curriculum and timetable supremo. Paul, the final member of the team, is absent. I am greeted with indifference. I feel like an intruder. This management team is clearly a tightly knit group around Trevor. I can understand why they don't relish an outsider, particularly one who isn't a teacher and who comes from government.

The main issue is how to improve assemblies. Trevor thinks these are noisy and not given enough attention. He believes they should be a symbol of the school's improved behaviour and that they should be done properly. He has tried to cajole staff into improving them, but now feels he needs to get heavier and introduce a new system, with kids lining up outside and then coming in and sitting quietly.

At 8.35 we go up to the staff room where Trevor and the senior management team give announcements to staff and staff respond with questions or notices of their own. The staff room, I am told, has just been redone. I enter the room. It has a modern, Ikea look to it: purple armchairs and wooden tables. Eighty teachers look at us as we enter, their slightly bleary faces signalling the beginning of term. There is a kitchen area. A bank of pigeon holes lines one of the walls and a coffee machine whirs in the corner. I look round trying to guess which one is John, the NUT rep.

Trevor begins: 'Hope everyone's had a good holiday. Let me start by introducing Peter Hyman who, as you know, will be working with us for a couple of terms. I am sure you will make him feel welcome.

'Let me talk about assemblies and the new procedures. Teachers should bring down the students five minutes early at 10.35. They should line up outside and then file into the hall when they are called.'

Trevor then takes questions. One teacher asks all teachers to look at the cover rotas for absent staff. Another asks staff to keep an eye on a new child who needs extra help because of some ghastly incident at home. This is my first taste of the frontline; a brief but essential operational meeting to ensure the smooth running of the school. There is a real urgency and practicality to it. It is very different from the Number 10 Monday morning meeting on sofas in Tony's study.

'You'll want a tour of the school,' Emma says after the staff meeting. 'I'll grab a prefect to show you round . . . You'll do Jackie,' she says, as a girl who looks about fifteen saunters past with a friend. She is carrying a handbag, and has a pretty, pale face. Her clothing has made only a passing acquaintance with school uniform. She smiles. 'Please show sir around the school.'

We start to ascend the six floors of the main school building.

'What's your name, sir?' she asks. 'Peter,' I say automatically, forgetting that no teacher is called by their first name. 'Mr Hyman,' I quickly add. This feels very peculiar. Sir or Mr Hyman. I've never had that kind of respect in my life.

On each floor Jackie bumps into friends who she stops to peck on the cheek, 'See you later,' and then continues the ascent. It is as if school is one big social club. I notice the stairs and all the classrooms are stained all over with black marks where chewing gum has been spat out and trampled into the floor. On the sixth floor I am shown the art room and the roof garden – which is more roof than garden, though there are a couple of nice looking pot plants. Then it's down to the other

# School uniform

School uniform is worn to encourage the development of self-confidence and pride in the school. All students in Years 7–11 are expected to wear full school uniform which includes black shoes.

Uniform is purchased at competitive prices through the school. All items should be clearly marked with the owner's name.

| | |
|---|---|
| **Blazer** | aubergine |
| **Shirt (boys)** | plain white cotton or cotton/polyester |
| **Blouse (girls)** | plain white cotton or cotton/polyester with collar |
| **Tie** | in office |
| **Pullover** | Black V-neck long sleeve (optional) |
| **Trousers (boys and girls)** | Black conventional tailored (black jeans are not acceptable) |
| **Skirt (girls)** | Black knee-length |
| **Shoes** | Black (leather-look) shoes only. Boots and trainers are NOT acceptable |

**Summer Uniform** – can be worn from May to October:

| | |
|---|---|
| **Polo-shirt** | with school emblem |

*School Prospectus*

buildings. Islington Green consists of three blocks: the six-floor tower with a corridor for each faculty, the performing arts block with the canteen at the bottom, and the oldest building where technology is housed and the area called the Learning Zone, which is for the most challenging students who are withdrawn from mainstream lessons and given special attention. In between the three buildings is a vast expanse of playground.

'What's your favourite subject?' I ask Jackie.

'Maths,' she says.

'Do you want to do A levels?'

'Don't know.'

'What do you want to do after school?'

'Don't know. Are you a teacher?'

Good question, I think. How best to describe myself? 'I'm on the senior management team,' I say.

I remember the chilling warning of another headteacher who told me: 'They either think you're OK or rubbish and have decided within a fortnight. No one is ever better than OK. Many are rubbish. You have to earn their respect.' I fear Jackie thinks I am rubbish. 'That's the smoking alley,' she says, pointing to a narrow passage-way at the side of the technology block. I am surprised this is a landmark on the official school tour. Or perhaps she thinks I am entitled to the 'rough guide' as I am joining the school.

Jackie drops me back at Emma's office. I feel I have made a first friend. I will now know one face in the school at least.

Emma has been here for eleven years under four heads. Her office has the best vantage point in the school, overlooking the playground. 'I spend a lot of time shouting at children through this window,' she says. 'I tell them to get to their lessons. They look through the window demanding things of me.'

Emma clearly likes the banter with students. A big, square man enters the room with a hooded teenager slouching beside him. This is the stereotypical monosyllabic pimply youth familiar to all those who have one or have been one.

'He turned up with no school uniform and has already had a bust up with a teacher. What shall I do with him? I don't want to send him home, because we are lucky he is in school in the first place.'

Emma is calm: 'Why doesn't he shadow your lessons today, Clive, so you can keep an eye on him?'

'Then,' says Clive in exaggerated I'm-speaking-to-someone-deaf-or-stupid tones, 'he will come back tomorrow with his school uniform, his full school uniform.' He looks the boy in the eye.

Emma tries to lighten the mood. 'We care about you,' she says, 'so when I bump into you later on today I don't want to see your miserable little face but a nice smiling one.' The boy grins for the first time before resuming his sulky posture. Clive and the boy leave.

'He only came to school five times last term,' Emma says. 'The trouble here is too many see school as an extension of their troubled life and then all learning is lost. Our job is to catch them doing something good.'

Soon it's time to be part of Trevor's new assembly regime. It's day one, I've got my first duty, and it's more onerous than it first seems. I am to stop kids coming into the hall from the back and instead make sure they go round the side, queue up in the playground and then go in. This is a new system and many of the children don't see why they are being told to go the long route. The task is going well until I lose concentration and gesture to a teacher to go into the playground. She looks taken aback before ignoring me and entering the hall.

The assembly is a collector's item. I feel transported back to a school of the past. Two hundred students sit on rows of blue plastic chairs facing an empty stage. A fierce-looking man in his early forties bellows orders from the front. He is a caricature army major. 'Now, you nasty oiks,' he seemed to be saying. In fact he is saying, 'The key to these assemblies is silence, listening, attention. I want you to be paying attention. You, cap off. When I say quiet I mean quiet. That doesn't mean a little noise, it means no noise. It means school uniform, full school uniform.' This goes on for eight of the ten minutes allocated for the assembly before he says, 'I should have wished you a happy New Year. Sorry, I forgot.'

There is a teacher hovering at the side of the hall, keeping an eye on his class. Could it be? Possibly? John the NUT man? I'm pretty sure the jeans, T-shirt and backpack, are a give away, but I'm not certain.

I'll find out later, but my next duty is to follow Trevor in the lift up to the exclusion room on the sixth floor. The exclusion room is one of Trevor's innovations. It is a place disruptive children can be sent during the day without having to suspend them from school. It is the way Trevor has used to cut the numbers of external exclusions. Trevor wants me to be on duty here a couple of times a week. The door is locked. No one has been excluded yet this term. Trevor finds a key and goes in. Desks are arranged in rows with a copy of the school rules on them in yellow laminated card. He shows me the file of offenders – each with their name, form, offence and teacher's name. On paper the offences look mild in many cases: uniform infringements, verbal abuse, the odd fight; I was expecting worse. I was expecting knives, assaults, drugs.

A few minutes later two dishevelled eleven-year-olds are brought in. 'Both weren't wearing their uniform,' says a breath-less teacher who has walked the six floors. 'This one came quietly,' she says, pointing at the taller of the two. 'The other put up a fight and went all stroppy. Unusual for him though. He's obviously come back after Christmas with a different attitude.'

'What lesson were you meant to be in?' asks Trevor. The aim is to give work to students in the exclusion room that mirrors the lessons they have been sent from.

'Dance,' says one.

'And you?'

'Dance,' grunts the other.

'Well we can't replicate that very easily up here,' Trevor says. 'We'll have to find something else to do.'

One of the offenders starts unscrewing a bottle of coke. 'Please put the bottle on the floor out of the way and face the front,' says the head sternly.

Tracey who runs the exclusion room enters. We leave her to it, but I am worried about spending time up here on my own. What skills do I have for the job? I've stood up to Alastair on occasions, admittedly not very often. I've tried not to be intimidated by Peter Mandelson's psychological warfare. I've jousted with a few *Daily Mail* journalists. Would this be enough of a training to face an irate and conceivably unhinged teenager?

I stop off in the library which is an airy, colourful oasis of calm. Flora is one of several librarians. Before she knows that I work with the headteacher, she starts laying into him. 'You enjoy books more than the headteacher,' she says cuttingly. 'This is the one part of the building he hasn't visited in the last year.' A statement I later discover to be inaccurate.

Flora is a middle-aged woman, with an engaging off-hand manner. 'It's the only department that's seen cuts.' She sees me as a captive audience and tells me some lurid stories. 'Someone nicked two shelves of books the other day. The fantasy section. We caught him selling *Lord of the Rings* on the estate.'

'How entrepreneurial,' I say. Education is perhaps becoming everyone's Number One priority. 'Better than selling drugs.'

'We got them back,' she says, 'but it took a while.'

I leave the library for the staff room and struggle to

remember the code for the door. It's a number that quite a few students seem to know and regularly prove it by opening the door, bellowing something and slamming it shut again. On entering I notice something I should have seen the first time: the NUT notice board. How could I have missed it? It is directly opposite the door for all to see. At the top in red pen it says 'John, NUT rep'. Underneath are several posters. 'No more lies Mr Blair' is the most striking. Is this a comment on education policy? No, it is a flyer for a demo in London protesting against the war in Iraq.

A teacher friend has told me never to go into the staff room empty handed, always bring something to read at the beginning. I forget this advice but dive for the *Guardian* which is lying on a table. Tony is beaming on the front page having just visited Basra in Iraq. I realise that up until that point I have given no thought to my previous job. Now it strikes me how much of a bubble the school operates in. I had arrived in a world, the real world, where people don't buy every newspaper every day and read every line of the news and comment sections; a world that doesn't hang on the verdict of the media each morning; a world that has space to breathe, space to try things; a world where what matters is something more immediate. Teachers have a breathless day with snatched moments to sit down to talk to colleagues. All the attempts that I made at Number 10 'to communicate better with frontline staff' presupposed they would have time to take in these messages.

The contrast in worlds is also about class. Whereas I felt I was walking into the establishment on my first day at Number 10, here I am entering a world stained by deprivation, an air filled with expletives and trouble. The accents have suddenly changed. I am used to middle-class or posh, from civil servants, business people, professionals. Here the students speak with strong streetwise north London accents. Many of the administrative staff, some of whom are parents of current or former students, do too.

I am ignored in the staff room. A few female members of staff are having lunch – I say lunch: eating small pieces of vinaigrette-drenched lettuce from Tupperware containers. I turn to the sports pages.

When I return to my room using the swipe pass that allows me entry to the administrative corridor, Grace is on the phone trying to track down a girl who has gone missing and is thought to have run off with her boyfriend to some squat. The girl is only fourteen, he is eighteen. Her sister, who is at the school, seems to know where they are but isn't telling.

Grace puts down the phone and introduces herself formally, shaking my hand and saying she is pleased to be sharing a room. She is tall and striking. I ask her to fill me in on the sort of students who come to Islington Green, and she replies at a gallop.

'What you've got to understand is the importance of family on the estate out there; the role of grandparents is immense. In 30 per cent of cases they are the carers of young people. The family structure is solid. It seems like there are only about twenty-five large families connected to each other. A lot of the parents may not be working, but some don't just have income from income support, they get money from the black economy. You should see what's in their homes: TV screens the size of this wall. There is infinite capacity to obtain mod cons in line with the Joneses. They have caravans on the coast, villas in Spain often. I've seen fireplaces worth £3,000 and you should see some of the wallpaper. While I'm off to B & Q they've got the most expensive you can buy. Just because on paper they don't have money, doesn't mean they don't have aspirations.'

She makes another phone call. I try to digest her summary of the school's clientele. She puts the phone down and resumes where she left off. 'I drive around, trying to round up kids and get them back to school – most of my time is spent on truancy – but there is a poor attitude to education. Most of the parents didn't get to college but the mother's got a job at the council. Now if you ask some of the Year 10s and 11s what they want to do at college they look at you sideways. The boys want to be builders or electricians or chippies, but working with their dad or a relative is less available than it was. Got to dash,' she says, and with a flourish she leaves the room.

I am discovering that there are a lot of snatched conversations at the school. The timetable drives everything. At break time you find most teachers in the staff room, but otherwise you have to look up their timetable on the computer and grab them in between lessons when you can.

Emma has given me a few lessons to sit in on to get a feel for

| **Timetable** | |
|---|---|
| Period one | 8.45–9.45 |
| Period two | 9.45–10.45 |
| Registration | 10.45–10.55 |
| Break | 10.55–11.15 |
| Period three | 11.15–12.15 |
| Period four | 12.15–1.15 |
| Lunch | 1.15–2.00 |
| Registration | 2.00–2.10 |
| Period five | 2.10–3.10 |
| School ends | 3.10 |

the school. I am to start with an RE lesson from Chloe, Head of Humanities Faculty, and one of the best young teachers in the school. Chloe's lesson plan is nothing if not ambitious. At 8.45

on a cold January morning, with a class of GCSE students, she is going for the big one: DOES GOD EXIST? is written in big letters on the white board. There are no blackboards at the school. Teachers write in marker pen on white boards, but a few classrooms do have the new interactive digital whiteboards, on which you can use software and project the Internet. I am perched at the back of the class with what looks like some of the cheekier students.

'We've covered this a bit in the past but never seriously, and you did find answering it hard in the mocks,' Chloe says breezily. This seems a bit harsh. Theologians have been wrestling with this question for centuries. It is asking a lot of GCSE students at Islington Green to crack it in the next hour, or in the mocks for that matter, but Chloe is going to try.

'Before we start properly,' she says, 'some feedback. I asked you all before Christmas to rate yourselves with the traffic light system: red, amber, green. I also asked you to give me feedback.' This seems to be exactly the sort of customer friendly service New Labour is advocating. Do these kids like her pally manner, the pink walls, the pot plants, the bubbly enthusiasm – and if the class doesn't like her, is there a 'choice' of alternative providers as advocated by the government? Will these students be able to do RE with another teacher?

'Well,' she says. 'You think I talk too much and go on a bit, and I don't do enough group work. So, in future I am going to make you work on your own a bit, and I will try my hardest not to talk quite as much.' I am impressed that the students had taken this seriously and that Chloe was going to adapt as a result.

'These are the two questions you need to think about,' she says. ' "How does the appearance of the world lead to a belief in God?" and "How does the search for meaning and purpose in life lead to a belief in God?" There are four people you need to know about: Paley and his watch, Feuerbach, Marx and Pascal.'

A boy enters the room noisily. Leaves again. Then comes in again two minutes later with a chair. Chloe begins with a description of several theories about God.

'Paley says God exists because life is so complicated that it had to be designed by God. Feuerbach, a German, said you need to believe in God because it gives you hope. Marx said it was the way the rich people put on poor people. Pascal said it was like betting, it was worth covering yourself just in case. It's like your GCSEs, it's worth covering yourself by doing more than the five you need.' She brings alive each example with current references including from *The Simpsons*. The class is quiet and gripped.

Chloe then breaks them up into small groups to go through a work-sheet giving more details of the different theories. I try to work out what gives her confidence and authority. The students seem to think she is on their wavelength. She is on top of her subject, and she seems very good at detecting nonsense.

'I want you to do a mind map of these theories for home-work,' she says as the pips go for the end of the lesson. Trevor wants to get rid of the pips. He says it makes the school more riotous because there is a mass scramble for the classroom door when the pips go. Far better he thinks that teachers let the students out on their terms at the end of the lesson. However, teachers have defended the pips in the past because it's easier to order your day around them. By 10.45 and the end of the lesson I've made up my mind that God probably does exist and, as Chloe rightly says, is it worth taking the risk in not doing so? You might as well believe in him just in case.

My renewed faith in God is soon to be tested in the science lesson. This is on the fifth floor of the six-floor block, and Steve, a science teacher, is at the door welcoming students to his room. Gentle classical music is wafting from a tape recorder on his desk. 'Coats on the pegs please,' he says as the students arrive. Black mini-skirts and black boots seem to be the uniform of the day.

'Today we are going to continue with human cloning,' announces Steve. He is short with glasses and wears chinos and green shirt, safari style. He carries a large bumbag round his waist. What is in it? Stun gun or felt-tip pens? All has not yet been revealed. The class is silent and attentive. Either this is a very obedient group of students or Steve has a natural authority. I am not yet experienced enough to know. I sit in the corner on a tall bench overlooking a basin.

The lesson has a pace to it. Steve first hands out a work-sheet on alleles which I discover are collective genes. He lets the students spend ten minutes working out the answers. It is multiple choice. Some students can't wait for the answer. They call out, 'Is it b? Is it a?' Then it's video time: a *Panorama* investigation into human cloning that went out a few years ago. Every few minutes Steve stops to go over the biology on the board. From his description it would seem that cloning is extremely simple. 'It's easy to do,' he says. 'The science can be done. It just hasn't yet worked in reality.'

The programme has an interview with a couple who cannot have a baby. The man says: 'I don't mind having a mini-me, if IVF doesn't work.'

Steve stops the video for a moral debate. 'Who thinks human cloning shouldn't be allowed?'

'Why isn't it illegal?' says one.

'I don't see what's wrong with it,' says another.

The answers become more sophisticated. 'It's different from identical twins, because this is a father and a son looking identical. That's freaky.'

Steve asks for a vote on human cloning. Nine are for. Eleven are against. The lesson ends. The hour has gone quickly. An hour strikes me as a very long lesson. Many schools have fifty-minute lessons, some thirty-five, but it's a good sign that this lesson went so fast.

It was now time for the next lesson. I enter Studio 3 in the arts block and I am greeted by the command: 'Think of the crisp, think of the crisp, think of the crisp.'

'Monster munch,' shouts out a round student who knows his crisps but not his music.

'No, quavers. Quavers are half a beat. Crotchets are one, minims are two.'

I am in Martin's music lesson. There are two double basses in the corner of the room. Written above the white board are the following questions:

> What I now know is?
> What I have learned is?
> What I found difficult was?
> What I found easy was?
> What I didn't enjoy much was?

---

### Staff Bulletin

#### WALKMANS, MOBILE PHONES AND HEADPHONES

Students should not wear headphones in class for Walkmans or mobiles. It is clearly not possible to concentrate on class work whilst listening to something else! Mobiles *are* allowed in bags or pockets but should be *switched off*. If a teacher confiscates any such item it will be put in a dated envelope and placed in the *school safe*. It will then *only* be returned to the student's parent from the school visitors' reception at the end of the school day.

---

'This is Mr Hyman, he is sitting in on our lesson today.'

'Hi, man,' say some giggling girls, delighted by their originality.

This is a Year 7 class. I am surrounded by eleven-year-olds. Many of them are notoriously difficult, enjoying the size and freedom of the secondary school too much. Martin takes the register verbally.

'I'm talking, you're listening,' Martin barks out. 'Mohammed if I have to say your name again, I'll give you a warning.'

Three kids have CD Walkman earpieces on at the back of the class. I am standing a yard or two away, and will look feeble if I say nothing, so I quietly tell them to turn them off. They reluctantly do so.

'Why have we started chatting? Ladies at the back. Let's clap the beats. Four beats in a bar. Nearly every piece of pop music is in 4/4 time.'

Martin confiscates a boy's coke can with his right hand while continuing to talk. I presume these are the sorts of skills that you acquire in the classroom and are not compulsory parts of the teaching training: '*And today we have a confiscation practical; will every teacher try to swipe something from the person next to them.*'

'Crotchets have one beat, like tea. Quavers sound like coffee. Tea one beat, coffee two beats.'

The students are given the task of writing their own music with four beats in the bar. The girls on the back row are lost so I explain it again to them. Without someone additional in the class, these students will not have been able to write anything in the lesson. I feel useful. A boy comes in and sits in the corner of the room barefoot and starts crying. Thirty heads turn to look at him then they turn back. Two boys come in with his shoes and give them to him. Martin is ploughing on.

'I've asked for quiet I will get quiet. Right, this half of the room clap coffee, this side of the room clap tea, and when I move my arms the other way, reverse.' Martin is now looking like a windmill. Right arm up for coffee, left arm down for tea. The students do this well, though some deliberately do too many claps.

Down the left-hand side of the white board is written an escalator of punishments.

> First warning
> U [on the register meaning unsatisfactory]
> Written work
> Detention
> Exclusion room

There are padlocked lockers in the corner of the room and sweet and crisp packets littering the floor. One boy has a huge yawn.

'Mohammed, second warning. Now, for homework I want you each to write sixteen bars, that's four lines of music. Use crotchets, quavers and minims, in 4/4 time, so every bar must have four beats in it.'

The lesson ends. I have finished my induction to the teaching in the school and it has been a great experience. In one day I have learnt how to count and write music, I have got closer to deciding whether God exists, and I know the basics of how to clone a human. If I had been an enthusiastic child paying attention that day, able to shut out the circumstances of my life and family, the rewards would have been fantastic.

However, the low-level disruption was striking too. Children sauntering in to lessons five, ten, fifteen, twenty minutes late with no explanation. Children without pens or notebooks. Children not removing their caps or putting down their hoods. Children turning round and distracting others, fidgeting, chewing, attempting to listen to their Walkman, screwing up bits of paper. In government we used the phrase 'on message' for politicians who followed a script, but most were reluctant to do so. In school the equivalent jargon is 'on task', and it is clear that there is equal reluctance from teenagers. As one teacher put it: 'These children have few social norms. Half the time it's not that they are deliberately disrupting; they simply don't know that when someone else, namely the teacher, is talking, you should not talk but listen. The job is to remind them constantly what is acceptable behaviour.'

We all think we know what teaching is like. We've all been to school. We've all had good lessons and bad lessons from good teachers and bad teachers – but observing teachers close up after a gap of nearly twenty years brings a fresh perspective. At a school like this, with a lot of difficult children, the sheer will-power from teachers is extraordinary. Each teacher I have seen – and I have seen some of the best – has a different style. Some are stricter, some more interactive, but all have a presence, and a command. Their lessons have a pace that carries you along with them.

To do this five lessons a day five days a week must require huge stamina. Teaching seems to me to be physically demanding, you are on your feet the entire time. I have never seen a teacher sit down. The need to control, animate, enthuse, whilst dealing with constant provocation makes teaching also emotionally draining. 'Teaching is a craft you know. No one would think of being a surgeon for the day, yet everyone thinks they can teach a bit. To do it properly takes real practice and experience,' says one teacher to me ruefully.

'Hope you won't report me to Tony Blair,' Paul says with a smirk. Paul is tall and slim, with short silver hair. He did history at Bristol as I had, and he sees himself as the intellectual of the team. He writes books about teaching difficult students and his view is that no one really appreciates or is honest enough to admit how difficult teaching can be in inner-city schools.

Senior managers take it in turns to do assemblies. This is Paul's turn and his theme is: 'Why the situation in Iraq is like Vietnam thirty years ago'. He stands up to face nearly two hundred twelve-year-old faces. For them Vietnam means nothing, but the polemic is about to begin.

'Today in Iraq we have a similar situation to Vietnam. Vietnam is sixteen hours flight time away and has a tropical climate. The West wanted a different type of government in Vietnam. They didn't want them to be free to elect any kind of government. The Americans wanted them to have what the Americans wanted. They decided to bomb the people who didn't agree with them. So they dropped bombs with acid in them. Let's hear a piece of music from Jimi Hendrix from the time. He was anti the war and a lot of American soldiers coped with the war by being in a drug-induced state the whole time, which is what this song is about.'

As the song fades out Paul produces a slide to go on the overhead projector. 'This is a picture of the pile of bodies at My Lai. An American platoon went into the village, went berserk and killed the whole village, including fifty, sixty, eighty innocent children. That was when the Americans realised they had to get out of Vietnam. Many people are saying that Iraq could be like Vietnam. The whole situation has that feel to it: getting bogged down, staying in too long. The lesson is that even if people think they are going to war to solve a problem, war leaves things worse – there is more cruelty, and bloodshed. So judge for yourselves, will it become like Vietnam, will they lose direction? The danger is they will kill too many people. Going in to cure a patient in fact results in killing the patient, then you have to make up your own mind if that is right. Let's end with a Doors' song. They were anti-war like Jimi Hendrix.'

As the song fades down a bit Paul leaves the students with a final thought. 'You are responsible young people. When you have the chance to vote in a few years it will be for you to decide your verdict on this war.' The music crescendos again and Paul floats to the hall exit on a cloud of left-wing propaganda.

'Who's going to put the other side of the argument?' I say to Paul afterwards. He smiles, implying that if I want to do a counter-Assembly I'm welcome to. I'm not sure that my first big appearance in front of the school should be defending the war on Iraq, so Paul scores something of a victory.

'One of your government's little schemes I expect,' Trevor says to me at an SMT morning meeting, referring to the female police officer we have on site three days a week. It is indeed part of Labour's 'Safer Schools' initiative. Though, as I am beginning to find out, these good ideas are all about implementation. The rhetoric of the policy implied the police officer would patrol the corridors. In reality the SMT are debating how best to use her time. She is sometimes called to intervene in playground fights, but soon teachers realise that this makes no sense – fights rarely get out of hand and teachers usually have a sixth sense about when they are likely to fizzle out, so don't get involved unnecessarily. But a police officer is trained to get control of a situation immediately. 'It would be irresponsible if I didn't – supposing the student did have a knife, not to go in with sufficient force would be a dereliction of duty,' she says to me. In reality it is going to be the presence, particularly on the street outside school, and the less visible work like using the police database to track down a missing student, or speaking to students on safety issues in small groups, that is likely to prove most effective. For the school's reputation though, the presence of a police officer, like any high profile crime prevention policy, is double edged – does it provide reassurance or merely create fear?

One prospective parent certainly knew which when she asked me in shocked tones as I was showing her round the school: 'Do you really need a police officer on site?'

On my way to a classroom after the meeting an Asian boy who goes up to my waist, blurts out: 'Do you know Tony Blair?'

'Yes, I used to work with him,' I say.

'So you were his little helper. What did you do for him?'

'Write speeches and other things.'

'Couldn't he write his own?'

'He did mostly.'

'So he was lying if you wrote them.'

'What do you mean?'

'Well if you wrote them, he didn't write them.'

'No he wrote most of them himself.'

'But if you wrote some, then he must have been lying.'

'No. Anything he speaks, he believes and has agreed.'

'So you correct his spelling.'

'His spelling's quite good actually.' Good public school education.

'Does he remember you?'

'Yes, I hope so. I've only just left.'

'Would he read a letter if I wrote to him?'

'Probably.'

'Would he himself.'

'Yes, depends.'

The boy seems satisfied and walks into his lesson. I walk back to my room. I'm stopped again.

'Wine gums, wine gums. £1.50 a bag, sir. How about it?' The impish boy delves into his bag and comes out with a giant pack of wine gums in an unmarked plastic bag. What should I do? This could be a teacher-training sample question. Am I meant to:

a) tell him off
b) tell him off and confiscate the wine gums
c) buy them
d) walk on and say no thanks.

My answer on the spur of the moment is d.

---

**School rules**

Listen in silence

Put up your hand to speak

Arrive on time to lessons with the correct equipment

Do as you are told when you are told

Keep hands, feet, comments and objects to yourself

---

At Year 10 Assembly things started kicking off in a big way. I am on door duty again, sending students round the long way, toughing it out when kids plead to be let in the quick way. I am practising a voice of teacherly authority. Nine times out of ten I sound like someone trying to be a teacher. I am quickly discovering that if I am walking about the school or see a play fight in the corridor and ignore it I get a reputation for being a soft touch. So I find myself saying a lot: 'And where should you be?' A question seems to be better than merely telling the students off. It is effective about half the time.

The assembly is about to start. Clive is standing up in front of the Year 10s, ready to entrance them with his tall stories and urban homilies. The way to get silence, I discover, is for all the teachers to raise their right arm in the air. All the children are meant to respond by doing the same and, as if by magic, the room quietens. This is obviously something they are used to doing in primary school. It always seems to work. In the second row from the back a scuffle breaks out. It is Darren who I had seen earlier in Emma's office. He is making a grumpy annoyed sound. Angela moves in and tells him to stop. She then asks him to leave. He won't. He starts shouting at her. I see Trevor standing outside the hall and go out and tell him to come back in case he is needed. Trevor tries his softly softly approach. Calmness is everything for Trevor. There is never any need to get aggressive.

He very quietly stands next to Darren, bends down and whispers in his ear, 'I want to talk to you about this outside.' Darren seems to be going along with this, but, as he stands up, he knocks the chair of the boy in front who spins round and a scuffle breaks out. Darren then refuses to go. His arms flail. Trevor insists on his going and tries to move him along. The boy begins to lash out at people around him and refuses to go quietly. Trevor pins his arms behind him in a kind of bear hug. He manages to get him up the stairs out of the back of the hall. He hands Darren over to the on-site police officer who takes him away for calming down. Trevor then returns to the front of the hall.

With impressive calmness he says: 'Congratulations to all of you for not taking part in that conflict or egging it on. You acted very responsibly. But you should all know that if you get into a fight with the headteacher, you won't end up coming back to school again. Now, you may be shaken up by this incident, so I want you to be particularly calm and responsible for the rest of the day and let things get back to normal.' Like Tony, Trevor is very good at judging tone. He leaves the hall. I catch up with him later and he is looking a bit flustered but remains calm. 'In more than twenty years I have never had to wrestle with a student,' he says. He is also angry. 'But then it was mad, whoever thought he should be put back into assemblies with all that provocation. He was never going to cope in that setting.'

At the 8.20 senior management team meeting the following morning there is a post-mortem about the incident. The consensus is that the full moon had something to do with it. Angela says the children are always a bit madder at this time of the month. She says that the incident was sparked by the girl in front who had said Darren looks like a spastic. He had called her a bitch. Then the girl's boyfriend had joined in.

There is less consensus about whether Darren will return to the school. Angela wants him to go to the Fresh Start Programme, which is an off-site pupil referral unit that provides one-to-one attention for a few weeks to get a disruptive student back on the straight and narrow. Trevor thinks Darren should probably not return, but be found a different school to go to.

I get a glimpse of the intense difficulty in making these decisions. They are all fine judgements, but ones that have a huge personal impact on the life chances and potential happiness of individuals. There are also competing interests: those of the one disruptive child who still deserves an education and those of the wider school. How many chances to give someone is almost a moral question. On one level there should be no limit, on another there has to be a cut off point eventually.

'I've got something for you,' Paul says as we sit in his poky office, surrounded by books and papers. The room has a low ceiling, an attic feel and the quirky and slightly revolting appendage of a toilet in the corner cut off from the rest of the room by very thin cardboard walls, the result being that when Paul relieves himself mid-conversation you can hear everything.

'There's someone I would like you to do some reading with,'

he says. 'His family have asked for some extra help. I've tested
him and he's got a reading age of about eight. He is Year 9,
about fourteen and needs some one-to-one help catching up.
You'd take him out of lessons for two periods a week and work
with him in the library.'

'I don't have any training, though,' I say.

'I've written about this myself, and there are plenty of
materials for you to look at. The key is to give him confidence
and plenty of practice.'

Later that day, Paul brings Jimmy to my room. He is a chubby
boy with pale skin and carrot-coloured hair. He is wearing the
obligatory baseball cap pulled over his eyes.

'Mr Hyman is going to work with you a couple of times a
week, I'll leave you two to decide which lessons are the best to
be pulled out of.'

'Right,' he mumbles.

I have Jimmy's timetable in front of me and let him see it.

'Dance' I immediately alight on as one to miss. This may be
deep prejudice that Jimmy's shape does not lend itself to ballet.
I am relieved that Jimmy readily agrees. However, the second
missed lesson is not going to be as easy. 'French,' he says, 'I
could miss French.' Jimmy has two lessons of French a week, so

if I take him out of one the other will become pointless. I agonise over this decision. I loved French myself at school and did it for A level. If Jimmy stops doing it now he will never catch up – but is this a sacrifice worth making so that he can learn English properly? I am paralysed by indecision. I have been part of so many big decisions in the last few years, and now faced with one seemingly small decision about a boy's life, I can't decide what the right thing is to do. It seems to matter so much more. I feel as if I have too much power all of a sudden and don't know how to exercise it.

I decide that the imperative must be literacy and so we agree he will come out of one dance lesson and one French lesson. I am not sure what he will end up doing in the second French lesson. I tell Jimmy I will see him next week and we will go from there.

I go to the library to look for some suitable books for low-age readers. A teaching assistant shows me the selection. 'Oi you,' she shouts across the library to a tall boy who looks about fourteen. 'You've got a reading age of about three. Come here and read to sir; show him these are for low readers.' The boy is unsurprisingly reluctant to take part in this exercise.

'I'm just going to a lesson.'

'No go on,' she says, 'read the first sentence.'

I say to him not to bother, and he leaves. I find a book on motorbikes, having been told that Jimmy has a real interest in them.

Every Monday at two I have an hour with Trevor, effectively a line management meeting, which he has individually with all his senior managers. I have never in ten years had any kind of line management meeting. That's not how the special advisers' network works, though it's common in the civil service.

Trevor's office is always spotless and paperless. Teachers

complain about red tape, but none of it seems to be ending up on Trevor's desk. Once he has done his papers, they either go straight back to his PA or he stores them in a little drawer. Alastair Campbell is the same. He is equally particular. He used to unleash ferocious broadsides in the middle of meetings if someone slurped their tea. He once told me off for reading his Sunday newspaper the wrong way. It had to be done in order, and then each supplement put back in the right place.

This is not my way of doing things. I am always uncomfortable around excessive tidiness. It's partly because I believe mess is creative. It's also because I believe life's too short to file things. I know this is contradictory and filing things would save time in the long run, but I never seem to manage it. I also think, by way of excuse, I can trace back my messiness to an incident at school, to a teacher, a fierce, strict Scottish teacher.

I was about nine at the time, enthusiastic and neat. The teacher set one of his long weekend assignments. We had to find out about different types of birds and write a project on them. I wrote about thirteen pages, including colour pictures. I remember quantity being as important as quality, having compared the maximum number of pages others had done on previous projects, and knowing that thirteen would be a record. I was very proud of my project, which had benefited from the number of encyclopaedias my father had in the house. I handed the work in and the teacher handed it back without marking it. I asked him why. He said, because I hadn't underlined the title. This was one of his big things: 'Always underline the title twice.' I'm not sure why I hadn't – perhaps I had got carried away drawing birds – but I hadn't and now a good piece of work was not being marked. I pleaded with him to mark it if I now underlined the title, but he said no it was too late. I was not just upset, but outraged by the injustice. I never worked hard on assignments for him again. I believe it had a lasting impact. I rebelled against neatness. Also, I now obsessively revise pieces of work before handing them in, then I wait with excessive nervousness until they are handed back with a comment. For every single note I wrote for Tony, I was on edge until it was given back, in case he didn't like it or, as the fierce teacher had done, he were to say: 'Sorry Peter, I'm not reading your strategy for public service reform unless you underline the title . . . twice.'

At this session, Trevor wants to discuss exactly what I will be doing. We agree that I will spend time in charge of the exclusion room, some time teaching politics and debating with a small group, some English lessons as a classroom assistant, some one-to-one reading and a few hours helping the key GCSE 'marginals', those students who are close to getting their five A–Cs, but need a bit of extra help. In addition, I will join in all the management meetings and help him with some projects. I am pleased with the variety; it will give me a real sense of the school.

'Sir, please let me out.'

Another child is begging to leave the premises. It is 1.15. Lunch hour has begun and I am on gate duty with Emma. In front of me are thirty faces, and thirty races: black, brown, white. Our task is to let out students only if they are in full school uniforms and have a signature in their school diary from their parents and their head of year allowing them to leave, but it is more complicated than that. Some are allowed out because they are on a reduced timetable. That means they are not coping with school and spend some of the time at home or in an alternative environment. Some are allowed out anyway, for a special reason. Emma, who recognises everyone, knows instinctively who's bullshitting and who's genuine. Unlike me, she can sniff a forgery too.

A girl appears with a scrap of paper saying her mother has given her permission.

# Languages spoken at Islington Green School

| | | |
|---|---|---|
| Somali | Portuguese | Serbo-Croat |
| Bengali/Slyheti | Arabic | Cantonese |
| French Creole | Urdu | Gujerati |
| Albanian | Swahili | Twi |
| Turkish | Ilocano | Greek |
| Tigrinya | Yoruba | Mende |
| Spanish | Persian/Farsi | Vietnamese |
| Luganda | Russian | Mandarin |
| Italian | Kurdish | Asante |
| Tagalog/Filipino | Pashto | Azerbaijani |
| Polish | Shona | Wolof |
| Patua | Bulgarian | Nepali |
| Dutch | Macedonian | Lingala |

| Ethnic Groups at Islington Green School | Percentage (%) |
|---|---|
| White British | 48.3 |
| White Irish | 1.1 |
| White any other white background (Turkish mostly) | 16.3 |
| Mixed – white and black Caribbean | 3.5 |
| Mixed – white and black African | 1.2 |
| Mixed – white and Asian | 0.1 |
| Mixed any other mixed background | 2.4 |
| Asian or Asian British – Indian | 1.0 |
| Asian or Asian British – Pakistani | 0.2 |
| Asian or Asian British – Bangladeshi | 4.3 |
| Asian or Asian British – any other Asian background | 0.2 |
| Black or Black British – Caribbean | 4.2 |
| Black or Black British – African | 9.9 |
| Black or Black British – any other background | 0.4 |
| Chinese | 0.7 |
| Any other ethnic group | 6.2 |

'Where's your diary?' Emma asks.

'Lost it so I've got a piece of paper.'

Emma looks at the paper. 'Whose signature is that?'

'My mum's.'

'So if I call her now on your mobile she'll vouch for you will she?'

The girl looks sheepish. While she is wrestling with this moral dilemma, three tall lads push past her and lunge for the gate.

'Diaries,' I say in full teacher mode. They scrabble in their Nike bags and pull out dog-eared diaries. I let them through.

'Where's your uniform?' demands Emma to a short girl with a ponytail.

'What do you mean? This is school uniform.'

'Shoes, ties.'

'Lost my tie.'

'Well go away then,' Emma says brusquely.

'Come on Jack,' a child shouts through the gate at a friend who hasn't made it out yet.

Ministers have just come out against what we were doing. 'Tipping out' is what they call it, and they say it should be stopped. Schools should not release their students on to the streets, only for them to cause havoc in the local area and return to school late. Instead, they should be in school, stimulated by exciting lunch-time clubs. This is one of many examples, I now start seeing, of how the school is on the receiving end of government pronouncements. This is exactly the sort of talking point I used to be in favour of at Number 10, and it's good popular stuff with the voters. Now that I'm seeing the announcement from the school's perspective, I'm wondering why ministers even bother to mention such micro issues other than to show they are 'in touch' with voters. The first implication of the government statement is that schools are releasing children out of stupidity. In the case of Islington Green

School it is to ease the pressure on a canteen that is too small to cope with 983 children getting lunch in forty-five minutes. The second assumption is that the children run amok. In fact there is very little trouble when ours go out. Where I am sure ministers are right is that there should be more clubs at lunch time and a longer lunch break.

The trickle turns into a rush as twenty students approach the gate in one go. This is where it gets tricky. 'Diaries,' Emma and I shout in unison.

There is a mass reaching for bags to produce diaries, but as the scrum approaches a twelve-year-old to my left squeezes under my arm, I lunge at him to haul him back but miss him. Emma spots the boy and shouts after him: 'Kieron, I'll get you later.'

We resume our check.

'Stop,' Emma shouts. She looks hard at the diary in front of her then looks up at a tall shifty-looking girl. 'So your name is Mark is it? Right I'm confiscating this diary. You are using someone else's as a forgery. You should tell Mark that your little game has been rumbled. He will have to come to me to get it back and explain himself.'

'But miss.'

'No buts. Right, gates closing.'

'Wait miss, wait miss.'

Two tiny Year 7s race for the gate, flailing their dairies. Emma lets them through. We close the gate with a padlock and make our way to the canteen where there is mayhem, but joyous mayhem. Hundreds of students are cramming their way between two red posts, loosely queuing to get their dinner. Nearly half of them are able to have lunch for free because their parents are on benefits. Others have a smart card or cash. A small hunched group of teachers sit surrounded by noise and flying chips. The smell could be worse. It's not the over-cooked cabbage that is still the dominant smell in a lot of hospitals, but

the aroma of cooked potatoes. Serving lunch to hundreds of
noisy teenagers in forty-five minutes must be one of the most
thankless jobs imaginable and the dinner ladies are clearly
exasperated by it. One shouts at a boy who speaks little English:
'Don't just point. Until you say the words I'm not giving it to
you.'

If this is representative, then the food children eat at school is
a scandal. It's not that it is not freshly prepared. It is. There is a

varied menu: lamb curry, cauliflower cheese, salads of all kinds, rolls and sandwiches, yoghurts. What could be better? The problem is that also on sale every day are pizza, sausages and chips, plus a machine with every conceivable chocolate bar, and a counter serving sweets and crisps of all varieties. So what do 95 per cent of children do? They march past the salads and choose, every day, pizza and chips. A minority have chips and salt and nothing else. Some make do with crisps, a drink and a sweet pudding. Given that primary schools don't sell sweets and crisps, why on earth should a secondary school? This is one of Angela's great crusades. 'Healthy food is a healthy mind' seems to be her motto. She wants free fresh fruit, fruit given out before exams, and unhealthy food to be weeded out. I would go one further. People should be able to eat what they like outside school but while in school, they should only be served healthy food. That means no chips, no sweets, no fizzy drinks, no chocolate. A school would not dream of showing violent or sexual films to pollute the minds of the students, so why should it serve junk food to pollute their bodies?

Teachers tend to push into the queue and thrust money at the cashier as quickly as they can. I hesitate but finally see an opening. My first school lunch for nearly twenty years is cauliflower cheese. I sit down at a table with Barry, a head of Year , who was a pop musician for ten years, touring the world, and is now a music teacher. He has long dreadlocks, and has a quiet but effective manner with the students. His favourite question to them after a lesson or assembly, is: 'What have you learnt?' Paul joins us as does Sally, a former actress, who is benefiting from the government's homes for key workers initiative. I am made to feel welcome. I am blending in – at least I think I am – spending my breaks and lunch times with staff, spending time in the playground.

'What's the food like at Number 10?' Barry asks. 'There

wasn't any,' I say to their surprise. In fact, gallingly, a café opened in the basement of Number 10 – the first ever – literally a month after I left. 'The Cabinet Office canteen which we often go to is not up to much,' I say. There is little choice at Westminster. We normally used to walk across St James's Park to Prêt à Manger or went to one of the departmental canteens. 'This is better,' I say enthusiastically. They look at me as if I'm mad.

I enter my office and get on with my work, looking at the weekly staff bulletin. It's printed on pink paper and goes to every member of staff. It contains Trevor's weekly diary. It is essential in a school for the head to be completely transparent with staff about what he is up to, Trevor has told me. 'Otherwise teachers think they are doing the hard work in the classroom and you are doing nothing.' The bulletin also contains useful announcements for staff, timetables for exams, names of children who will be absent on trips, messages from Trevor about the need to award merits this week or continue to focus on homework.

Grace's passion for the virtues of education, and her zero tolerance of absenteeism are starting to make me feel a touch old Labour. As she foams at the mouth about fines and prison sentences, I meekly proffer some good liberal objections for why this kind of approach might prove counter-productive.

'Banging them up sends a signal,' she says, and reveals that they prosecute both parents for persistently-truanting children.

I'm shocked. 'Why do both have to go to prison? What happens to the child?'

'Yes you have to do both or it's unfair. Both are responsible. Oh, they've normally got a relative to take them. It's only for a week or two. Very few are taken into care,' she says. 'Fixed penalty notices come in soon. That will shift the dead wood. That will deal with those who take a day off school because it's nice weather. The piss-takers I call them. Those that rock up when they feel like it. They will have one month to pay the fine, then we will prosecute them. They'll get a higher fine or a prison sentence. I know it sounds horrible, but all they have got to do is go to school. They get a free meal there and everything. It's a good deal. The parents need to be more responsible for their children's education. The children complain that it's boring. I say: who told you life's a party? Life is mundane. You'll know boring one day, when you've got kids and a mortgage.

'They need structure and discipline, and it all starts in primary schools. Too many leave not being able to read. What have they been doing for the last three years? Oh yes, circle time. Once you've taught a child to read, that's it, everything is unlocked. I say start them young, stretch them, give them Shakespeare, expose them to things just out of their grasp and make them get there. Encourage them and challenge them.'

By now I am bobbing along on this wave of evangelical fervour.

'Kids have not got any gumption any more – parents don't spend time with them. I had one parent who phoned me and said their child was not reading. I asked her: "Do you read with her? Why don't you take her to the library?" "Oh yeah, suppose I could," she said. But it's a bit of a hassle. She'll go shopping instead. Everything is too easy for them. "I want, I want, I want." They get, they get, they get. It's all one way.'

---

### Weekly newsletter

We are very pleased to welcome Peter Hyman to Islington Green this term. He has settled in very quickly.

---

Cecilia Darker is a plain-speaking, flamboyant dressing, former dance teacher, and now owns a chain of local pubs and a local theatre. She has spiky hair and a flowery jacket. She enters the room with a flourish and greets me with a cheery 'How's it all going?'

'Great,' I say. This is my first governors' meeting, and she is the Chair.

Fifteen governors have assembled, including a timid-looking Liberal Democrat councillor. I don't know whether he will pounce on my presence or ignore it. At least six of those present are from the senior management team or teaching staff of the school. The meeting starts and Cec chairs with an attractive informality.

Trevor begins with the headteacher's report. This is the sales pitch to governors on how well things are going. Few of the issues that we discuss at SMT meetings are aired here: 'Our website is now up and running and very impressive. Islington has implemented the required workforce changes. Staff are now offered a free lunch on the last Friday of each month, one of a number of schemes to show our support for staff. We have got money to become an extended school. The SMT have all been on leadership training.'

Trevor concludes and Cec spins round and says: 'I'm going to put Peter on the spot now and ask him what he thinks of us all, what do you think of the school?'

I am hibernating in the corner and look up with a start. I hate it when this happens. I become shy and gibbering. 'I've been made to feel very welcome here and am impressed by how positive and upbeat everyone is. I am grateful to Trevor and the SMT. I am truly impressed by the staff, but shocked by the state of the buildings. I'm really enjoying myself.'

The governors look pleased at my assessment.

And it's the truth. I am delighted to be doing something

different. I hadn't realised how much I needed a change. There had been long periods at Number 10 where from day to day I had barely left the building, had little contact with the outside world. It is hard to describe quite how liberated I feel. I am released from the meetings, the internal politics, the frustrations of government.

Word is spreading slowly of my past life. About twice a week a child stops me in the corridor or in the playground: 'Are you Tony Blair's mate? Do you know Tony Blair?'

It was usually followed by a bewildered 'Why have you come to this dump? You must have been paid more in the last job. Why are you doing it?'

My answer always sounded corny as soon as it had left my mouth: 'I want to work with students like you' or 'Because there is nothing more important than education' or 'Because this school is on the way up and I want to be part of it.'

In my first weeks I had seen fights and witnessed the difficulty of controlling lessons and assemblies. I had also seen inspiring leadership and dedicated teaching. Most of all I had seen real lives, and real emotions. I was coming home every night elated by the day I'd had. The thing that surprised me most was how much the new job was opening me up. I had always been reluctant to talk about my previous job.

The other reason I was becoming more relaxed might have been the fact that I had not yet taken on any responsibility. I was not yet teaching, which I knew would be stressful. I had left a world where, however used to them I was, I always felt I was on show. There was nothing easygoing about a room of Tony, Gordon, John Prescott, Alastair, Peter or Philip. Now there is more of a team atmosphere, The senior management team share duties, back each other up, stand in for each other.

With all the column inches written about education, from funding problems, to truancy, to debates about selection, no one had prepared me for the single most striking feeling of my first weeks at the school: exhilaration. Schools are vibrant, thrilling, fast-moving places to work. They are places where you can make a difference. Each day I feel lucky. Best of all, no one has held my previous job against me. At least, not yet.

# IN AT THE DEEP END

I finally bump into John, the NUT rep, Socialist Workers Party activist and politics and media studies teacher. I had been right. The T-shirt, jeans and backpack had only been half the give away. A look that said, 'You are a sell out,' was the other half. His reputation has preceded him. Not just that he likes a political fight, but that he is a dedicated and conscientious teacher.

The encounter starts innocently enough. I am walking into the humanities department office, looking for another teacher. The room is empty apart from the person I am pretty sure is John. As I am leaving I decide out of politeness to introduce myself. I have been at the school several weeks and have not had a conversation with him.

'I'm Peter Hyman, it would be good to have a chat about history teaching when you've got a moment.' I thought it possible we might bond over the suffragettes or the role of the judiciary, even if the invasion of Iraq proved a no-go area.

'No, I decided to be civil, not say anything offensive, but I opposed you coming from the beginning. Tony Blair is a war criminal and I don't want anyone associated with him at this school.'

I flinch, slightly taken aback by the ferocity of the attack. 'Well,' I stutter after what seems like a lengthy pause. 'I hope you will not condemn me before you have had a chance to get to know my views. Just because I worked for Tony Blair doesn't mean I'm not an individual with my own opinions.' As the words leave my mouth, I realise how pompous and disloyal to my former boss they sound.

John wishes to talk. This is a juicy opportunity – a New Labour apparatchik standing before him; the school day finished; only a bit of boring marking to be done. I can see the glint in his eye. I am in for a serious tongue lashing.

'Let's not talk about the war now,' I say. 'I'd be interested in your views of the school.'

John leans back in his chair. 'This school was damaged by being put into special measures totally unfairly in 1997 for what seemed like political reasons. I am sure it had something to do with Tony not sending his children here and so the government had to prove that this wasn't a good school. Labour got elected on the day Ofsted left here. We were celebrating their departure with a bottle of Champagne. And another thing, I have always resented David Blunkett's attack on teachers. He never understood teachers.'

I agree with him that the government has too often in the past appeared to berate teachers rather than support them.

'I don't come from some far left sect or something. I was taken to see Nye Bevan when I was five. I was always in the Labour party. I come from a working-class background, only went to university at the LSE because of free education. So it sickens me that a Labour government is stopping working-class kids going to higher education.'

I slip effortlessly into 'defend the government' mode. I have had seven years practice and only four weeks in the real world. It hasn't yet dawned on me that I am allowed my own views. 'But why should the 50 per cent who don't go to university subsidise the 50 per cent who do go, who will get better jobs and earn more in any case? Isn't there a good left-wing case for the government's views?'

'All the kids in my class are put off going to university,' he says, as if conclusive proof of his point of view.

I counter with my own equally small and unrepresentative sample. The previous week a journalist from the *Independent* had come in to talk to twenty sixteen-year-olds about tuition fees. Despite her prompting all of them, they said that while not wanting the fees, university was important, and if you could go you should go and money wouldn't put them off.

'Higher taxes for the well off would be more progressive,' he says. 'I don't mind paying more taxes.'

'I agree higher taxes are one option. Though I wouldn't have said paying for university places is the first call on that money.'

I do not share Tony's views on taxation, particularly direct taxes. Or, put another way, I can see the tactical and political reasons for reassuring people, particularly before 1997, that we would not make a move on direct taxation, but I do not believe, as a point of policy principle, that a higher tax rate on the very wealthy would do any harm. I would cut taxes at the bottom and raise them at the top.

John moves effortlessly on to the next item on his shopping list of betrayal. We were on to the cold cuts counter. 'This school hasn't benefited from funding.'

I know from the head that this is nonsense. Of the possible attacks on the government this is the most preposterous. 'But I know for a fact spending has gone up at this school.'

'Come with me,' he says. He gets up from his chair and heads for the door, jangling his keys. Where was I going to be taken, a leaky roof, a broken window? He unlocks the classroom opposite and shows me some textbooks. 'Look,' he says, 'there is one between two for geography and history. In my day we had one each.'

'But that is surely a choice. The department and the school have chosen to invest more in computers, but it's definitely got the money for books,' I say.

After more arguing John concedes that resources have risen, but only to the same levels as at the end of the last Labour government.

'What about teachers' salaries?' I say, believing I'm on safe ground given that they have gone up dramatically in the last few years.

'Well mine has gone up a lot,' he says – an unadulterated positive statement. 'But not for ordinary teachers. One teacher here, with London prices and everything, was on the breadline. Sounds funny but that's the truth. She left because she couldn't survive to the end of the month. Labour never run the economy well,' he goes on. 'There are always cutbacks under Labour.'

'But hasn't that been one of our great successes? Full credit to this government. We've got stability and now we are pouring money in.'

'No, you inherited a strong economy.'

Then, like a DJ linking the Beatles to Eminem without missing a beat, John manages to turn teachers' salaries in Islington schools into a reason for condemning the war on Iraq.

'Take the war – look at all the money spent on Afghanistan and Iraq. What do you think of the war then? What are your views?'

I say: 'It was a very difficult decision, but the only justification would be on humanitarian grounds. I believe there are some good reasons why the Left could support this kind of action, however much they dislike Bush, because getting rid of Saddam is good for the people of Iraq.'

'Don't tell me about "humanitarian". I was one of those who protested when Saddam Hussein gassed those people at Halabja. I was there at the beginning. I can just see this for what it is. It's not why we went to war. We went because of weapons of mass destruction.'

He pauses momentarily for breath.

'This is just an imperialist white invasion of another country. People always dress things up in high-minded moral reasons,' he says. 'They are not exactly going to be honest about wanting to take over another country. There won't be free elections. If there are and a theocracy develops, then the West won't stand for it.'

'Time will tell,' I say. I try and draw the conversation to a close. Apart from his initial outburst it has been friendly, though combative, but John, suddenly realising, I suspect, that he has been fraternising with the enemy, turns to me and rediscovers his glare.

'If it's to be believed that you were Tony Blair's speechwriter, then you have been part of the propaganda machine taking Britain to war on a lie.'

'Well,' I say, 'let's talk about teaching some time.'

John gives me a half-smile and I leave the room, thinking what I usually do after listening to veteran politician Tony Benn. It's all very plausible, but there are so many leaps and assumptions in the argument that when one flaw emerges the whole house of cards comes tumbling down.

While the unions are less strong in Islington, I get the sense that there is enough self-censorship, occasions when Trevor would tip-toe round them, to suggest that the unions could hold back the chances of turning round the school.

*

My honeymoon period has been short. Up until now I have been scratching the surface: sitting in on lessons, watching assemblies, on gate duty with another teacher – dipping my toe in. Now the challenge really begins, the first of my hour sessions in the exclusion room in sole charge of some of the most disruptive pupils in the school.

Exclusion rooms are more common now. They are sometimes called the 'inclusion room' because they are a way of taking children out of lessons without excluding them from the school.

Tracey is in the classroom, ready for me to take over.

'Hello, sir,' she says. Being called sir by other members of staff as well as by the pupils still jars with me. Tracey is an inspiring figure. She also runs the 'little house' which was formerly the caretaker's house, but has been transformed into a counselling place where the mentors, psychologists, home-school liaison worker and social workers meet with students, individually or in groups, to work through problems. She has a natural way with the students, and they respect, trust and, in some cases, totally rely on her.

'We have two today,' she says, 'Not our regulars.'

Samantha and Carl are getting on with some work at separate desks. Both are in the exclusion room for minor disruption in the classroom. Samantha has a longer sentence because she is not wearing school uniform.

For a child to be sent to the exclusion room a teacher has to get the Head of Year or Head of Faculty to sign a form, and write down the reason and the length of time they want the student to stay there. It is meant to be a sanction that comes a long way down the line after verbal warnings. Samantha's entry reads: 'Refusal to follow teacher's instructions and not following school uniform code. Period 2 and break and period 3.' Carl's reads: 'Refusal to follow teacher's instructions.'

Tracey reminds me of the procedure. 'You first get them to write out the page in front of them on the desk which tells them the school rules. Then they write out answers to the three questions on the board: Why were you sent here? Was it fair/unfair? What will I do differently next time? Then they are meant to get on with the subject that they are missing. If they haven't brought any work, we have appropriate work-sheets and books in the cupboard for each year and most subjects.'

Just before Tracey leaves me to it, another client bursts through the door. It's Jamie. I had seen him the day before in an English lesson I had been observing. He had been disruptive throughout. Tough looking, he has a thin comb stuck in his hair. Tracey removes it in a friendly way and hands it to him. He puts it straight back. I am dreading this. Samantha and Carl are not going to cause any trouble. Jamie is a different matter. Before she leaves I ask Tracey where she will be if I need her and make sure I have her phone number.

For the first time at the school I feel alone and scared. The responsibility for what happens in this room in the next hour is all mine. This is a situation where teaching skill and experience would help enormously. I have no experience. As for skills, I could write a strategy for the students. I could draft a press release about them. I would be able to judge whether they were on message. But control them? That will be a challenge.

I debate with Trevor and with Paul at regular intervals the school's approach to inclusion. Nationally 9,000 children are permanently excluded each year and 10,000 are 'missing' from the school system altogether. Trevor is passionate that we should do all we can to include children. I don't know how much that is because the LEA and government seem to want it, and how much this is his own educational belief. Paul, who sides on most things with teachers, has a firm and unwavering view: we should give them numerous chances, everything possible, but eventually with the 'nutters' it should be 'offski'. They should go to a special school or special unit elsewhere. His view is that the majority have to be catered for and teachers simply cannot teach if the thirty known 'head cases' remain in the school.

I remember from government how contentious our exclusion policy has been. In 1997 we sent out the signal that schools must do more to include children, but Tony got increasingly annoyed by this because every time he met parents and teachers they complained about it. He then got passionate about excluding them, because he thought this was essential to improve behaviour. The result had been mixed messages.

I look at Jamie's paperwork. His crime. 'Repeated use of bad language first period.' He is sitting the other side of the room from Samantha and Carl who are chatting quietly whilst trying to answer their English SATs paper on Alice Walker's 'The Flowers'. Jamie, to my surprise, is silently writing out the rules when a new customer appears accompanied by Jess, a dance teacher and Head of Year 11.

'We're just keeping him up here for one lesson,' she says breezily, 'so there isn't another clash with his teacher.'

Terry sits down at a desk in the middle of the room. The teacher had written a mini-essay in the box marked 'Reason': 'Terry refused to remove his hooded top before going into assembly. I asked him at least three times before I removed it myself. Once I did this he lashed out at me with aggressive language.' With expletives watered down with asterisks she has added for emphasis in brackets: (f**k off you p***y hole!).

'What lesson are you missing?' I ask him.

'Science,' he grunts. He is small, surly, fed up, like a hamster who has run out of toilet roll to chew. He starts scribbling on a piece of paper.

The room is calm. My client group has doubled. The atmos-

# EVENT LOG

| Time in exclusion room | Report – offence |
|---|---|
| **1 period** | Very rude – shouting at staff 'prick and dickhead', truanting |
| **1 period** | Staff confiscated phone as using in class, swearing, 'give me my f★★★ing phone' |
| **1 period** | Refused to sit down, walked out without permission, kicked cupboard, threw objects |
| **2 periods** | Eating polo sweets during exam, passing them to pupils who threw them around |
| **1 period** | Hit pupil on bottom, deeply upsetting pupil – apologised and made up |
| **2 periods** | Throwing clay around refused to clean up, rude to staff, extremely disruptive |
| **2 periods** | Climbed fence and left school without permission |
| **1 period** | Threw pupil's jacket in bin, despite being warned, refused to apologise |
| **3 periods** | Bullying another student during registration |
| **3 periods plus lunch** | Creating havoc on the second floor |
| **Referral unit for 5 days** | Caused extensive damage to the lift |
| **1 period** | Jumping on and off table, kicked pupil, pupil fell back and hit his head |
| **Excluded one day** | Headbutted another student and refused to give explanation |

phere is tenser, but I am sitting at my desk getting on with my own work, and looking my most serious and, I hope, professional. The situation is under control. This is not quite as hard as it seems.

I begin to flick through the bumf Trevor has given me on *assertive discipline*, his area of expertise. He gives talks on the subject at other schools. He believes it is the key to a calm, ordered school, which is his number one priority.

I read his bumf on the subject: 'You have a right to teach and your students have a right to learn in a classroom free from disruptive behaviour. Teachers today do not receive the respect from parents and from society that they used to. More students come to school with behaviour problems than ever before. Teachers are not sufficiently trained to deal with behaviour problems. The myth of the "good teacher" keeps teachers from asking for assistance. Good curriculum and stimulating material is not always enough to motivate students to behave.'

Trevor's solution is that students need to know the expectations, they need limits, they need positive recognition and support and they need to be taught how to choose responsible behaviour.

Trevor identifies different teacher styles to deal with poor behaviour. *The pleading style*: wishy-washy with students, one day not responding to disruptive behaviour, the next reacting firmly. This, unfortunately, is the style I recognise in myself. *Aggressive style*: treating classroom as a battleground, 'us and them', determined to score a victory over the children. The ideal is the *assertive style*: telling students what behaviour is acceptable and what is unacceptable, what will happen when the student chooses to behave and what will happen when the student chooses not to behave. No questions. No room for confusion.

To back this up Trevor has clear rewards: verbal praise; written praise; merits; merit certificates; attendance prizes; head-teacher's commendations.

Trevor believes in cash prizes for those with the most merits and the best attendance. These are up to £20 for a student, and £600 each term for the best tutor form, which they usually put towards a trip to a theme park.

The sanctions have a similar hierarchy: verbal warning; a letter home to parents; report card – which means teachers monitor each lesson; breaktime detention; lunchtime or after school detention; exclusion from class or school.

The exclusion room is low down the list, even though teachers quite often use it as a first resort, understandably in some cases, in order to get an irritating child out of a lesson. Angela's analysis of those sent to the exclusion room shows that boys get sent far more than girls and the younger students more than the older. The most common offences are disruptive behaviour, truanting or bunking lessons. Trevor remains optimistic that the most difficult students can be reached, and it is true there is more support for them than ever before. The question is how many children can get the one-on-one help and how the benefits can be sustained. The BEST workers (Behaviour and Education Support Teams) – part of the government's Behaviour Improvement Programme – appear to be making a difference. They're targeting the children who need the benefit of several different services, whether it is a clinical psychologist, a health visitor or a social worker. Joined up lives, lives with many problems, do need joined up solutions. At government level I saw how hard it was to get departments to work together. This project has the potential to be more successful because all the practitioners work out of the same building and start from the individual they are dealing with.

The door opens, flung as far as it will go, hitting a desk. A large boy with short spiky hair comes towards me at pace. He reaches into his pocket, gets out a crumpled form, flings it at me and bellows: 'Fucking teachers!'

He slumps in the front desk a yard from me and puts his head in his hands.

I uncrumple the piece of paper and start reading the entry. 'Matt consistently refused instructions: school uniform, made remarks, walking about in classroom.'

Matt gets out his Walkman from his bag, puts the headphones in his ear and starts listening. This is a direct challenge to me. He knows it's not allowed. I tell him to put it away, which to my surprise he does immediately. Even he must think this is a bit cheeky. Then, to my surprise, he starts writing out the school rules as he is meant to. It's as if this is second nature. I get the impression the exclusion room is a home from home. I flick through the file of past customers and realise that Matt is virtually a season ticket holder. He is overdosing on bad behaviour.

'How many times have you come here?'

'This is my thirtieth. I'm going to get an external exclusion now.' He doesn't seem to care. After fifteen there is usually an automatic external exclusion.

The difficult part of the exclusion room is what to do after students have written out the rules. They are supposed to get on with working alone on their subject, but very few can be bothered. This is when they get bored or angry and look for distractions. Carl needs help. 'This English stuff is boring,' he says. 'This book is boring. I missed the lesson we did it in anyway. All this stuff is about mood. Poetry, description, all that. It does my head in.'

Jamie pipes up: 'I did it yesterday.'

'So can you help him?' I ask.

Jamie gives the answers that he has learnt from the lesson the previous day. He has obviously absorbed more than I imagined, given his disruptive behaviour. He is pleased to be helpful. 'Thanks a lot,' I say to him.

Bolstered by our friendly exchange I try to cement the relationship. 'How was your birthday then?' I remember it had been the previous day.

'Cool, got this jacket.' He is sporting a grey hooded top.

'It's nice.' Forty minutes later I realise my answer should have been: 'Where's your school uniform?' I've not yet got that teacher's eye for the 'rules'.

Terry is not bothering to write the lines. 'You know everyone has to complete this before they leave,' I say.

'You never told me that, sir, I'll never do it in time.'

'Yes you will if you start now.'

Carl says, 'I'm bored. This stuff's rubbish. I'm tired.' He yawns and leans back. Jamie starts chatting. I don't know the level of strictness that is required in the room. Is it an achievement that they are not having a go at each other or walking round the room? Or should I be insisting they work in silence? Jamie is now a stream of consciousness. Does this matter? I content myself with trying to get through this first session.

Five minutes before the end Matt finishes writing out the rules so I say, 'Let's get you some science work.'

'But there's only five minutes to go, sir.'

'Well let's at least make a start,' I say, but rummaging in the back cupboard I fail to find any. Terry has now finished his writing. The bell goes. Matt and Terry can both go, I say, and they rush to the door and are off. Three remain. Jamie, Samantha and Carl start chatting.

'Do you live with your mum?'

'Yes, just my mum.'

'See my dad every Wednesday and some weekends, that's as much as the court allows.'

'Why is it your dad has all the money, yet everyone lives with their mum?'

'My dad has a criminal record, that's why.'

'I live with both my parents.'

'You're lucky.'

'Yes.'

'So where's your uniform?'

'I've got a note,' says Jamie. He gets out a note: 'My washing machine is broken so for one day Jamie is without uniform – from Jamie's mum.'

'Who forged that?' asks Samantha.

'No one.'

'What else did you get for your birthday?'

'Money.'

There is something streetwise, yet vulnerable about these teenagers. Underneath a layer of bravado these are children like any others, but children who, in the words of one teacher, have just seen too much. It reminds me of Mario Cuomo's great line: 'Children growing up, hearing the sound of gun-fire before they've even heard an orchestra.'

Tracey relieves me of my duties. I have survived my first hour in the exclusion room. I am drained. I retire to the staff room to queue up for a cup of tea and Kit-Kat. I sit down and chat to some of my new friends.

I have heard three times in a week similar comments from teachers about the students. 'They could all be in *Oliver Twist*.' 'They all look as if they could be Fagin's little helpers.' 'Urchins, every one of them.' Another teacher gives more details. 'You and I are socialised when we are about four. We learn to share, to respect others, all the basic tools of society. Many of these kids haven't, so we are teaching it to them now.'

I am enjoying the staff room. There is a far more equal gender balance in teaching, in fact overall more women than men. Politics is still very male, very macho. Teaching is now a profession with many attractions. There is more chance to develop professionally. It is far better paid than it used to be, with the head at Islington Green on more than £90,000, the senior management team earning £50,000 plus, and most classroom teachers earning £25,000 and above. I started off sharing the predudice of a lot – that the thirteen weeks holiday teachers get is a luxury. The longer I am at this school, the more I see the physical and emotional demands of the job, the more deserved I think it is.

I gradually discover that a lot of teachers have almost drifted into the job. I'm sure this is different from other professions. It's hard to drift into being a doctor, let alone a surgeon, but when I ask 'why teaching?', almost every teacher talks of trying something else first and either not enjoying it or not being good at it, or not being fulfilled. Of the SMT, Trevor was in marketing before teaching; Emma and Paul wanted to be journalists; Eileen and Angela were both in the private sector. Angela has worked her way up to deputy head having left school with no qualifications, aged fifteen, worked as a typist and receptionist then in public relations, before doing a degree in education. Eileen had a spell at NatWest.

Ted is a maths teacher, who after a career as a property developer went sailing round the world. Then he decided he wanted to do something different rather than drift into retirement, so he retrained as a teacher in his fifties and now seems to be loving his new life. He enjoys doing the statistics for the department, looking in detail at which students are performing, and where the department should put most of its attention. For him the culture shock was enormous – going from a big office, secretaries, to a 'grotty' classroom, rude students and all your own paperwork.

Alan is a teaching assistant in his fifties. His daughter Chloe is Head of Humanities. He's a working-class, London lad, and for the vast majority of his life has been a butcher, becoming, to his great pride, a master butcher. He then did a degree at Middlesex University where his daughter was also studying, before coming to Islington Green as a teaching assistant. 'The first day teaching in school I thought I was taller than what I was. I felt I was floating,' he says.

This is the first time since I've been at the school that someone has described how I feel. '"Is this right?" I say to myself. Should I feel like this? It's pure gratification. I am elated. Seeing those kids' faces and thinking that I've taught them something.'

Alan has strong views about the lower standards today and the benefits of his secondary modern school, even though he is certain he passed the 11-plus but was kept out of grammar school because of class prejudice. 'Discipline is different today,' he says. 'There was corporal punishment then. Didn't do me any harm. No noise in the class – that would be painful for you if there was. Numbers, geography, history, were all better in the Fifties than now. Did you see that programme where they gave A★ students at GCSE the 11-plus exam of thirty years ago. Only one passed it. Computers, calculators, it's not up here any more.' He points to his head. 'Pencil and paper, they were the best. It's now all out of a book for the curriculum. I wasn't taught that way. It was all put on the board. No one knows their numbers these days.'

Alan is giving me an insight into the path that many Islington students will be taking, and that's if they are lucky. There is an argument that for some students comprehensives have been worse than the secondary modern. The secondary modern might have been unfair, and lowered the expectations of some who happened to fail the 11-plus, but, so the argument goes, the good ones at least prepared students for practical work when they left. By giving students an academic education, which results in 72 per cent at Islington Green failing to get five good

GCSEs, too many leave school without either qualifications or practical skills.

I soon have another exclusion room session, and this time reach the room late and out of breath. My heart is pounding. It then sinks. A pounding, sinking heart can't be good for you. I see before me three of the worst, most uncontrollable kids in the school. I have encountered them once before in the Learning Zone; they're quite a team. It's hard to be sent here from the Learning Zone. They must have done something really unpleasant.

Tracey hands over to me with a knowing smile. 'I've put Alex's drink and crisps in the drawer down here,' she says, pointing to the bottom of the teacher's desk. 'Have fun!'

'Why are you here?' I ask Alex.

'Because we took a fire extinguisher and let it off in Miss Gartland's face.' I'm sure Angela will have enjoyed that.

'Why did you do that?'

'Because our maths teacher said he didn't want us in lessons. If he had said he wanted us we wouldn't have done it.'

Tom joins in: 'Sir, have you ever got beaten up in the street?'

I don't answer.

'Sir,' he tries again, 'would you dare punch me?'

'No,' I say, 'punching doesn't usually resolve anything.'

Hamid, the third of the gang says: 'You mean if someone beats you up you just stand there and take it?'

This is going to be a very long hour. Hamid starts to blow huge bubbles with his pink gum and then lets off a rasping pop as one collapses on his face. Tom gets up and walks towards me. Alex follows.

'Could you sit down please Alex.' I am ignored.

'Could you sit down please Tom.' I am ignored.

I stand up from my chair and approach them. 'Could you sit down please,' I say more firmly.

They side step me and go for the drawer. Alex takes out the fizzy drink. Tom takes out the crisps.

I ask Tom for the crisps, but he eats them ostentatiously in front of me.

I ask Alex for the fizzy drink, but he hides it between his legs and pretends he hasn't taken it. Both swing back in their chairs, smirking, knowing that round one has gone to them.

This is humiliating. I simply don't have the tools to control them. If I try to stop them doing something, they ignore me, which means I lose authority. If I don't ask them to stop doing something which they know they shouldn't be doing, they know they are getting away with murder and I also lose authority.

They should never have been put in the exclusion room as a group. The rule is you split up trouble-makers. What adds to my difficulties is their sentence is too long. They are in the exclusion room for eleven periods which is more than two days. This defeats the purpose of the room which is as a place to cool off. I suppose it is a way of not externally excluding them, but it drives them potty, and I am going to suffer as a consequence.

A mobile phone alarm goes off.

'Could you turn that off,' I say. This one I've got to win or I will look a complete fool.

They sit back and laugh.

'I haven't got one,' says Tom.

'Nor have I,' says Hamid.

'I know it's yours,' I say to Hamid.

'It's not. Check my coat if you like, sir,' he says, handing over his duffle coat.

There's no mobile phone in the coat.

'It's in his bag,' shouts Tom.

Alex gets up and grabs the bag just before I reach it.

I sit back down and say, 'The more this goes on, the longer you will end up staying in the exclusion room.'

As in a prison, there are only two approaches: time off for good behaviour, or time on for bad behaviour. This seems to do the trick and Hamid turns the mobile phone off.

A fourth boy arrives. You can only be accepted in the exclusion room with the right paperwork, but this student has none.

I phone Tracey and tell her the situation and ask if she wants him accepted.

'Send him back. By the way, how's it going up there?'

I don't want the students sensing my unease so I whisper: 'It's quite difficult, they're egging each other on.'

Alex says, 'Quiet everyone he's called for help. Let's show whoever comes that he's been lying, that he doesn't really need help.'

For a couple of minutes they get on with their work in silence, but the boredom sets in again. Bill, the new boy, has refused to leave, despite my attempts to send him back to his lesson. Tom throws chewing gum at Bill.

'Is it all right if I fart, sir?' asks Bill. He's got the hang of baiting me and he's only been in the room a couple of minutes.

'Hamid have you ever kissed anyone?' asks Bill. He's not just going to bait me, it seems.

'Yeah,' Hamid says nervously.

'Yeah, I bet you have,' says Bill goading him. 'You've kissed your mummy goodnight.' He smacks his lips together.

Alex leaves his seat again, walks to the corner of the room, climbs on a desk and announces: 'I'm going to climb out of the window.'

I size up the window. We are on the sixth floor. It is a 100-metre sheer drop on to concrete. However, the window is small and opens only slightly. I'm pretty sure he's not going to manage it. I won't let him faze me. 'Go ahead then,' I say.

He continues to try. I begin to worry that he might, at a push, succeed, but I use all my will power to ignore him. He's annoyed by my indifference. It works. He climbs down. Late in the day I've won a small victory.

Paul, the deputy head, walks into the room. 'Do you need some help, sir?' he asks. This is well-meaning but I know that now any shred of respect they still have for me has gone. 'Right, I'm going to talk to you three, Tom, Alex, Hamid, one at a time, and see what we can resolve. Who wants to go first?'

Alex stands up and bolts for the tall metal cupboard at the back of the classroom. He opens the door, dives in and closes it behind him. The class is silent. There is a part of me that is secretly pleased that Alex is playing up to an experienced deputy head and not just me.

'Alex, it looks as if you have nominated yourself,' Paul says . . . 'Alex come out of there.' . . . 'Alex I'm losing my patience.' . . . 'Alex . . .'

Alex steps out of the cupboard and swaggers towards Paul and the door.

'Right sir,' Paul says to me, 'I will be back to see the others shortly.'

The two of them depart.

With Alex gone and the triumvirate broken up, things become a little calmer and I stagger on to the end of the period. Tracey comes up to relieve me. I couldn't be more delighted to see her.

I can't remember this feeling before: a deep sense of power-lessness and stupidity. Perhaps it's just the unsettling feeling of being back on the bottom rung trying to learn a new set of skills. My ability to argue or reason that I have used for years, rational discussion leading to rational conclusion, counts for nothing.

Here it is about fronting it out, showing your own power and control, getting beneath the brave exterior and trying to connect with the child inside. There's something deeply depressing about Hamid, Tom and Alex. All have a spark to them, but it's a spark that has become a wildness. Yet they have the intelligence, and the opportunity, the caring at this school, to get on. They seem so completely indifferent to rules and boundaries. They are only thirteen yet they don't care about school or the consequences of their actions. Have their parents let them down? Has society let them down? Has the school let them down? Or have they let themselves down? I leave school that day, for the first time since I arrived, depressed and pessimistic. What a task Trevor has to improve this school. How is he possibly going to achieve it?

The following day I bump into Tracey in the corridor. 'They've written to you to apologise, sir,' she says. 'It was their own idea.' I don't believe they have written to me off their own bat, and I never get to see the apology.

I go into the playground. Members of the senior management team are encouraged to help out with the lunch queue, to make sure there is not too much shoving. I am starting to get used to the pattern of the day, and used to the melee of the playground – so much so that students are starting to treat me like their other teachers, demanding something or having a laugh at my expense. It takes me several minutes to realise that the student greeting me with a slap on the back and a friendly 'Hello, sir' has planted a 'kick me' sticker on my jacket. He rushes off with a cackle of satisfaction. I've obviously got 'mug' written on my forehead too.

Another student, of fourteen, asks me if I can get her a tie because she has lost hers and her mother wouldn't pay for another one because she said she 'could get bread and biscuits for the same amount of money'. I find her a tie and, although I should charge her for it, I let her have it for free.

One sad-looking, fragile eleven-year-old is stalking me. Every time I see him he mumbles a long story about how he was sent to the exclusion room by mistake and got in trouble at home for it, and the teacher must now tell his parents that it was unfair. I shudder to think what happened to him at home to make him so relentless in pursuit of a 'school pardon' but no matter how many times I direct him to the relevant teacher, he returns to me for help.

One tough looking kid teaches me some of the subculture of the playground, an amazing education into what's really going on. There are effectively two tribes, 'safes' and 'sweets'. The safes go up to other safes and go 'safe'. The sweets go up to other sweets and go 'sweet'. If the 'safe' says 'safe' to a 'sweet', then they say 'sweet' back. 'Safes' are distinguished by having trousers that sag down to their knees, they are normally black students and they wear flat baseball caps. The sweets are normally white, sometimes Turkish, and they wear baseball caps with longer peaks. 'Heavy', 'class', and 'ream' are the words for cool. 'Jam' and 'kick out' mean go away. 'Your mum' is a big insult – even though it is only the beginning of a sentence, the end is obviously implied. 'Buff' means something great. I feel I am being let in on a big secret. I wonder how many teachers know that the size of the cap determines what gang you belong to.

The next time I'm in the exclusion room, I'm in for a big shock. There's no one there: ten empty chairs, ten empty desks. Has Trevor's magic suddenly worked? Have Islington Green's children suddenly seen the light? Have children been taught right from wrong and have now en masse chosen right? I sit down at my desk and look around the room. I can hear an English teacher in the classroom opposite, trying to control the class.

'I'm talking,' he keeps saying. He isn't. He's shouting. 'So why did Romeo want to marry Juliet? . . . Was Friar Lawrence a good influence . . .?'

The sun is dazzling through the window. The turquoise notice boards are illuminated. A large poster entitled 'emotional intelligence' – about social skills and getting on with others – catches my eye on the left wall. White piping hangs from the ceiling. The radiators are painted in the school colours. The phone is broken. I have one hour sitting in an empty room, knowing that at any moment the door might be flung open and some thunderous entrance might be made. Nothing stirs. I have an hour of surreal calm.

The exclusion room turns out to be good preparation for my first real classroom experience.

I am a classroom assistant in Sally's English class with some Learning Zone students. These are students taken out of mainstream lessons because they either have disruptive behaviour or poor literacy or both. There are only between eight and ten in the class with two adults – a teacher and an assistant. Our classroom is in the old technology block. It has a shelf running round the perimeter to put books on, leaving an inviting gap underneath. Lessons are at a single high table with chairs resembling bar stools around it. There is a sofa in the corner. This is meant to create a more relaxed primary-school feel and give students a place to read.

This is a typical lesson:

I enter the room. Sally is already writing the lesson objective and date on the board. The classroom appears to be empty. But I see arms and legs poking out from under the shelf.

'By the time I turn round I want everyone sitting up at the desk or there will be detentions.' One boy rushes out from under the shelf. The others do so more half-heartedly. One remains in the corner under a sink, thinking he hasn't been spotted.

'Stuart, I will count to three and then I will get angry. One, two . . .'

Stuart scrambles out and sits down.

Kelly enters the room. She is the only girl. There are meant to be three or four in the class, but they have not turned up for weeks. So she is outnumbered eight to one. She's a bit of a tomboy which helps. She wears glasses and neat school uniform with socks pulled up to her knees. She shouts at Dave for no reason and sits down.

Neil saunters in, shoulders slouched: 'Got to give a note to my Head of Year.'

'Can you give it to her at break, the lesson's starting,' I say.

Neil walks out ignoring me. ' Neil,' I call after him. 'Please come back. You can go at break.' He looks at me contemptuously and walks away.

' Neil,' my voice trails off. Neil is on anti-depressants. I have never seen him smile, though he did laugh once when he was picking on another student.

Simon shuffles into the room. He has mild learning difficulties and a motor disease and moves slowly. He has charm and an ear-to-ear smile. Getting from the sixth-floor of the tower block to the technology block between lessons takes a lot of stamina, even though he has a lift key.

'Sir, this is boring,' says Stuart.

'We haven't started yet,' I say.

'But I know it's boring, it's English.'

'Oi, four eyes,' says Dave to Kelly.

'Don't call me four eyes.'

Kelly takes off one of her shoes, holds it in her hand like a club, with the heel pointing outwards, and approaches Dave who is spraying the insults.

'Kelly stop,' Sally says. Kelly hits Dave feebly with the heel.

'Kelly put that down.'

'Why are you picking on me, Miss?'

'Don't be wound up by him. Dave, apologise!'

Dave mumbles: 'Sorry four eyes.'

'Miss.'

'Dave.'

Kelly picks up her rucksack and leaves the classroom with a swagger, slamming the door behind her.

'Right she's getting a detention.'

'Hello Simone,' Benny says entering the room, fifteen minutes late and tipping Simon's chair backwards. The group switches between being motherly towards Simon and treating him to the same aggressive and mindless behaviour as everyone else. It's not always clear which is worse.

Sally: 'Benny, leave him alone and sit down, you're late.' It's like musical chairs. One in one out. 'Right, I want you to write about your favourite thing. I have written the instructions on the board. What is your favourite thing, what does it look like, what does it smell like? When you close your eyes what do you imagine about it? Well done Dave, well done Stuart, you're starting immediately.' Sally is good at praising the students to encourage others to follow them. If she can, and this class tries this theory to destruction, she always prefers to praise the good ones rather than tell off the bad.

There is momentary calm as the students realise there is a simple task to carry out. Sunil, who is clearly quite bright, missed lots of his primary schooling through illness, and although he speaks perfect English, he cannot write a word. I have never met someone before who cannot spell his own name. The class has an extraordinary spread of reading and writing abilities, from next to nothing to pretty good. Teaching such a range in a way that benefits all is difficult. I sit next to Sunil and help him with the assignment. He is due to get some additional one-to-one help soon.

Every time I am in this class I am gripped by the dynamics being played out. The three toughest kids are vying to be top dog. A couple of the others know they will always be too weak to dominate, so use verbal niggling as a way of asserting themselves. Kelly receives grudging respect because she is a feisty girl. Ngu and Sunil, both foreign, are treated as acceptable outsiders, and are respected when they join in the larking about. To all of them the lesson is a game: how much can we get away with before the teachers snap? There is no sense in which they are there to learn, or because they believe the lesson or school is for their benefit.

Stuart breaks the quiet with fury. 'He cussed my mum,' Stuart says and gets up and whips Nick, who has been sitting quietly, with his tie.

'Put your tie on and sit down please,' I say to Stuart. He ignores me the first six occasions I ask him.

'He called my mum a bitch, that's b . . . i . . .,' there's a long pause, '. . . c . . . k.' Emphasising a word by saying the letters is usually effective, but the power can be lost if you can't spell.

'Don't get wound up by it, just sit down,' I say.

'Oi, sir why are you looking grumpy?'

'Can I have a pen sir?'

'Yes sir, I need a pen.'

'Sir, gis a pen.'

'Oi sir, pen.'

'Can you bring a pen in future please,' I say giving out pens. 'I can't give out new pens every lesson.'

Matthew, who refuses to work most lessons, has not had much attention. He attempts to remedy this by climbing on the shelf and banging on the window.

'Get down,' Sally and I shout in unison. Two instructions for the price of one, but it has no effect. Matthew laughs and throws a pen at Simon. At least he's got a pen.

'Get out of my lesson,' Sally says snapping. Matthew slowly

obeys. He leaves the room but disrupts the next five minutes by banging on the door.

'Just ignore him,' Sally says. I go outside to see if I can reason with Matthew. He has disrupted several lessons.

I sit with him in my office and ask him what the matter is. He opens up very quickly: 'My dad says he hates me and never wants to see me again. You know last time I saw him we drove around in his car and he wore two pairs of sunglasses so that he couldn't see and then he tried to run people over. My stepfather keeps telling me I'm the devil and have 666 written on my head.'

Other teachers tell me afterwards that he makes up a lot of stories and it is very hard to tell which are true. True or not, it's worrying that he should be telling the stories at all.

'Do you like this school?'

'No. It's boring.'

'Did you like your primary school?'

'Chucked out 15 times.'

'What can we do to make it better?'

'Stop the teachers picking on me.'

I convince Matthew to come back to the lesson and try to behave.

On the way back to the lesson I notice Jason, who has left the class and is now in the corridor sobbing. I leave Matthew and try to find out what's up.

'Why are you crying Jason?' Silence.

'Can I help?'

Five minutes of trying gets nowhere. So I go and ask his form teacher to have a word. He has no luck either. I return to the lesson.

Simon has decided the way to make friends is to copy the worst behaved students. It is a pitiful sight. He has shaved his head recently to make himself less cherubic. Now he clambers over to the corner of the classroom, with a slow painful bending movement he manages to position himself under the shelf so that he is doing something naughty. He looks round for approval from his peers. He gets some.

'What on earth are you doing Simon, you're normally so good?'

'Do you fancy miss, Sir?'

'She fancies you.'

'Are you two married?'

'You know Sir, she dresses to impress you.'

'That's enough Benny, that's inappropriate.'

'Miss do you like sir?'

'Enough.'

'Any more and we will start putting names on the board.' Sally draws a smiley face and then a sad face. This usually works. Those who get their names put under the sad face then need to be good for the rest of the lesson to get it rubbed off.

'Listening arms please,' Sally says. 'Good Stuart, good Benny, good Ngu. Who's not got their listening arms? Right I want you each to read out what you have done.'

Dave sucks on a long stick of sherbert. Stuart gets out his mobile phone. The latest craze that the school is cracking down on is hitting someone or abusing them and then using the new video facility on expensive mobile phones to record the student's reaction, and then texting the video images to a friend in another class as a trophy of the dastardly deed.

Dave reads out his contribution. There is a lot of giggling.

'My favourite thing in the whole world is bed because it's big it looks nice. It smells nice and it makes me feel relaxed. It makes me tired. When I close my eyes and imagine I can see pillows and nice cover and comfortable bed.'

'Applause please, that's very good,' says Sally.

There is a smattering of clapping. Sunil has managed to write a line but doesn't want to read it so Sally reads it for him. ' "My favourite thing is my brothers, mum, dad, sisters and me." Good, who's next?'

Stuart slowly edges towards the front. 'My favourite thing in the whole world is my phone. The reason is because you can make music. I like it because it looks buff, it smells like strawberry and it makes me feel happy.'

'How sweet,' Sally says.

Ngu reads out very slowly and deliberately: 'My favourite thing in the world is God, Allah, (both have been crossed out) Mum because she only looks after me and takes care. It smells like perfume and it makes me feel wonderful. When I'm with my favourite thing the best day. When I close my eyes I can see me and my mum have so much fun.'

'That's lovely,' says Sally. 'What a good piece of work.'

'Can I sit on the sofa now I have finished my work?' asks Dave. Benny leaps on to the sofa without asking.

'Arsenal, Arsenal, Arsenal,' chants Dave at full volume for no reason.

'Dave, quieter please! Right, let's finish off with a story. Those listening nicely can go first to break.' Sally likes to end the lesson by getting them used to stories. Four of them squeeze on to the sofa, elbowing each other to secure more room.

I notice perhaps the strangest, most poignant sight since I have been at the school. Benny, the tough guy of the class, starts sucking his thumb. None of the other students notice and he seems unembarrassed. This is listen with mother, and the teenager becomes a vulnerable child within an instant.

'Right, off you go,' Sally says. The students leave. I feel sucked of emotion, reeling from an hour of non-stop battling. You need to come to these lessons prepared, fighting fit, on top bantering form or you can easily get very despondent, and very angry.

Back in the staff room after one of the Learning Zone lessons, a teacher tells me that schools like this find it nearly impossible to raise standards amongst what he calls 'the lumpen' group of white working-class kids. He regales me with the words of a teacher he used to work with: 'You can't polish a turd. Remember that phrase.'

I do. It's a memorable phrase, and it sums up one attitude to the students at the school. It is an undercurrent I have picked up in some teachers, those who call students – admittedly with wry humour – nutters, head cases, ragamuffins, oiks. 'You can't polish a turd.' What a graphic, disgusting, depressing phrase.

Is that fatalism justified? My experience in the exclusion room has shown me just how hard it is to turn round a school like this. Can you blame some of the teachers for seeing their job as just coping, 'babysitting the students for five years' until they go out into the world as cheap labourers, layabouts or criminals. Is that all that can be expected? Is it too late by the time they have reached secondary school to make a real difference? Is all that research, that shows that from birth to five are the crucial years, right? Is there any chance that Trevor can deliver at a school like Islington Green with the intake that it has to deal with?

# DELIVERY PAINS

They seem a world apart: Prime Minister and Headteacher, policy and practice, Westminster and the frontline. Big judgements are made in the glare of publicity: the Northern Ireland peace process, the European constitution, the raising of taxes, a new asylum policy. Big judgements on a smaller scale are made with no fanfare and no publicity: the expulsion of a child for violent conduct, a confrontation with an irate parent, the timetabling of the curriculum to get the most out of students. Yet the people making them are strangely, uncannily similar.

A dog-eared photo from the Seventies tells the story. Trevor is pictured in velvet jacket, flared jeans and multi-coloured V-neck sweater playing the guitar in a band. His flowing red hair and beard complete the image. He looks like the young Tony Blair of Ugly Rumours fame. Tony and Trevor both rock legends . . . in their own bands at least. Trevor more successful with a group called Press UK. He signed a record deal and toured the clubs and bars of Northern cities. Tony, by his own admission, had less success.

Tony and Trevor have a lot in common, not just the guitar playing. Both are baby boomers, both middle-class, but both strangely classless; both tall, upright, charismatic; open-minded, lacking ideology and dogma. Both are driven and ambitious, both optimistic. For both, delivery is the key. Delivering for Tony means turning round vast swathes of Britain's public sector. For Trevor it means transforming an inner-city school.

I am now seeing for the first time what delivery means on the ground. I am witnessing the hundreds of micro-decisions that build into delivery. I reflect now on the hours of meetings I had attended in government to develop the right strategy for public service delivery.

The government's reforms were nothing if not ambitious. The reform of 24,000 schools, 400 general hospitals, 48 police forces, the criminal justice system, the asylum system, the railways. For those who at different points in the last ten years have had doubts about New Labour, and worry about where the 'project' is heading, the renewal of public services provides the answer. For in the end, there is nothing more radical, more progressive, or more in tune with our values than the re-invention of collective provision, to strengthen and modernise the services that we all rely on. I have always believed that the great governments all had one overriding mission, one reason they were given such strong mandates. For Attlee after the war it was to build a welfare state that gave working people proper minimum standards and genuine peace of mind. For Margaret Thatcher it was to tackle the unions, and make the private sector more dynamic. For Tony Blair it was, after years of neglect and under-investment, to make the public realm more creative and responsive as a driver of equality and opportunity.

Tony made two gambles, both of which were courageous. The first was that, despite the huge clamour from the Right to abandon the traditional tax-funded public services and move to a private or social insurance model, we would keep them in place and in the second term raise taxes to fund them. This offended Tony's New Labour instincts, but he realised that it was essential in order to achieve the modernisation of public services and, if explained properly, would be supported by the public.

The second gamble was that there had to be root and branch reform of the public services. They could not remain vast bureaucratic monoliths of the 1945 model. Tony repeated in private, mantra like, that 'We will end up suffering not for reforming too much but for doing too little.' He would do whatever it took to make the public services more responsive. This was controversial within the Labour party. There are many who believe that Labour is trusted so much more than the Tories on the public services that we can afford a quiet life. Put the money in, sing the praises of staff, and we will be fine. Tony thought that wasn't enough and my instinct, even when I disagreed with individual policies, was that in the long run the changes being made now – to open up the public services to greater diversity, to make them more responsive to a demanding public – will be seen as commonsense in ten years' time. In most social democratic European countries the diversity the government proposed in health and education – the use of private and volentary sectors – has been the norm for decades.

Focusing on 'delivery' – with the introduction of numerous targets – was controversial. It came about, as many things did, in part because of our sensitivities about Labour's past reputation. To prove that money was being well spent, and that we were not open to the charge of being wasteful and tax spenders, Gordon believed that having public service agreements with departments – specific targets and outcomes – would ensure that the money was spent on the real priorities. The other important reason was that we wanted to change the culture of the civil service away from just policy formation, judging success by the number of White Papers or Bills in the Queen's Speech a department produced, and instead focusing on tangible results.

Politically, targets were a rod for our own back. If we set ambitious targets and just failed to meet them but still made great progress, we were accused of failure. If we set unambitious targets then the frontline had nothing bold to aim at.

Delivery proved harder than any of us imagined. The size of our majority made it no easier. It made it no quicker to train the doctors or easier to repair the railways. It didn't make it more likely children would not truant from school. However, the size of our majority had done something else. It had inflated expectations. Our rhetoric often made things worse. The result was that from as early as a few months into government we were worrying about delivery. Could we deliver quickly enough to satisfy people?

An ongoing debate between Tony and Gordon was how much to 'boast' about government delivery and achievements in order that the public heard and believed them, and how much to let people experience the changes for themselves. Our paranoia was that we would not get credit for improvements or the media would convince people that they hadn't happened. For instance, we kept hearing stories from MPs that our Sure Start programme, successfully helping under-fives, was popular, but few thought it was a government initiative.

All our training, the popular wisdom of government communications, was that repetition was the key. I spent a lot of time preparing briefing notes for ministers on the basic achievements, for them to repeat in interviews. Tony got increasingly frustrated that good news was never reported.

As early as January 1999 I wrote a note to Tony outlining the problem and trying to find solutions to what had been nagging away at all of us:

## Why is delivery so hard to get across?

Our problem on delivery is deep-seated:

- A media that is not interested.
- Eighteen years of cuts and despair in the public sector has left a culture of complaint. Professionals don't work with government, but instead lobby to get more resources and higher pay.
- Undermining of the five key pledges by ministers, opinion formers, departments who see them as the wrong ones.
- A 179 majority leads people to believe that there is nothing to stop us delivering more quickly.
- A perception that we have overclaimed instead of spelling out the time it will take to turn things round.
- Turning round huge bureaucracies takes time. e.g. we are short of cancer surgeons. They take thirteen years to train.
- Raw data often fails to translate into anecdotal evidence.
- The public act as consumers of public services, no longer as passive recipients.
- We have convinced ourselves that we have allocated historic sums of money. We have not. Over the Parliament [1997–2001] the money going into education and health is not a quantum leap.

I went on to describe what I called 'failure as folklore'. There were certain public services that had 'chronic problems spanning many years which have resulted in collapsing trust amongst the public'. I named the three most obvious ones: inner-city schools, particularly in London; the London Underground; and

A&E waiting times. Each of these needed special attention and long-term solutions if we were to convince people we could crack the worst areas of public service decline. I argued for special attention on London, not least because the problems were often worse and had the power to pull down overall delivery for the whole country. I then advocated some solutions, or partial solutions, that included ten-year plans, greater honesty about the length of time it would all take, and making sure the five key pledges were delivered quickly.

Tony's frustration showed regularly. It was partly the impotence that every Prime Minister feels when the departments over which he has some, but not much, control do their own thing. At bilateral after bilateral meeting with Secretaries of State, Tony would return to the obsessions which in his view needed immediate attention. Why can't we do whatever it takes to get rid of bad headteachers? Why can't we build free-standing units to do thousands of routine operations to clear NHS waiting lists? Why can't we target the persistent criminals? Why can't we find a quicker way to turn round asylum applications? There was sometimes a lack of nuance in these requests, and Secretaries of State who knew more detail would often wince at the crudeness with which Tony wanted to act, but he was usually right.

In February 1999 Tony's view was that: 'The basic problem which I guess is not new for Prime Ministers is control. How do we drive our will down through the system, monitor progress and then achieve delivery? A stronger centre could give more direction and keep on the job until we are sure people are moving in the way we want.' He would often say: 'Why does all the radicalism come from Number 10? Why aren't the departments trying to push us into more radical positions?' Tony's criterion for a good minister was the boldness with which he or she carried out reform.

At the beginning of the second term I remember Tony saying, 'We did the symbolic and easy things like the minimum wage, now we are on to the really hard stuff.' It was genuinely difficult. The irony of government is that at the point when you have learnt the ropes and know how to effect change, you are losing popularity, your honeymoon is over and people expect results to be showing. Thatcher only got going in the second term, Tony kept reminding us.

By the start of the second term, the building blocks for delivery were being put in place in a serious way. The delivery unit was set up under Michael Barber who had been head of the Department of Education's successful Standards and Effectiveness Unit. Michael was one of the most impressive and talented people I worked with in government. Quietly spoken but authoritative and reflective, Michael was an academic, a former teacher, one time NUT official, Liverpool football fanatic and an authoritative voice on education. I was sceptical at first that he would be the man to bang heads together in Whitehall and drive through delivery, but his relentless focus on outcomes and his collegiate way of working with departments, as well as his close working relationship with Tony, ensured that he was just about our most effective operator.

The Prime Minister's Delivery Unit was to monitor seventeen priorities, each of which was to have a named official in each department, working to ministers and in charge of delivery plans. There were to be plans for each of the seventeen objectives and they were to be monitored by the Prime Minister in stocktakes every six weeks. I worked with Michael and others to narrow this down to the eight key objectives that were most relevant to the public: NHS waiting times; cancer/coronary heart disease; the patient experience; railway reliability; the tube; secondary school performance; crime, especially street robbery; and asylum.

These stocktakes were gladiatorial in appearance but rather softer in reality. They would take place in the Cabinet room. The Prime Minister would sit in his normal chair, the Secretary of State would sit opposite him flanked on one side by his Minister of State and on the other by the Permanent Secretary. Assorted special advisers and officials would be present on both sides. On Tony's side of the table were normally the Cabinet Secretary, the principal private secretary, the key policy advisers, Michael Barber, Sally Morgan and myself.

The aim was to check delivery was on course and to focus on a few key issues where the PM had been briefed in advance that in the eyes of the centre, a department was not making enough progress. Michael used to start with a quick presentation before drawing out the key issues. On education, for instance, we would focus on a different plank of reform each time. How was the Key Stage 3 strategy (for eleven- to fourteen-year-olds) working? Was teaching reform making a difference? Were classroom assistants being used properly? How do we make more dramatic improvements in GCSE results?

By the second term we had a better framework for what we wanted to achieve, with Tony thrashing out the four principles of reform: high minimum standards, devolving to the frontline, flexible professions, and more choice. I sent Tony a note in June 2001, just after our second election victory, with some thoughts about what our fresh mandate meant and the key questions facing us.

We should reinforce the sense that the election was a turning point in the battle of ideas, and that the centre of gravity of British politics – on investment, reform of public services and Europe – has moved to us.

We must define expectations on public services early on, so that there is agreement on what we mean and what we think the public means by delivery.

Now is the time to ask if our public service reforms are radical enough.

But the main point of the note was to make the case for big investment in public services, not more incremental change.

We need to be honest about the position on investment.

First, we have not found a magic formula that allows us to cut taxes (because we think this is the worldwide trend – Tony's view) and produce European levels of investment in public services.

Second, the money that has gone into public services so far has been modest. The first three years of the last Parliament saw virtually no increase in spending in key public services and schools and hospitals are heavily under-funded.

Third, the current spending review plus one more at the same sort of level, is not going to undo thirty years of underfunding of our public services. We should not convince ourselves that it will.

Fourth, investment, and not just reform, is key to delivery. One of the yard-sticks by which we will be judged is whether we have put the funding of health and education on a more secure long-term financial footing.

Fifth, there is a tax credit agenda which has the potential to swallow up a lot of cash. We need to decide how much we want to spend on credits this Parliament.

One of the debates between Number 10 and Number 11 was on a matter of serious policy substance. What proportion of extra spending should go into public services and how much into tax credits? Gordon's case was that tax credits were essential if we wanted to meet what was, after all, the Prime Minister's pledge to end child poverty in twenty years. The Number 10 view was that tax credits should not divert too much money from health and education. Passionate as I was about education lifting children out of poverty in the long run, I believed that we also had to tackle poverty and inequality head-on in the short term through tax and benefit changes. However, education was my priority and I ended my note with a passionate plea for more spending.

Why aren't we more ambitious about investment? The spending review does provide consistency of funding but does not put the public services on a new financial footing which will be essential when we want to convince people we have delivered.

The last Ofsted annual report made clear that 25 per cent of secondary schools had both unsatisfactory accommodation and insufficient learning resources. To remedy these deficiencies will take large-scale funding. Yet we should want to do more, we should want to develop secondary schools that provide real opportunities for teenagers.

Most secondary schools are in charge of more than 1000

teenagers between 9 p.m. and 4 p.m. These teenagers need stimulation and excitement to keep them engaged. Yet unlike many other countries, only a fraction of schools have theatres, orchestras, playing fields, swimming pools, etc. The most run-down private schools would have all these things. Investment must mean not just clearing up past problems but providing the facilities, the well-paid teachers, the well-stocked libraries that in the end is at least half of what delivery is about for pupils and parents. We should decide what we want secondary schools to provide and then work backwards to find the resources. That will make us more ambitious and long term in our funding, not constantly providing £200m or £500m here and there to solve immediate problems.

I was buoyed up by Tony's note to the office, after the summer break in 2001, which said: 'We need detail on how much money we need to fulfil the Peter Hyman definition of delivery.' I felt my badgering was paying off, but I wasn't yet sure I had enough allies in the building to make this count.

The key meeting was the Number 10 Policy Unit away-day before the spending review, when the specialist policy advisers in each area were saying what they thought was needed in order to prepare Tony for discussions with Gordon.

All ministers, and particularly the Prime Minister, have many voices in their ears. Tony was blessed or cursed by advisers most of whom wanted the last word. In all the time I worked with Tony, advice was never agreed between advisers before he was approached with it. The system was that Tony heard a range of views and then made up his own mind. Everyone was too individualistic to have it any other way. Philip would never have wanted his memos to be pooled; they were sent straight to Tony. Peter, who favoured handwritten notes to Tony, with no copies made to anyone else, would never have done otherwise. Alastair, Anji and Sally wrote less down, but knew they could bend Tony's ear whenever they liked. I, like Philip, enjoyed the idea that I was writing a well thought-out note that would have influence. I guessed that Tony liked this system; he never complained, though at times it must have been deeply frustrating.

I came armed for this meeting with a plethora of facts, because I knew I would be up against economic advisers and policy advisers all wanting to show constraint on spending. The facts were these. For sixteen out of eighteen years between 1979 and 1997 the Tories spent more than 40 per cent of GDP on public spending, in four consecutive years more than 48 per cent – this despite Thatcherites even now saying that 35 per cent is the ideal. In contrast Labour has spent under 40 per cent in six out of seven of its years in office. The government's argument would be that a lot of Tory spending went on waste – mass unemployment and rising benefits – while ours is going to health and education. But despite our rhetoric, despite some generous spending reviews, no one looking at the facts could accuse Labour of being profligate spenders. Similarly on tax take, the Tories, despite claiming to be big tax cutters, ended up after eighteen years taking more in tax as a percentage of GDP than they inherited. As for education spending, it was 6.3 per cent in 1975, dipped in the Eighties to under 5 per cent, remained under 5 per cent under Labour but was creeping up. Growth meant that 5 per cent was more money than the same figure thirty years ago. But there had not yet been a step-change in spending.

Halfway through the meeting, following an economic presentation in which the recommendation, contrary to what Tony wanted, was that spending could barely increase, and then education and health presentations which were modest and to my mind lacking in ambition on investment, I made my case for more education spending. 'This is absurd,' I said with my normal understatement. 'Education spending is only going up by a fraction of 1 per cent of GDP. France has spent more than 5 per cent of GDP since records began. Our aim surely is to get education spending up to almost double what it is now. Why are we refusing to back our number one priority with money?'

The factual approach seemed to work. Tony had convinced himself that spending was broadly on the right lines and was now confronted by the fact that it wasn't. Over the coming weeks the battle raged at Number 10, and with the Treasury who were happy for more education spending but only if defence got a bit less. Defence was another of Tony's priorities, because he thought Britain needed more-flexible and well-resourced defences, and because he believed Labour needed to be strong on defence.

In the end, with the department and others weighing in with the Treasury, education got a billion more than it might have and a big increase in capital spending, and I considered my small part in this victory to have been one of the best things I had done in government.

In parallel to Michael Barber's work on delivery policy, I was charged with the communications strategy for making it work. There was nothing harder in my job. The dilemmas, questions and issues mounted up. Should we keep quiet about delivery for two or three years while it happened, or constantly flag up our plans? Should we emphasise the radical cutting edge of policy which showed momentum and proved we were on the case, or did that frighten the unions and frontline staff too much? Were we better off aggregating health, education, crime and transport into 'public service reform', or better off talking about them separately? Was there a danger that slow progress on transport contaminated the other areas which were doing better? How could we convince people that crime was falling – which it plainly was – when no one seemed to believe it? How did we get away from reciting a litany of statistics which washed over people's heads?

Then there were the big intellectual arguments that we had to win with those in the service and with opinion formers: tax-funded public services were better than social insurance funded services; you could have choice *and* equity; 'more does not mean worse': you could get 50 per cent of pupils into higher education without reducing standards.

Most of all, I tried to work out what the key elements for delivery were. I kept saying to people that we could meet targets, but no one would notice if we hadn't done the other key things that matter to people, like rebuilding the infrastructure and improving customer care.

The best example of delivery in the first term was primary school results which shot up from roughly half of eleven-year-olds reading, writing and adding up properly to three-quarters, with the poorest children leaping forward in a way that had not been seen before. This was real delivery and we wanted to replicate it. I wrote a note to Tony, following discussion with Michael, about how we could repeat this in other areas.

We believe the following factors were key to the success in primary schools:

*Strong focused Secretary of State and Dept*. A strong Secretary of State pursuing reform relentlessly with a clear message: standards. Reform agenda shaped at an early stage with tough decisions taken early. Real dialogue between frontline and ministers giving reform momentum.

*Public and professionals support the priority: we set the hurdle by which we are judged*. 11-year-old primary school test results agreed by staff and opinion formers as the single best judge of success.

*Symbolic policy.* Literacy hour an easy to grasp policy.

*Personal experience.* Personal experience chimed with statistical fact: primary school results being symbolic of wider visible change – better school buildings, smaller class sizes.

*Struggle.* Struggle to achieve the changes with teachers initially opposed.

*Professional support.* Teachers confirming the changes because they were won over and because they were given proper training on literacy and numeracy strategies.

*Third-party endorsement.* Ofsted giving trusted third-party endorsement of the changes – particularly when even a sceptic like Woodhead admitted there was big progress.

*Trust stats.* The way we measured success, though occasionally under fire, had credibility when the target was met.

I was concerned that these ingredients were not in place in other key areas. For example, the fact that there were two sets of crime statistics – one of police-recorded crime, one the reporting of victims – made it impossible to get across the clear message that crime was sharply down, even though it was. However, this new infrastructure, led by dynamic Secretaries of State backed by Michael Barber's unit, slowly began to turn round delivery and grind out the results we needed. But as Tony kept saying in stocktakes, the key was not just to flog the system harder but to make the structural changes that would mean we could sustain the improvement in results.

\*

One of the things Trevor is big on is the reputation of the school and getting it a good press. I am notionally meant to be helping with the school's media, but I soon discover Trevor is a natural at it. He has a good eye for a story and presents the school's case with great skill. He has, dare I say it, presentation skills that New Labour would be proud of. It is surprising how many requests the school gets. There is always some TV company, local media, wanting 'just a few fifteen-year-olds to talk about drugs', or 'a handful of sixteen-year-olds to be interviewed on tuition fees'.

My first assignment is to sit in on an interview for *The Times* that a journalist called Wendy is conducting with Trevor, and then show her round the school.

It is a good glimpse into his story. When Trevor, an economics and psychology teacher, became head of his previous school, he was, at thirty-five, one of the youngest heads in the country. He transformed the school with exam results nearly doubling. He says, 'I was warned off coming here. Some said it was too different from Essex, that London had too many of its own problems. That I wouldn't succeed. It was the school Blair allegedly refused to send his children to. My daughter worried the stress might kill me.'

The 'allegedly', I'm sure, is for my benefit.

'There was a sense of chaos, and of course the school was in special measures. The truth was the school had lost its way in terms of organisational strategies. The problem was not the staff. I couldn't have had a better or more willing group of staff. The problem was lack of organisation.'

'But,' the interviewer asked, 'how will you attract middle-class children back to the school?'

'I'm not head-hunting wealthy children. There are some 5 per cent from quite wealthy backgrounds, 40 per cent in employment who are quite aspirational, 50 per cent on benefits in social housing. Some join the school with a reading age of six.

My aim is to improve the success of the school and the reputation of the school. I am not per se trying to attract back parents who want to send their children elsewhere – but I hope my youngest daughter, who is nine, will come. I like that idea – keeping it in the family. I want to see other teachers putting their money where their mouth is.'

'What are the most intractable problems?'

'Nothing is intractable. Every problem has a solution. The main thing here is that children come with a range of their own challenges in their heads, and the danger is that you can be distracted from the main aim and you end up trying to keep the plates spinning, forgetting that you need the plates to eat dinner. The reality is that it's not rocket science. You have to keep putting the systems in place and stick to them doggedly. Almost any will do as long as they are kept to properly and the boss means it. It's all about the ability to get things done and deal with challenges. Take an example. A third to a half of children join the school not at the start but throughout the five years of their school life. That means every week there are half a dozen new children. It was only quite recently that we introduced a system for integrating them properly. Before that it added to the chaos.'

'How are you doing for money?' asks the reporter.

'It's quite clear that the Labour government is putting more money in – apart from the blip last year. There has been a huge increase of about two million pounds in budgets since I was first a head, eight years ago.'

The interview comes to an end and the journalist wants to be shown round the school – my job. I am under strict instructions to show her the best bits.

I spent a lot of time in the last ten years thinking about events for the PM. Control, nothing unexpected, smooth choreography were all important. Only occasionally was there a 'Sharron Storer moment'. This was the time when during the last election the irate partner of a patient confronted Tony outside a Birmingham hospital.

'I want to see the big tower block,' Wendy says. This is not one of the best bits, but I give in.

The tower block has long narrow corridors. I have already discovered that at lesson changeover time there is five minutes of mayhem, whilst children flood out of ten classrooms and move to a different floor, before lessons resume. Unluckily for me, I am showing the journalist round at precisely this time. As we reach the second floor a student rushes down the corridor with another student on his shoulder, making loud grunting noises. Wendy, a quiet, middle-aged, middle-class woman, takes in a sharp breath but attempts to remain calm. 'They get a little boisterous between lessons,' I say meekly, before ineffectively telling the student to dismount.

I skip down the stairs, herding Wendy to the opposite end of the school. 'We've done the tower block,' I say definitively. 'Let's see the Learning Zone,' I'm hoping I can still save the day.

The Learning Zone is usually calm, but, because it is designed for some of the most difficult students, it always has the potential to boil over. We climb the stairs of the old building and I ask the journalist to wait outside the classroom. I go in and, to my horror, see several children attacking each other. One is already lying on the floor gasping. A teacher is sitting on a chair, watching but not intervening. I panic. I'm going to let Trevor down. *The Times* is going to say that Islington Green is a sink school.

For the first time since arriving at the school I raise my voice, and it's not at a pupil. 'Can you get them to stop fighting,' I shout aggressively at the teacher. 'I want to show a journalist round right now.'

'They're not fighting,' the teacher says calmly. 'They are acting. This is a drama lesson.'

I want to bury my head in a hot vat of school custard until the embarrassment subsides. I apologise repeatedly and return to get Wendy.

'Come in,' I say to the journalist, beaming. 'There's a lovely drama lesson going on.'

Trevor's optimism had shone through. 'Nothing is intractable,' he had said. But that wasn't what it looked like when I delved further into the school's history.

Margaret Maden, the thirty-four-year-old head who took over the school in 1974, told me that she faced high levels of truancy with year 11 running at 60 per cent attendance and many leaving before exams. Literacy was poor. Behaviour was challenging. In short, exactly the same issues as now. She wrote that apart from doing a lot of PR her main priorities were to:

- establish some clear systems, procedures for staff and pupils e.g. staff handbook, pupils' code.
- improve staff quality.
- establish a Friends of Islington Green association for parents, staff, governors, primary schools heads. (This became very important for the school image and morale.)
- establish an integrated studies programme for first year pupils.

One article about her at the time said: 'Being head of a modern comprehensive is probably, on balance, a slightly more difficult job than being leader of the Labour Party.'

When I showed Trevor the account of the school in Margaret's day, he wrote on the top of it: 'Brilliant, thirty years on and still the same problems!' Only this time he is optimistic that the money, the accountability, the staff will make a long term difference.

There is a sense sometimes, not of ever greater progress, but of going round in circles. Many of the things we were trying now, branded as 'innovations', were in fact tried in Margaret Maden's day. The exclusion room, the learning zone for the more challenging kids – all had different names but were around then as now. At a national level those on the receiving end of policy from different governments must regularly have a sense of déjà vu. Teachers saw grant-maintained schools, set up under the Tories, abolished under Labour, and now hear of Labour's new idea of independent state schools, which albeit in a different guise will, like GM schools, also be independent of LEA control.

One thing though has changed dramatically since Margaret's time. She went out of her way to attract middle-class parents, to balance up the intake. Her contacts, and the poor state of schools in the neighbouring borough of Hackney, meant this was at least in part successful. Today Trevor is resigned to the fact that he will have less success. Houses in Islington are too polarised between the very wealthy and the poor estates, so there is not a young professional middle class as there was thirty years ago. Hackney schools are improving, so fewer escape across the border. And of course, league tables and Ofsted, introduced since Margaret's time, mean that there is far more information about schools, and middle class parents are very unlikely to pick any school until GCSE results are above the magic 50 per cent mark.

I reflect on what Trevor has told the interviewer. He, like Tony, needs to play many roles: an education visionary, a good personnel manager of demanding staff, a first rate administrator and systems man, as well as having good personal skills to deal with parents, students, LEA, the community, and other schools. He has to run a £4–5 million budget, recruit and retain more than a hundred staff, deal with the heating, lighting, equipment, the problems of large, old, buildings, and be able to use and channel initiatives from local government, national government, the voluntary sector, education agencies, local volunteers, the police, the health service and the local media. Of these, the two biggest skills needed on the frontline are operational and personal.

As I watch Trevor and the management team, I start to get a fuller picture of what the job entails. Operationally there are a hundred decisions a day. Each of the following happens while I am at the school.

*Problem*: There has been snow overnight and the playground is icy. Can it be cleared in time for break? If not, will it be a hazard and should the school be closed? *Decision*: Trevor closes the school so as not to risk students and staff injuring themselves.

*Problem*: The heating is not working and classrooms are cold. John, the NUT rep, has complained at staff briefing. Should students wear coats in lessons, or should they go home at lunch time if it hasn't warmed up? *Decision*: The school warms up and the problem goes away.

*Problem*: Students have been caught stealing books from the local Borders bookshop during school hours. Is this a matter for the school or the police? If the police are pressing charges, should the school punish the students anyway or is it none of its business? *Decision*: The truancy part is the school's business and the pupils are punished accordingly. The theft is left for the police to act upon.

*Problem*: The canteen is closed for refurbishment. It was meant to have been completed over the half term so as not to disrupt the students, but has run over time. How do 950 students get served lunch? *Decision*: Packed lunches are provided to students queuing in the school hall.

If these are the problems a head faces, then there are plenty of people, I found out, who want to 'help'. There is now an army of outside organisations who want to be part of a school's life. Whilst I've been at the school they have included:

> Mentoring schemes by city banks.
> Lawyers who want to teach human rights classes.
> University visits and partnerships.
> Shakespearian actors coming to help fourteen-year-olds with *Macbeth*.
> Howard League for Penal Reform doing workshops.
> Arsenal programme helping with literacy – using materials connected to football.
> Skillsforce, an MOD-based initiative, helping with vocational courses.
> Journalism course at the *Guardian* and City University.
> Hugh Masakela teaching students to sing African songs so that they can back him in a concert.
> Speak Out, a group that helps give reticent students the confidence to speak in public.
> Joined-up Design for Schools – a project working with students to help improve the school environment that led to the redesign of the playground.

All are worthwhile, all are in theory giving a new experience to the children, but, having dealt with several of them myself, it can be exasperating and fiddly to get them in at the right time, round up the right students, and make sure the event runs smoothly. Then I worry that a one-off intervention, as opposed to a real connection over time with the students, may be of little lasting benefit.

I use my one-to-one 'line management meetings' with Trevor to pick his brains. How is he going to turn round this school? What are the priorities? What is the key to success? I think he finds this useful as a way of clarifying his thoughts. He might, of course, find it intensely annoying. I ask him straight out how much he is importing the systems he has used at the previous school and how much he is starting again.

I am surprised by the answer. 'Ninety per cent is what I did before.'

I reflect on how different the Prime Minister's job is from any other. Trevor and most other leaders have several goes at running different organisations. They can learn and move on, getting better the whole time. For a Prime Minister, however, there is no real practice or training, other than running a department, which is not the same, and it either works or it doesn't.

Trevor has real self-assurance. He believes he has learnt the craft of headteacher. He was effective at raising standards in his last job. The task here, with a few adaptations, is to perform the same trick again. He admits that his style is collegiate rather than tough or aggressive. He tells me he has worked with some really tough heads who made a difference to their school even though they were unpopular. He talks admiringly of what they achieved but says that he could never be a 'bastard type', it simply isn't his style. Trevor is very focused and very determined, but I wonder whether he has made enough changes in his first two years, or whether he's simply trying too hard to be liked. That was certainly the criticism of Tony, before he broke loose in the second term.

The cliché about leadership is that the main test is how good you are in a crisis. This is important, of course. A crisis can blow you away. But as I saw in government, with the fuel protests or the foot and mouth crisis (where better planning might have been made), these things will always come along. and the best you can do is deal with them as calmly as possible. In a school there are individual incidents that may be shocking or difficult, but they do not usually amount to full blown crises. I'm not sure this is the real test of leadership.

I believe that two much more mundane tests are the real essence of good leadership. The first is what I would class the 'bread and butter' test, the consistency test: are the right systems in place to ensure the organisation can replicate and produce high standards day after day? This is the key, particularly in a service industry. If you go into a café on any day of the week, will the sandwich be the same quality as the day before? If you have a hip operation, can you guarantee that it will be more or less the same quality whether you are first in line or fiftieth? In fact there is some academic research that shows that surgeons who do 150 or more of the same operations a year are the safest. At a school the key is to ensure that children are in the right place at the right time for the smooth running of the building day in day out. Good schools will ensure there is some consistency in lesson standards throughout the year.

The second essential is 'driving an agenda'. In this Number 10 and the school have equal problems. In government there are hundreds of distractions. It is almost as if there is a conspiracy against you setting your own agenda. There are day-to-day calls on the Prime Minister's time. There are media inspired crises, real or imagined, to deal with. It is very easy to become a problem solving Prime Minister rather than an 'agenda setting' Prime Minister. I thought quite frequently, for example, that education was becoming less of a priority because it was not in crisis. An area like health got more attention because the media spotlight on it was stronger and the potential political damage of failing was greater. At a school, just staying focused on the big picture and not getting distracted by the disruptive students, or the day to day running, is hard. Once the school term starts there is frantic activity, driven by the tyranny of the timetable, that exhausts staff and frazzles the senior management team. The task is not to be swept along with the trivia but to make sure that standards have been raised in the school.

In *Good to Great*, Jim Collins looks in detail at hundreds of companies and asks what turns a good company into a great one. His answer, perhaps surprisingly, is that it requires a leader who embodies two things: 'personal humility and professional will'. It is this duality, 'modest and wilful, humble and fearless', that characterises the great leaders: those who channel their ego into their organisation and not their own riches or standing, who live up to American President Harry Truman's dictum that 'You can accomplish anything in life provided you don't mind who gets the credit', those who match their humility with a relentless focus on outcomes and goals.

I ask Trevor whether he feels pressure from government. He says, 'No, not really.' For all the initiatives he receives it is somehow too remote, and Trevor is confident enough in his abilities to get on with the job. I ask whether he feels pressure from parents or governors or the LEA. Again he says, 'No, not really.' I am surprised. Tony, all politicians, feel three giant pressures: the media, the electorate and unforeseen events. Here at the frontline there is stress, and plenty of it, but far less pressure to perform, at least for Trevor. Some in government would argue that this is the problem with public services; that the consumer pressure is not being felt by frontline staff. Trevor, I sense, would quite welcome parents complaining hard about a department's performance. It would give him a greater lever to reform it.

He seems to have two passions: positive discipline, on which he gives seminars around the country to earn money for the school, and systems, which he believes are essential for the smooth running of the school.

He believes that the key to turning round a difficult school is getting the behaviour right, becoming a calm school. For him there is a hierarchy. Behaviour first, attendance second, then achievement. A calm school, he believes, in which children turn up on time every day, will lead to results going up irrespective of anything else. Most difficult is to get the learning right. This is, he says, because it is very hard to hold teachers to account day-by-day in a systematic way.

If Trevor is a systems man, then other members of the SMT seem to have different emphases. Paul is the teachers' advocate. He believes the key to everything is what goes on in the classroom, and what will make life easier and more effective for the teacher. He believes in removing disruptive pupils, and thinks that unless you do this, it becomes impossible for teachers to teach. Emma and Angela are both motivated by the pastoral side, by ensuring that every student is properly cared for and that they don't fall through the net. By their own admission, the danger at a school like Islington Green is that so much time is spent on dealing with the difficult children and coping that not enough focus goes into learning. It may be the stage that Trevor is at in the change programme for the school, but learning and achievement seem to be too low down on the agenda. There is no member of the management team obsessively talking and acting to improve what actually goes on in the classroom.

I think about this as I attend a key SMT meeting in Trevor's office. This is the key strategic meeting of the week, and I learn there is always a full agenda. I notice a card on the bookshelf: 'Chinese Proverb – Those who say it can't be done, shouldn't interrupt the person doing it.' The meeting usually runs to time. In other words, Trevor is a good chair. This is a big, and perhaps surprising, contrast to the number of ramshackle badly chaired meetings I sat through in government.

The meeting always begins with the same items: minutes from the last meeting; any other business, devoted to Trevor's late additions; and then something I find fascinating called 'quality circle'. This is the chance for the senior managers to recommend members of staff – teachers or admin – for a letter of commendation from the headteacher. This seems such a simple and good idea. Why was something like this never done at Number 10? The answer seems to be that everyone worked hard for a common goal and being there was seen as a reward in itself. The result was that people didn't always feel valued.

Recommendations start flowing: 'I think Bettina, should get one for running a brilliant conference, and Debbie for organising cover so well.'

Trevor then moves on to the real business on the agenda. This is a mixture of the strategic and medium-term and the operational and immediate. On the agenda are:

Lunch time: should it be staggered or changed to make the school calmer?

House system: should the school move to a house system or not?

Building works: when is the school going to be refurbished? When are the electric works going to be done?

Homework completion: how do we ensure that teachers are setting homework and children doing more of it?

Staff absence: why are so many of the support staff taking so many days off and what can be done about it?

Education Action Zone events: upcoming events between Islington Green and its partner primary schools as part of the action zone.

I am struck by how many initiatives Trevor has to juggle at the same time. Each small chunk has big implications for the smooth running of the school. Also, all the items are practical. I spent much of my previous job crafting rhetoric, shaping messages, suggesting how the government is positioned. All the decisions here have an immediate effect on children's lives.

The big discussion of the meeting is on the timetable. This almost seems a deliberate strategy to make me feel at sea. It is very complicated. I am in awe of what Eileen, the deputy-head, has to sort out.

There is a debate about how many staff are leaving and therefore how many additional hours are needed. There is another debate about how we get rid of staff in subject areas where we have too much teaching. I pipe up once. I preface my words cautiously by stressing my ignorance, but ask whether we can focus more attention on literacy in Year 7, the first year of secondary school, given that 40 per cent of children arrive at the school with low reading ages.

I have opened a can of worms. Trevor is sympathetic, but thinks it is hard to timetable. Eileen looks as if I am about to cause her a lot more shuffling of rooms and teachers. Trevor suggests another period of English and maths for Year 7s. But then what should give? There is a debate about whether, legally, we have to do as much citizenship in Year 7. I quickly find out that any tampering with hours is fiercely resisted by the department involved. The timetable, it seems, or the difficulty in changing it, is one of the forces of conservatism within the school.

Trevor is good with staff and he's got an inclusive style. One unusual touch is that he buys them food – he provides all staff with a free meal on the last Friday of the month. He also pays for a big event at a restaurant once a term. Once or twice a term he holds what he calls, in true Bill Clinton style, town-hall meetings. This is a staff meeting to discuss strategic matters. The upcoming one is important. It is to outline the strategy for the school. I have sold Trevor on the idea of telling it as a journey. The only way for staff to make sense of what is important is for Trevor to boil it down into a few clear objectives. He is good at the vision thing. I have suggested that each term has a key theme. We have come up with a calmer school in the summer, a higher attending school in the autumn term, a higher achieving school in the spring term in the run up to exams. Trevor has boiled this down to 'Abide, Attend, Achieve'. I can't stand the abide bit but am overruled.

Trevor holds the meeting in the largest of the new performing arts studios. He feels it is a more upbeat venue – polished wood floors and white walls – than the run-down assembly hall. The staff appear in dribs and drabs between 3.30 and 3.45. Trevor has a powerpoint presentation.

'When I got someone in recently to speak to the senior management team and other members of staff about our vision and aims, I was surprised that not everyone said the same thing.

'Well, I think the bottom line is to raise exam results. I have been here two years. We have had a successful Ofsted last year, positive national and local publicity, the school is on the way up. So what now? Where are we on the journey? Well, this is the most exciting job I've ever done, and I am excited by what our youngsters can achieve. I am perfectly happy for my daughter to come here. I want us to go from 30 to 50 per cent getting five good GCSEs in the next three years. It is ambitious and challenging but realistic. Fifty per cent should not be out of our grasp. Also, every child on our roll should get one A to G grade GCSE. Schools of a similar kind to ours, with the same intake, can get up to 55 per cent achieving this. I want to be the best. I want to be head of the best school.

'The way to do it is by improving our organisational capacity. It's as if we have a big urn, we've got the sugar and milk, but we haven't switched the urn on. The systems are crucial.

'I'm also clear we need new buildings, and my personal pledge to you is we will rebuild them.

'We have boiled down our message to abide, attend, achieve. I know it sounds evangelical. We've done fantastically well. Now, as they say in politics, we need a step-change. For the next half hour I want us all to have a 'thought shower', or what some people call a brainstorm, on the calmer school for next term.'

Trevor is into Post-it note 'thought showers' in a big way. It was one of the tools recommended at a national college of school leadership training session, and, though sceptical to begin with, he now thinks it's a winner. So staff break down into different groups, each with a pad of Post-it notes, with a flip chart in front of them. The aim is for each group to write down three ideas for making the school calmer and the children better behaved. The ideas flow: get rid of fizzy drinks and chocolates that hype them up; more teachers patrolling the corridors; get rid of the pips which make people rush for the door at the end of lessons; staggered lunch hours so the canteen is calmer. At the next SMT meeting we decide which are the best ideas and allocate someone to action them. Then I write it up into a calmer school plan for the next term.

Speaking as an outsider, I say at the meeting, the key question for a calmer school seems to me to be deciding what is the acceptable level of behaviour and then being consistent about enforcing it. The trouble, as I see it, is that the senior management team has not really decided how heavy to be. Is the aim silence in class, in which case those who aren't get punished? But, as Trevor and Paul believe, silence is not necessarily a sign of learning. 'On task' talking about issues can be useful, as long as it is directed. Similarly, on uniform or running in corridors, are we going for a zero tolerance approach or a laissez-faire approach? The problem at the school seems to be a clash between two cultures: a street culture (baseball caps and hooded tops and Walkmen and truancy and playing up in lessons) and a learning culture (reading, doing homework, turning up on time and paying attention). The school is at an in-between stage, edging towards a learning culture, but still accepting large elements of the street culture. Moving faster to the learning culture, accepting far less of the street attitudes, seems to be essential to moving forward.

After the SMT meeting I get talking to Trevor about which of the many initiatives coming from government he feels are effective. The school's strategic plan highlights a bewildering array of them:

> Extended school plan
> Behaviour improvement plan
> Education action zone
> ECI regeneration project
> Key Stage 3 strategy
> Leadership improvement grant
> Pastoral support plan
> Healthy school action plan
> Plans for Citizenship lessons
> Citizenship action plan
> Work related action plans
> Creative partnerships
> Schools sports co-ordinator
> Homework plans
> IT plans

These are major plans. But which are meant to have priority? Or are they all equally important? Should a head be more concerned about the healthy school plan because there has been so much on obesity in the press, or is the citizenship action plan, given the talk of respect and responsibility by the government, a higher priority? To be fair, the government has reduced the number of tiny initiatives that were a feature of the first term, though there remain overlapping policies like Excellence in Cities and Education Action Zones.

Trevor's attitude, which I am sure is common to many heads, is that if there is a pot of money being offered by government then the school should apply. That is why he applied to be an extended school – which is a new government push to have schools open from morning to night and at weekends to serve the rest of the community. As the school was already doing much of this, Trevor successfully applied for the £200,000. He was then able to use the money more or less how he wished.

'This is a charade,' says Trevor. 'The real power government has is resources. Day-to-day government cannot be involved in running public services, and changing law or guidance takes a long time. So what they do is come up with an idea, put money up and get schools to chase after it. There is asymmetric information as they used to say in economics. Both sides – government and schools – don't have information about what the other is doing. Ministers don't think we know what's important. Schools say that ministers don't know how to run education. The result is that the government has pots of money for different things which we bid for and then adapt to the things we were always going to do. Of course the system breeds a bureaucracy of mediocre administrators and bureaucrats and educationalists who don't work in schools, who inflate their role to perpetuate their existence. Take the extended schools meeting I went to the other day. There were only two heads in the room out of fifty people. All the rest were from quangos I'd never heard of that don't actually do anything. They don't work with teachers or children or managers. I left early. I couldn't stand it.'

I ask him again what initiatives have worked. 'The literacy

strategy in primary schools worked because it was a good idea, it was something that a school had to do and was not optional, and there was money and training for it. The Education Action Zone works because the money is broken down into specific areas. Most initiatives are not simple enough. The money is spread over too many things.'

My experience in just a few short months reflects what Trevor says. I am spending a lot of time bidding for pots of money to do things the school already wants to do: small sums from charities, regeneration projects, Lottery funds, each with laborious, but I suppose necessary, forms to fill in. Unlike for primary schools where the message was clear – to get the basics right – the number of things secondary schools are being asked to do is staggering. It reminds me of a comment Estelle Morris, former Education Secretary, said to me once: 'We expect a school to be an oasis of order and calm when all around it is mayhem.' In the time I have been at Islington Green, government had suggested schools should have: house systems, uniform, not allow children out of school at lunch time, attract more maths teachers, deal better with behaviour, be inspected by Ofsted without warning, step up the Key Stage 3 strategy, not allow students out on study leave before their GCSEs. Some of them are micro, some more strategic. A headteacher needs to be confident of his or her own strategy, and relaxed about the volume of orders from on high, or else they would spend their time in permanent irritation at what they are being asked to do.

Trevor gives me a manual that he has used in previous jobs. It is called *School Improvement Reports*, edited by Tony Attwood. It is a practical guide for teachers and headteachers, a trawl through all the research available to produce an easy-to-understand series of measures to turn a school from failure to excellence. Its philosophy is stated at the beginning.

The power to change is in the school. This is of course a most radical view at a time when power in education has been devolving away from teachers for so many years. Our view is very clear: schools improve because teachers decide to improve them, not because of government initiatives, curricula, inspectors, naming and shaming or anything else imposed from without.

The report goes on to describe why it makes this assertion, giving a fascinating account of the history of education over the last forty years from the perspective of the teacher.

Modern educational endeavour started in the 1950s with the unexpected announcement by the Soviet Union of the launch of the sputnik. The immediate view of the United States and in Britain was that we were behind the USSR technologically. The only way to catch up was through education. The education in question to be not just of a gifted elite but of all pupils.

The first revolution was in the form of better curriculum materials, produced by the top educationalists of the day, but it did not produce a great rise in standards. The result was that fashionable thinking in the Sixties believed that schools couldn't change themselves because capitalism threw up too many inequalities, and poor housing and poverty had to be tackled first: 'Western society had within it such deep divisions that it was quite impossible for schools to do anything about anything.'

This view was then finally contradicted by the late Seventies when the pendulum swung back and academics started showing that it was the implementation of the curricula ideas that was at fault and not the idea that schools could change themselves. Since then there is a growing consensus that schools can make a difference, and that there are definable attributes to a good school: dynamic leadership, high expectations, acquisition of basic skills, continuous monitoring of progress and an ordered well-run institution.

Reading this manual reinforced what Trevor was saying. It was beginning to challenge a lot of my thinking too. Instinctively I believe in the power of government to make a difference. I believe in intervention. I believe government can and should intervene on behalf of the public to improve services. However, there seemed to be an almost parallel world, under the radar of government, of dedicated public servants who were humouring government – going along with their schemes, alive to the fact that government changed its mind regularly, or a new political party would gain power and change things – but continuing to do what they thought was right; and if government wanted to claim credit for it, or thought its plans had made a difference, so be it. All the time these heads and teachers knew that it was in fact their strategy and their plans that were doing the delivering. I was seeing things now from the school's perspective. Government had to hand down policy that applied to 4,000 secondary schools, yet each school was at a different stage of reform, and needed different solutions. Government policy-making was simply not suited to the individual needs of schools, just as politicians believed that schools were not paying enough attention to the individual needs of students. What good heads were doing was to take the policy and implement it at a pace and in a way that suited *their* school.

Policy-making in government was complicated. There were four power blocks: Number 10, the Treasury, departmental ministers, and civil servants. Number 10 would see the big picture and the Prime Minister would have lots of instincts and hunches. The Treasury would want money spent wisely and therefore have its own independent thoughts on the policies that might achieve this. Ministers, who were reshuffled a lot, would have their own thoughts on how to make a difference. Civil servants would have to control all these outpourings and would often be world-weary about what could be achieved.

The answer, as Michael Barber was trying to persuade departments, was to see reform as having three types. His analogy is that of a computer. There is hardware, which is the funding, the capital for building works, the qualifications framework. Then there is the operating system, which is the performance management framework and choice and diversity. Finally there is the software, which contains the strategies for improving teaching and learning. Government plays an important role in the first two, and should encourage best practice in the third. It should try to curb the endless 'software' announcements that are about the small details of running a school and teaching. This is where government must let go.

For Tony and Trevor, their fortunes both depended on delivery. For Tony, after the Iraq war, it was essential that public services got better. For Trevor, the school needed a step-change in results, having gone up from 24 to 28 per cent of pupils getting five A–Cs in two years.

As Trevor said to me, 'I'm not the bastard type. That's not my style of leadership, but if things don't improve dramatically this year, the gloves will come off.'

In a few weeks' time those results would come through, but for now I had my own personal bit of delivery to see to. I was about to try my hand at real teaching.

# TEACHER

'Education is not the filling of a pail but the lighting of a fire,' said the poet, W.B. Yeats. From what I can see, the students here need both. There seems to be a gaping hole in the bottom of most students' pails, where information has seeped out. Indeed, it may never have been put in. Similarly, the fire has not yet been lit for many students for whom school is a bore, and in some cases agony.

I have been a classroom assistant, now it's time to find out if I have any of the qualities needed to be a teacher. Paul says I should take a handful of gifted and talented Year 10 pupils, take them out of the citizenship lessons, and do debating and politics with them. This will require a lot of preparation. I will need to speak to each student individually to find out if they want to do it. Then I will have to book a room to teach in, and plan the first lesson.

The students I pick from the Gifted and Talented list all seem keen. Citizenship lessons are a good idea. Children need to be aware of the world around them, political choices and what it means to be a good citizen. The trouble in schools is that these lessons can be boring and are often not treated seriously by teachers. If you are a maths teacher, for example, it's a bit of a chore to be talking about the European Union or promiscuity with your form for an hour each week.

I decide that it is best to pick a classroom in the new performing arts block. They feel different from the classrooms in the old block, where most other lessons are held.

I think about the lessons I have observed and the crowd control techniques I have read about. I remember using a quote for a Tony speech from a Ministry of Education *Teaching as a Career* leaflet that was produced in 1945 and was aimed at recruiting 'men and women released from HM forces and other national service'. I re-read it to see how the profession has changed. There is a refreshing honesty:

Teaching is an exacting profession and though it can and does afford a happy and satisfying life to those who are well equipped for it by disposition and attainments, it is a misery for those who choose it and find that they have missed their vocation. This warning is necessary in the interest of the children in the schools as well as in the interests of those who are weighing the question of becoming teachers.

On the other hand it would be foolish to regard teaching as some 'mystery' profession which only the very elect should pursue. There is no ideal teacher and there is no list of select gifts which every teacher must possess. For instance, it is no doubt desirable for a teacher to be patient; but this does not mean that no impatient person ever became a good teacher. One thing however must be emphasised. The chief characteristic of all children and young people is that they are growing; growing in body, mind and spirit; and any adult who does not possess, and cannot acquire an understanding of this characteristic and an appreciation of what it means in the daily life of a school had certainly better give up the idea of teaching. Again, those to whom little children are, and are likely always to be, a perpetual exasperation should not dream of teaching them.

Every child should have a good general education, and in particular be able to read, write, speak, and listen to his own language intelligently. A teacher must be an educated person. But this does not mean that he should necessarily have amassed a great amount of knowledge, though obviously he cannot teach what he does not understand. The hall-mark of a good teacher is that he is himself always learning and always developing his knowledge and understanding of children and young people. In short a teacher should be a person who because his attitude to knowledge, to ideas, to his fellows and to life generally is better educated today than he was yesterday and will tomorrow be better educated than he is today.

This seems to be the perfect description, and I am reassured that impatience is not necessarily a bar. As for children being a 'perpetual exasperation', that seemed to be common to most teachers.

My aim is to teach them a bit about debating, a bit about writing and performing speeches and a bit about politics and the media. I start to plan the lesson. Preparation is everything. I feel I need to tell them where I have come from, partly because it might interest them, partly to explain why I am teaching this subject. I have also read that you should set the ground rules early, so that the students don't see you as a soft touch.

The second period on Tuesday approaches. I photocopy materials, get some spare pens ready in case they don't have them, and head for Studio 4 of the performing arts block. The lesson is meant to start at 9.45. At 9.50 there is no one there. I convince myself this is because the arts block is a bit of a walk from the main building, then in ones and twos they start arriving.

One of the Turkish boys says, 'Hi, sir, I've brought my mate, he's a good debater too, is that OK?' I've no idea if it's OK or if he has only been brought so they can mess around together. I feel I'm out of control and the lesson hasn't even begun. 'Yes it's fine,' I guess.

Shona, a pretty girl with long blonde hair arrives. 'What's this all about, sir?' she asks nervously. I have forgotten they must be as nervous as I am. This is new for them too.

I soon realise that I have picked a silly room for my lessons. Being a music room, and having a cupboard full of instruments beside my desk, I get a trickle of students barging into the room: 'Can I borrow a guitar, sir? I'll just be a second.' I am flustered. There are too many distractions. Will they listen to me?

I've soon got seven in the class. The eighth and ninth haven't turned up. I ask if anyone knows where they are. No one does. I decide to begin. My first ever lesson. Admittedly only with a small group, but it's a lesson none the less. I have prepared a short introduction.

'This should be exciting and fun. There is nothing better than a good debate or argument. You have all been picked because you have done some of this before and are really good at it.' I know some have done a public speaking course in Year 9.

'This week we will do four things. We'll talk about public speaking and what you have done before, and have a short debate just as a trial run. We will discuss the elements of debating, and then we'll talk a bit about the media and what media you read.

'I used to work at Number 10 for the Prime Minister. I used to help prepare for Prime Minister's Questions where you have to debate against your opponents and make the best possible case for what the government is doing.'

I then set out the ground rules. 'Passion is good, but respect other people's views. When they are speaking please don't shout out or interrupt. Say what you think, don't be afraid to offer opinions. That is what we are here for. I want everyone to take part, which is why it is a small group. Please turn up on time. It's hard to get involved in a debate if you haven't been here at the beginning. Enjoy yourself. You should have fun and you will find this useful for your GCSEs, for job interviews, for any job you might do that involves presenting or making an argument. Now, who knows the key to good public speaking? Some of you have done some of this before.'

'Eye contact,' one shouts out.

'Yes, good.'

'Speaking clearly.'

'Passion, diction,' says another.

'What's diction, then?' says a third.

'It means speaking clearly.'

'Yes, so why did you just repeat what he's just said?' Anyone who uses a big word at school is usually pounced on and called 'a boffin'. It is not cool to be clever.

'Let me tell you another couple of tricks,' I say. 'First of all, we used to use what we called killer facts. Key facts that are hard to dispute, that make your case for you. The other important trick is to tell stories, connect with people emotionally not just rationally. It is far more powerful to say my uncle, or someone you know, is suffering from cancer and tell the story, than just giving the statistics about cancer sufferers.'

Another student joins the class. I now know what teachers mean when they say that one child can change the whole balance of a lesson. He is a nice kid, but a very talkative one. Barely having sat down he asks: 'Sir, why is Michael Jackson persecuted? I mean everyone knows he's innocent. Someone like him would never have done what they say he's done. You think he's innocent don't you, sir?'

'Let's not talk about Michael Jackson now. We are about to start our first debate.'

But he's not deterred. 'Sir, just answer the question, do you think he's innocent?'

Another student tells him to shut up. 'You're obsessed,' she says.

'It's a question of human rights,' he insists.

I try to move on swiftly. I have decided to get them going on the topic of the moment: Iraq. It is going to be interesting because there are both Turkish and Kurdish students in the class. I am sure that the Kurds will back the war, even if the Turks are more sceptical. I write on the board: 'Was Britain right to invade Iraq?' This starts an immediate debate.

'Of course not,' shouts out Ian, a student with shoulder-length blond hair.

'Let's have a vote at the beginning,' I say, 'and then we will take another one at the end and see if your views have changed. Who says Yes to this question?'

No hands go up.

'Who says No?'

Seven hands go up.

'Who says Don't Know?'

One hand goes up.

'Right, I've got some hand-outs for you to read. I want this half of the class to argue Yes and the other side to argue No,' I say, making sure the students divide into two groups. 'But No's easier,' says one of the Yeses.

'The point of debating, is to be able to argue for each side. It's good practice.' I hand out some sheets. One is the political broadcast to the nation that I helped write for Tony Blair on the eve of war. Another hand-out is by left-wing writer John Pilger in the *Mirror*, saying the war is a Western conspiracy. A third sheet contains some first-hand accounts of the brutality of the Saddam Hussein regime. They start reading the sheets, but want to talk about it immediately.

'What do you think, sir, did you support it?'

'I think there is a good case for saying Iraq is better without Saddam,' I say.

'But that Bush guy, he's mad, he's a warmonger. Why is Blair so close to him?'

'Yes, why is Blair creaming him,' says another. 'Is he gay?'

'Yes, tell us, sir, have Blair and Bush got a thing? Is that why Blair does whatever he says?'

'I bet that Blair would never have gone to war if he had to fight himself,' says Ian definitively.

'We can debate this all in a minute,' I say. They are busy writing. 'Remember what makes a good speech. Make sure you have a good beginning and a good ending.'

'Can I write about George Bush?' asks Ian.

'Yes, if it makes the case,' I say. I give them a few minutes to write. 'Right, has everyone written a short speech? Who wants to go first? Right, Ian.' Ian shuffles to the front. He says with passion: 'George Bush – idiot son of an idiot. George Bush is a liar, a warmonger, a cowboy, an idiot, a cheat, a murderer, a fool, a redneck. Do you want this man as the most powerful person on earth? He has ruined billions of lives. He has killed more people than all the terrorists.'

I'm taken aback by the ferocity of the onslaught. Now I am torn. Should I commend him on his great delivery and imaginative use of adjectives or defend George Bush. 'Very good delivery,' I say. 'But successful debating has to be about argument as well as insults, forceful though the insults were. Right, who wants to argue for Yes then?'

Shona stands up. She makes a good case for the war using the eye-witness accounts.

I take a vote at the end. It is now 8-0 against. Even the Kurdish student has voted against the war. This is not good news for Tony Blair, but at least I have enjoyed my first lesson.

Next lesson I decide to continue the political theme. I try to teach what the political parties stand for so the students can write their own debates.

I give them each hand-outs on the main parties' beliefs with photos of Tony Blair, Michael Howard and Charles Kennedy. None have heard of Howard or Kennedy or know which party they belong to.

I break them down into pairs to write their speeches. 'You do Labour, Sir, we'll do the other parties.' I agree and deliver a short speech on Labour's belief in strong public services.

Then it's their turn. They are all getting the hang of political rhetoric and the effective use of repetition. Timor, the Michael Jackson fanatic, stands up for the Conservatives:

> England our great country, threatens to be ruined by this
> horrible excuse for a government. Labour: all mouth and
> no direction. Lib Dems' and Greens' policies are unde-
> liverable. Retain our glorious past. Keep the freedom that
> is ours. If you're clever enough to realise this country is
> going to waste, you are clever enough to vote
> Conservative.'

'Very good end line,' I say. 'You're a natural.'

Zeki, who shares Ian's loathing for George Bush, gets passionate about the Greens:

> Today is the day when you have the power to change
> reality for the better. Today is the day when we make

history together. Today is the day when you will be not frightened to speak your mind. We, the Green Party, say there is more to life than money. Whatever your race, whatever your colour, we promise we will treat you as equally as any other human being. So vote for the Green Party for a better tomorrow.

It's Shona's turn. She has been struggling to find out what the Lib Dems stand for:

We are the Lib Dems. We exist to bring independence and equality to our society. A vote for us is a vote for empowerment, liberty and individuality. We believe in our community and the people that live there. We stand above all other parties. While they argue and shout we listen. Labour have made seventeen different tax rises only to spend the money on the war in Iraq and tuition fees. Education, education, education. Most of the new student population can't afford to pay for the education they have been promised. Conservatives have made a decision to move backwards and destroy the unity that our country has worked so hard for. Give the people independence, free us from the state. Vote Lib Dems. The state shouldn't own the people, the people should own the state.

I enjoy these lessons and find the students stimulating and good fun. One says to me, rather forlornly, that he wishes he was at a school where he wasn't called a 'boffin' for being clever. The danger in a school like ours is that the high fliers are dragged down, and that not enough is laid on for them. My lesson is meant to be the kind of session that may stimulate them. The school attempts to provide a rich 'gifted and talented programme' but it is hard not to spend most time on the most needy students.

These lessons give me a real insight into the extraordinary alchemy of teaching. One day it all works, I'm in good form, the students are focused, I think they are understanding the point, thinking for themselves. The next time, perhaps because I have done less preparation, perhaps because the students have had a bad day, the lesson is lacklustre, the students less sparky. For that hour, though, the class is in my hands. I am in charge, I can inspire or bore, shout or cajole, laugh or get fed up. It's all about pace, interest, variation. I can tell after a few lessons that I have stuck to the same formula for too long. I am becoming predictable. Instead of this being a different type of lesson which they look forward to, it's becoming a routine and I will have to change things round.

In teaching, like politics, the same question arises – is it charisma or solid determination that leads to better results? The debate among the senior management team is interesting. Trevor is a big advocate of active learning, and the use of a wide variety of tools – from mind mapping to memory games. He is often impressed by dynamic lessons of this kind. Eileen's view is that this is all very well but proof of the pudding is in the results. You can be very active and engaging but are you delivering the GCSE results? Her view is that some of the steadier, less flashy teachers are actually turning out the results. Teachers vary immensely. Some are comfortable with a variety of techniques. Others swear by traditional methods of 'chalk and talk' – standing at the front of the class and engaging students in a subject they are passionate about. What seems to be common to all teaching is the need for meticulous planning and pacy lessons that sweep the children along.

Paul says he has an assignment for me. He wants me to take three of my debaters to an event at Islington Town Hall.

The following day I leave the school with Ian, Shona, and Zeki. We are on our way to the Islington Pupils' Parliament elections.

'So why did you come to this school?' asks Ian.

'Yes, I was going to ask that,' says Shona.

'I care about education, I've written so many times in speeches that education is the future, I wanted to see for myself.'

It's strange walking out of the school with students for the first time. I feel responsible for them, yet they are fifteen and can do their own thing. It's hard to know how pally to get with them and how much to hold back. I like them and want to get on with them, but know I shouldn't try too hard.

'Well,' says Zeki, 'our school can do with all the help it can get.'

'It's getting better, isn't it?' I say.

'Yes,' says Shona, 'they're spending money, but not a lot of it is going on students themselves.' It's the first time I have heard the students' views of the school. There is a student council, but my sense is that it is not taken very seriously – and of course students are the consumers and they know better than any expert, inspector, teacher or parent whether the hours they spend at school are fun, stretching, interesting. 'Teachers are going on more training courses, but there's not much evidence in the lessons,' says Shona.

We enter Islington Town Hall, famous in the Seventies and Eighties as the home of one of the looniest of loony left councils.

'Committee room one please.' The man on the door points up the stairs, and we go up a grand staircase, past the council chamber, down two corridors and open a tall wooden door into a committee room.

There is Gemma, the organiser, surrounded by small, in some cases tiny, primary school children. 'Where are you from?' she asks, her glasses perched nervously on her nose, her bob bobbing, her woollen jumper as pink as candy floss.

'Islington Green School,' I say with great pride. It is the first time I have named my new employer in this way. It doesn't have quite the same ring as Number 10, but I am proud of where I am. Then I realise that the look of horror from my three students says it all. Here are three streetwise fifteen-year-olds having to debate with primary school kids. I feel guilty about what I am letting them in for. They turn to me for answers. I have none.

'I hope you all know,' Gemma begins, 'what today is for. We are going to elect a Prime Minister.'

'There is no vacancy,' I mutter to myself, still showing admirable loyalty to Tony Blair. I look round the vast oak committee table. All I can see are cherubic faces just tall enough to peer over the top. No bodies, just faces. Faces with plaits. Faces with smiles. Serious faces and happy faces. Innocent primary school faces. Faces that want to be Prime Minister.

Gemma continues: 'We will have one contest for primaries and one for secondaries – so we will end up with two Prime Ministers,' she says with a flourish.

It is a eureka moment! Gemma unwittingly has found a solution to the problem dogging the Labour Party for the past ten years. Make both Tony *and* Gordon Prime Minister. Together, at the same time. A joint leadership. Perhaps a job share, so they can both spend more time with their families as well. Tony could do Prime Minister's Questions on a Tuesday and Gordon could do it on a Thursday. They could both occupy Number 10. They could run the country from neighbouring rooms. What an example it would send! How family friendly! It would be a huge vote winner.

I am grinning to myself at the brilliance of the idea when the committee room doors are flung open and in walk four tall, spick and span, secondary school girls. Their mouths glitter with state-of-the-art braces. Confidence oozes from behind the steel and rubber bands. I haven't been in politics for ten years for nothing. I know the enemy instantly – and this is the enemy. A rival secondary school. Forget the primary schools. My students now have serious opponents. I am used to tribal fights. I have always relished giving the Tories a pasting. Now for 'the Tory party' read 'Highbury Fields School'. My campaigning juices are flowing.

The Highbury Fields girls sit down at the table in a neat line. They take off their coats with synchronised smugness and the lead girl puts a piece of paper in front of her. Her eyes do a tour of the table to size up the competition.

It is clear that all the other schools have known about this event for a while and have prepared speeches. None of my students have. I ask them if they want to get involved. They shake their heads and say No. They will just listen. I am disappointed that they will not be taking part. It's as if Labour has decided not to fight an election.

'Let's wait for the last stragglers,' says Gemma.

Another three secondary schools appear. 'Line up, line up, all together,' says Gemma shepherding primary and secondary candidates to the end of the long room.

'Are you all sure you don't want to make a speech?' I say to my three. 'You could scribble something now. I'll help you with it.' They shake their heads. My desperation is showing.

'No last-minute entrants?' asks Gemma. 'OK, let me read you a quote that might tempt you.' A tempting quote, something I've been trying to write for the last ten years. 'The last finisher is always ahead of the non-starter,' Gemma proclaims in her best Judi Dench voice. The primary school faces look blank, but someone is stirring beside me. Gemma's words are having the desired effect. Like a scene from a Hollywood weepy, the hero steps forward. Shona from Islington Green School rises from her seat with a whimsical grin on her face.

'I may be mad but I'll give it a go,' she says.

The legendary Islington Green School fighting spirit is still alive. She joins the group. Real courage. Real guts. Out of these small steps great political careers are born. 'She'll just have to make something up,' says Ian, in admiration at his classmate.

The hustings begins. Holly steps up from a primary school whose uniform is a red pullover with an embossed school badge. She has long plaits and a face that could launch a new range of Barbie dolls.

'Speak loudly and for no more than two minutes,' says Gemma officiously. Perhaps noticing my smirk she thrusts a watch into my hand. 'Can you do the timing?'

I have no choice. Holly has begun.

'When I am Prime Minister I will make sure we discuss children's problems and make sure they feel they can come forward.' Like any modern politician Holly is equipped with a five-point plan. '1. Children are able to talk to teachers. 2. Safety in winter. 3. Tuck shop to sell healthy food. 4. Children can talk through issues. 5. If I was PM I would pledge to listen and act on behalf of everyone.'

She sits down abruptly. A good opening bid, but a little flaky I think. Will she be good in a crisis? If the muesli bars run out in the tuck shop will she crumple? If a nasty boy in class 5e, dressed as a cowboy, wants her to launch an unprovoked raid on 5f's play dough, will she go along with it or resist this new doctrine of pre-emption? The jury is still out.

Then the first of Shona's competitors appears. It is one of the Highbury Fields girls. She unfurls her script, puckers her lips and begins. 'I have been Prime Minister of Highbury Fields,' she says, 'and this will be a fantastic promotion.'

Promotion, promotion. You don't become Prime Minister as

a promotion. You do it because you want to change the country and serve the people.

'I will be a voice for pupils.' A smug one, I mutter. 'Who says children should be seen and not heard?' she says with a flourish and sits down.

'I want to be Prime Minister,' says the next primary school girl, visibly shaking, 'because I am completely at ease with public speaking.'

Then the primary school star arrives. She's only ten, and with the clarity, diction and confidence of a born performer: angelic yet tough; girly plaits, yet professional fringe; casual trousers, yet sophisticated swagger. She gives the performance of her life.

'First issue, school dinners,' she says. 'This is *the* big issue. Why are there no vegetarian options? Why aren't the cooks nice? I've spoken to the head and the cooks and nothing has changed yet, so I have written to the inspectors and asked one to visit our school.' Dynamic or what? 'Number two: school toilets. Why are they so dirty? Why do children behave so stupidly in them?' She pauses for effect. Her timing is immaculate. 'Perhaps the two are connected. We need to sort it. I will lead by example,' she finishes. 'I will encourage debate. I will have small strong focused groups that will report back to this Parliament.' This girl is Prime Ministerial material.

The next girl looks as if she is out past her bedtime. She is tiny, her voice twitchy and high pitched. What she needs is a bath, breast feed, a quick rendition of 'Wheels on the bus' and lights out. What she wants is to be Prime Minister. That, I suppose, is what democracy is all about. 'Children should be made as safe as possible,' she says with feeling before petering out.

Now it is Shona's turn. I look nervously at Zeki and Ian and give Shona a warm smile.

'First thing to say is I didn't prepare a speech, but I just wanted to tell you why I want to be President.' There were one or two sniggers. This is a gaffe. Why has she said President not Prime Minister? But she recovers well. 'This is not about what *I* want but about what *you* want and how I can represent you as best I can.' She is charming and she's going down well. 'I want more events and shows to bring schools and the community together, more chances to talk about the real issues. So vote for me as someone to make your views heard.'

I am so proud of this off-the-cuff performance, but the competition is getting tougher: there she is in green stockings and full school uniform. I can tell immediately she is one of those people who loves following rules, like a friend of mine who, rather than protesting against the poll tax, queued up to pay it early. Her long blonde hair is so shiny and straight.

'This is about the passion within you, not written speeches,' she says. 'When the war on Iraq started there was lots of talk on television about whether it was right or wrong, but the voices of children were never heard.' Very true, very thoughtful. So what is the answer? How is this dilemma to be overcome? More than twenty under tens are on the edge of their seats, wanting to know the answer. (It's just possible they merely want the toilet.) What was this eager girl going to do about it?

She takes a deep breath, straightens her pristine blouse and says: 'That's why I joined the Liberal Democrats.'

I know it's churlish and competitive, nasty even, but I cannot bring myself to be pleased for her. Here is someone defying the cynical age, a young person engaging with politics, giving up her time not for booze and sex, violence or computer games, but *politics*. I should be happy. I try to be happy. I find it impossible to be happy.

'I now go to Lib Dem committee meetings,' she says with the gleam of someone who has just discovered peanut-butter for the first time.

'Get a life,' I want to scream at her. 'Do something naughty.

Hit me, go on hit me. Swear. Say a rude word. Anything. But please don't waste away your childhood at Liberal Democrat committee meetings.'

Ian snaps me out of it. He is gracious and puts me to shame: 'She didn't join the Tories so what are you complaining about?'

Shona shows why she is so nice. 'She's getting involved – that's a good thing.'

However, my instincts are right when the voting begins. The electorate – the kids in the room – share my view. That earnestness chip is embedded just a little too deep. The Lib Dem isn't getting their vote.

Gemma's counting system is elaborate and everyone chats amongst themselves whilst she tots up the votes. Then she coughs and says: 'We have the results.'

Nervous faces look intently at her.

'The primary school winner is Molly and the secondary school winner is . . .' She pauses. 'Shona.'

Shona is shocked. I'm shocked. She smiles a broad grin.

'Well done,' I say. 'You've done brilliantly. No prepared speech. Off the cuff. Aren't you good?'

'And,' Gemma says, 'the Prime Ministers will be able to pick their Cabinet and then we will get down to discussing some real issues.'

On the way out of the meeting, Ian ponders what role he might be offered by Shona. 'I could be deputy Prime Minister like that big Northern bloke,' he says.

'John Prescott,' I say.

'No, Alastair Campbell.'

I try and correct him, but he's having none of it.

As we leave the town hall I congratulate Shona again and ask her whether her parents will be excited. 'Is your family interested in politics?' I ask.

'No,' she says, 'they're just a normal family.'

Next week I get Shona in the local paper, under the headline 'New Islington PM vows to listen to students.' Trevor is pleased with the good publicity.

In the staff room the next day Paul suggests I come and see a 'mad' Year 8 class in action. He says they are uncontrollable .

I have read Paul's book *Surviving and Succeeding in Difficult Classroooms*, in which he writes:

> The first and most important lesson for any teacher in a tough secondary school is to get your overall thinking right. Start by disregarding the current 'inspector speak' which says that pupils behave badly when the quality of teaching is insufficiently stimulating. They often behave badly when lessons are brilliantly planned because they prevent the teacher from starting properly; they often behave badly because they have poor skills in the subject areas they are being asked to study, but most importantly they often behave badly because they have a very thin layer of motivation and a low level of concentration. Do not be demoralised. The vast majority of teachers would, and do, struggle when faced with large numbers of poorly motivated and badly behaved pupils.

We start to argue over it. I know Paul is trying to reassure teachers in difficult schools and counter what he sees as the lack of understanding shown by politicians, but realism can easily turn to defeatism. Though the point of Paul's book is to give teachers a series of coping strategies, the underlying case is that no one has ever truly been successful in these schools. He keeps saying to me: 'The starting point is the reality of these class-rooms. It's how you deal with the bottom sets. That's what people don't get.'

I go into Fraser's Year 8 class and immediately see what he means. It is mayhem. Kids are wandering about, throwing things, talking incessantly. He is pleased to have help. The topic of the lesson is Muslim traditions and hallal meat in particular, but few are listening. Fraser, a newish teacher, is using one of the techniques from Paul's book: a smiley-face stamp. Every time a student gets an answer right he comes up to their desk, opens their exercise book at the back and gives them a smiley face stamp. Once they have got ten stamps Fraser promises to write home to their parents, saying how well they have done. This positive praise scheme, however, has not stopped the disruption. I notice one boy whose back is turned to the teacher. Fraser has not told him off or asked him to turn round. I go up to him, thinking I am being useful.

'Could you turn round please?' I say quietly and politely.

The boy spins round and looks me in the eye. 'Can't you see this is a conversation between A and B. I'm A he's B. You're C, so get lost.'

I am gob-smacked by the rudeness, but obey his instructions. I ask Fraser what's his problem.

'I've already sent him out once this lesson. He's out of control.'

I spend the rest of the lesson standing next to Fraser at the front, looking stern. Fraser puts it down to the fact that he does not have them regularly enough to bond with them.

After the lesson Paul says he has an experiment for me. He wants me to work with key marginals. These are the students taking GCSEs in a few months' time who need five A–Cs to get to college but who are one or two grades short. The idea is that I work with them to help them complete coursework or to revise, and help them boost their grades to a C. This is exactly the same principle, even the same title – key marginals – as we use to plan general elections. The seats which we are most likely to lose or win off our opponents are the ones we put most resources and most effort into. 'This is cutting edge stuff,' says Paul. 'We will see if your intervention has any effect.'

The government measures secondary schools on the number of pupils achieving five A–Cs, so it is in the school's, and Trevor's, interest that we boost these. This is an example of public services responding to the way things are measured, and if one measure is chosen, this does not seem to be a bad one. The only consequences, though, are that those who could do really well, who could convert Bs into As, are given less attention.

Paul has arranged to interview the key students with their parents and ask three or four if they are willing to work with me on an intensive basis.

The first interview I sit in on is with Abdul. We are in Paul's office amidst the clutter, sitting on plastic chairs. Abdul and his mother sit opposite Paul and me. Paul looks at a sheet with the mock exam results on it. 'Right, Abdul, which of your Ds do you think you can turn into Cs?'

In a sullen voice he says: 'English maybe, health and social maybe, science I suppose.' His mother looks at him with an irritated frown.

Paul ploughs on. 'Would you like Mr Hyman to work with you on your coursework, so that you get it all in on time?'

'Hmm.'

'Is that a yes?'

'Don't need help.'

His mother turns on him. 'What do you mean you don't need help?'

'I'll do it myself.'

'Well, shall we at least give it a try?' says Paul.

I am not thrilled to have such a reluctant customer. Let's hope the next one is more receptive.

The next customer doesn't turn up.

'Right, I'll phone her,' says Paul. 'I'll do the interview on the phone.' He calls a girl from the Packington estate across the road.

Her mother answers. 'Yeah, sorry I couldn't come,' she says. 'Monica has a dreadful tummy ache. Can I phone you back in a minute. I'm just doing the cooking.'

She calls back a few minutes later. 'Monica's had this tonsillitis for ages,' she says. The illness has changed in the space of a few minutes. This doesn't look promising. 'Oh yes, please give Monica some help.'

The next couple of interviewees don't seem suitable. but the following day Paul finds me two more. I now have four.

Abdul needs help in health and social studies, as does Humeyra. Monica needs support in English, and so does Vanessa, a Nigerian girl. None of them need help in history, my own subject. I'm not sure if I will be any use on health but English I know I can have a crack at. 'Get alongside and see if you can make a difference,' says Paul.

It starts well with Humeyra. She is a bubbly, optimistic girl with a big toothy smile and flowing brown hair. She sets out competently what she is doing in each area to get her course-work in on time. She is confident, clued in. Her teachers, who I talk to, confirm this.

I speak to Jane, Vanessa's English teacher, about how I can help. Jane makes the point: 'Why give her special treatment when she never turns up for my lesson, never does her work, whereas I've got plenty of them who are keen, like little rodents listening to my every word? They're far more deserving.'

I go back to Paul, who agrees with the point but says we have picked Vanessa because she is a marginal. The students Jane has mentioned may be keen but are not marginal. However well they do in English, they are not on course for five A–Cs.

So I persevere. 'She needs to do her *Romeo and Juliet* coursework,' Jane says. I meet Vanessa, but only just. I try and meet her twice, but she doesn't show up. Then, I finally catch up with her in the playground and we arrange that she will come to see me twice – first period on Monday and first period on Tuesday.

On Monday it becomes clear that Vanessa doesn't do first period. She rolls in at 9.20 instead of 8.45. Jane says: 'I told you, you're wasting your time.'

Vanessa has no time to read Romeo and Juliet so I am given a short cut: the film starring Leonardo di Caprio. We spend the next five lessons, or the bits of it that Vanessa turns up for, sitting in the English department's office on leather armchairs, surrounded by textbooks and exam papers, watching Romeo and Juliet on video. It's a bizarre cinematic experience: irritated teacher and naughty pupil. After each twenty minutes I turn to Vanessa and ask her if she understands what's going on. I'm a bit rusty myself. Via the antics of Leonardo we grope for an understanding of the play.

I'm given a choice of two essays to do with her. One asks who is to blame for the tragedy. This is meant to be the easiest essay title for those who don't really get it, or, like Vanessa, who are clearly bright but have got behind in their coursework. The other essay, which is more difficult – for both pupil and this particular teacher – is about the role of Friar Lawrence and is for those who want to aim for a higher mark. I decide to try the Friar Lawrence one.

On lesson six we finally get to the end of the film and I tell Vanessa that next lesson we will be ready to start writing the essay. Come next lesson she is nowhere to be seen. I'm annoyed. She's watched the film, Now, when a little bit of work is required, she's off.

When she appears at 9.30 I sit her down and ask her what the problem is.

'We've moved out. We don't live near the school any more.'

'Where do you live?'

'Finchley.'

'I know the Northern Line,' I say. 'That is just a few stops from the Angel, about twenty-minutes tube ride. It must take you ten minutes at most to walk down from the Angel tube. That's a thirty-minute journey at the most. If you leave the house at eight you will always be here on time.'

She doesn't answer.

We get on with the essay in the remaining ten minutes. I am using the English department's essay plan which gives lots of clues to the answers. I'm quite grateful. So is Vanessa. We decide that Friar Lawrence is a meddling fool but can't be entirely held responsible for the deaths of Romeo and Juliet. We agree too that providing a potion that imitates death is asking for trouble.

We are halfway through writing the essay together when Vanessa stops coming to lessons again.

Meanwhile I'm trying to focus on another marginal, Monica. Monica has a permanent 'I don't want to be at school' expression. I soon discover that *Romeo and Juliet* is the coursework that she needs help with. We go to the library and she produces the question that she needs to answer. 'Who is to blame for the tragedy of Romeo and Juliet?' The idea for the essay is to go through in turn who it might be and then plump on two likely suspects. Monica seems to be happy to sit down and do the coursework on the spot. She has obviously paid attention in class because she has no trouble remembering the plot. She decides that Tybalt has stoked things up by being so aggressive and the two families are also to blame for not resolving their feud. I encourage her and she writes down her analysis well.

We've had a good lesson, but, when we next arrange to meet, I go and fetch her from the English lesson and she refuses to come. 'It's OK, sir, I'll type what we done myself.'

Next lesson I go up and ask her if she wants me to look at her typed-up version.

'Computer crashed. Anyway, stop hassling me, I'll do it myself.'

'Is there any other coursework you've still got to do?'

'*Time Machine*,' I think. *The Time Machine* by H. G. Wells is coursework for most of the students.

'Have you done it?'

'No, don't like it.'

'Why don't we do it now in the library? We can do it quickly in one lesson, then you'll get some marks for it at least.'

'No, I'm not going to do it, whatever you say.' With that, she returns to the classroom.

I mention this to Paul and, without telling me, he writes to Monica's parents to ask them why she is not co-operating. The next time she sees me she shouts angrily: 'What you doing telling my mum, I told you I'm doing it. Anyway, I've got things to worry about at home so leave me alone.'

My fourth marginal is Abdul. He's been reluctant from the beginning and seems to have taken a lethargy pill. His teacher tells me he sits at the back of the health and social studies course doing nothing, writing nothing, saying nothing. I take him to the library to have a quiet chat.

'I cannot work at home,' he says.

'Why? Is someone stopping you?'

'No, I just do other things, can't get down to it.'

'Well, we can work at school,' I say. 'How are you doing on your coursework?'

'Got a lot to do.'

'Shall we write a list?'

I find a piece of paper and get him to describe to me all the pieces of work he is missing. It is a daunting list: 'Science coursework, lost last year's piece. Need to do last practical. English teacher's lost my essay. RE don't know if I've been entered. Health, still got big project to do.'

'I've written all this out. Will you go to each teacher and discuss it all with them please?'

He looks pleased to have a timetable. I chase him up every three or four days. His teacher for health and social policy says she has phoned him at home and tried to get him to come in for special sessions to complete his coursework, but he doesn't turn up.

Having waited for thirty minutes on another three occasions for Vanessa, I decide to confront her properly. I find her in the playground, take her into the meeting room, sit her down and get tough. This is the first time I have had the confidence to be firm with any student since I have arrived, but I am convinced she needs a jolt to get her focused on her exams.

'Just because your sister is at college and just because you are clever does not mean you are going to get good GCSEs if you don't do any work. You have not finished the Friar Lawrence essay that you started. You never show up for my lessons. The exams are in a few weeks' time, you are not going to get the grades you need unless you get your act together *now*.'

She looks crestfallen. I don't know whether I have gone too far. She protests a little: 'I am, sir, I am.' She saunters out. I hope I have done the trick, or at least made her realise how important the next few weeks are for her.

I talk through my four marginals with Paul. He seems pleased that I am finding it so frustrating. 'You see, these things are hard. Here you are, an intelligent person, willing to work one-to-one with them, yet you're finding that difficult. What does that tell you? It tells me that even our marginals, even those we hope will get good grades, in many cases don't want the help or don't come to school. It shows you just what we are up against.'

Trevor has a different take. 'I find it absurd that coursework is not finished by Christmas. Why are teachers letting course-work drift into the spring term when the student should be revising?' His plan for next year is to make all faculties finish all coursework by Christmas.

All I can do now is chivvy my marginals along one more time and then wait to see how they do in their GCSEs, see if I have made any difference at all.

Next time I am in the library Flora, the librarian, takes me to one side with a conspiratorial glint in her eye. Am I in trouble for failing to return a library book? Is she about to complain about a child? 'They're in Syria,' she whispers to me by the science-fiction shelf.

'What are?' I say, taken aback.

'The weapons. My friend works for foreign intelligence. She says it is well known Saddam got rid of all the weapons two weeks before the war and sent them all to Syria. That's where he put his airforce during the first Gulf War, so that the Americans wouldn't destroy it. Look in Syria. Why don't people look in Syria? I hate to see Blair in so much trouble,' she says. My association with Tony is making me increasingly a figure deserving of staffroom sympathy. Since Labour's defeat in the local elections, since the horrific pictures of the brutal treatment of Iraqi prisoners by the Americans and with the Butler report into intelligence imminent, I am being asked regularly whether my former boss is on the way out. Until now no one has come up with a strategy for saving him.

Flora's theory sounds plausible and, given the painstaking but unsuccessful work of Hans Blix, the hundreds of inspectors searching for weapons since the war, the best minds in more than a dozen countries poring over the evidence, I like the idea that it is a librarian at Islington Green School who has tracked those weapons down.

'He comes in for such attack, but it's not his fault the weapons were moved.'

I am touched by her motherly concern. 'Thanks for the tip off,' I say before leaving the library.

My next big project is to try whole-class teaching. I have had a few little asides in the staff room, teachers asking me when I'm going to do some proper teaching as opposed to my small groups, and I am determined to have a go. So I ask Jane if I can take one of her lessons to do debating, 'persuasive writing' as the GCSE syllabus calls it. She says I can come and take a lesson with her mixed-ability Year 9 group.

I am keen to find out more about the craft of teaching. Fortunately, now that behaviour is beginning to improve, Trevor is spending more time on learning and how to teach imaginative lessons. Though, perhaps surprisingly, Trevor says that he has only spent about two weeks on the theory and techniques of learning in a teaching career spanning twenty-two years. At one of the staff meetings he hands us all a sheet to test whether we are left or right brained. The aim is to tick a series of questions and see which headings we fall under.

I am, it turns out, very right-brained. I am bad on filing, bad on detail, bad on reading instructions and DIY. I am better on ideas, energy, spontaneity. The ideal, Trevor says, is to be a balance of both right and left-brained. Right-brained people are basically intuitive and impulsive; left-brained people are more detailed, logical, thorough. Trevor says that exams are generally based on left-brained skills. The children at a school like Islington Green are broadly right-brained. That means, in his view, that teachers should be more imaginative about how they teach lessons, using different learning styles rather than just the traditional, didactic teaching of facts and lists. Some extrapolate this and say that girls are generally more left-brained and boys more right-brained, so that each need to be taught using different techniques. Trevor says that one of the problems he has faced in management is being surrounded by too many right-brained, ideas people and not enough detail people who relentlessly pursue an issue until it is completed. Government is the same. It needs the sticklers and those who relentlessly focus on the detail as well as the big picture people. Trevor has written out what that means for lessons:

- Plan your lesson
- Talk for twenty-five per cent of the lesson
- For seventy-five per cent of the lesson students should be active

Active means:
- Reading
- Presenting
- Solving problems
- Assessing each other
- Practising exam work
- Organising their own work
- Using mind maps
- Evaluating homework
- Making work fun
- Using visual and sound stimulus
- Assessing regularly and using it
- Building study skills into the lesson plan

Trevor goes on to talk about what makes a model lesson. He is worried this will sound as if he is telling the teachers what they know already. The deputy heads suggest it is still worth reminding them. When I see the list it looks impressive, but I know, from watching teachers and from my little experience, just how hard this is to pull off every lesson of every day with all the provocations.

# A model lesson

**At the start:**
In the first few minutes students arrive and you are there
to greet them
The first task is written on the board, as is the homework
and aims of the lesson
There is a meaningful activity on each desk for the
students to begin as you greet and usher late arrivals.

**In the room:**
The school rules and special class directions are clearly
displayed
Students know your routines and have the responsibility
to get appropriate equipment out ready for the lesson
They get out their homework diaries and place on desk
Students sit in their a–z places
The room is tidy, colourful and has recognition of
student achievements on the walls

**You begin the lesson (10 mins)**
By reminding students of the aims on the board
By instructing them to write down the homework/this
should be a mind map or presentation, prep for a test,
notes they can bring to use in class or reading
By collecting in last week's homework/it might need
presenting
A brief review of expectations and positive discipline
An exposition of between 5 and 10 minutes of the tasks
for the day
A question and answer session may be in the form of a
pop quiz to review students' knowledge

**Students work independently for 20 minutes**
They brainstorm ideas in groups of 2 or 3
They seek out their own knowledge (don't give them the
page numbers let them learn to use contents and index)
They reinforce by looking in reference books
They prepare an explanation to give back to groups

**You call for feedback**
Each student group speaks about their findings
They evaluate each others' findings and suggest
improvement.

**Individual task (10 mins)**
At least once during the lesson:
Individuals read
Work on an individual assignment in silence/exam
conditions
In Year 9–11 this could be an exam question

**Last 5 mins – exit routines**
Q and A review of lesson
Reminder of homework
Chairs up
Reminder of homework
Stand behind chairs
Leave when you say
Praise those who have done well/behaved
Remind those who haven't of the consequences
Put marks, P for praise and U for unsatisfactory, in the
register.

Trevor finishes with a bit of theory. It is, by coincidence, from psychologist Mihaly Csikszentmihalyi who inspired me when I first read his book *FLOW: the Psychology of Happiness*. The book is based on his detailed research about what makes individuals happy. His conclusion is that happiness or flow comes from activities that make you forget where you are because you are so absorbed in them, and you only get that when the challenge of the activity and your own abilities are in harmony. His example is a game of tennis. Playing someone slightly better than yourself gives you flow, whereas playing someone it is easy to beat ends up being boring, and playing someone a lot better makes you anxious or fed up. He has used this theory for education. This chart shows that when a student has learnt skills and is given a challenge at, or just beyond, this ability he reaches flow and enjoys the lesson. When he has more skills then the challenge demands he is bored and starts messing about. If he hasn't learnt the skills and is not challenged, as happens to some who have poor literacy, he becomes apathetic or, worse, destructive. When they are challenged but their skills are not up to it they become anxious. The teacher must strive for high challenge and high skills for every child – a tall order.

<br>

High challenge

| **ANXIETY** | **FLOW** |
|---|---|
| Challenge too great for skills | Challenge and skills in sync |

Low skill ———————————————— High skill

| **APATHY** | **BOREDOM** |
|---|---|
| Challenge and skills low | Challenge too low for skills |

Low challenge

I now have more than enough to be going on with. At the moment keeping order for a few minutes is going to make me happy enough.

I meet Jane in the staff room to plan the lesson for her mixed-ability year 9 group. I soon realise that the planning I have put into my debating group so far is not nearly good enough. Jane grills me as to what each five or ten minutes is going to be about, and educates me in some of the realities. 'They won't all be there for the first ten minutes,' she says. Then she asks, 'What is the objective for the lesson?'

The first requirement of any lesson is that it has a clear objective. At the end of the lesson there is meant to be a review of the objective to check that people have understood it. 'To understand how to make a speech and debate an argument,' I say.

Jane suggests we start the lesson with a warm-up. We then try to break it up into chunks. For each chunk Jane suggests a handout or a way of grabbing their attention, so I go away to plan them, to find some fact sheets for the debate off the internet and prepare photocopies for the lesson. She has agreed to remain at the side of the room to help with the crowd control if I need it.

I recall one of Trevor's favourite statistics. 'You remember 10 per cent of what you read, 50 per cent of what you see and hear and 80 per cent of what you say.' One of the things I had noticed was the emphasis put on reading and writing but not speaking or oracy, to use the jargon. This is not the same in other cultures. In a fascinating book, *Culture and Pedagogy*, Robin Alexander describes in detail the different teaching and learning methods in primary schools across five countries: France, Russia, United States, India and England. One of his most striking conclusions is that there is a 'yawning gulf' between England, where there is very little emphasis on speech, and the other countries where speech is 'in balance' with reading and writing. Despite a National Oracy Project between 1987 and 1991, there has been little done to correct this. I know that those who devised the literacy and numeracy strategies for primary schools assumed oracy would naturally become part of them, but it hasn't. It is another 'yawning gulf' between the political world – where there is endless talk and debate, where people are loquacious to a fault – and here at the school, where speech is being eked out of a tiny vocabulary and there is only one form of speech – street slang. Yet if these students are truly going to compete, if the opportunity and mobility we want for them is to be real, they need to become more articulate, be able to structure argument and thought, 'move between scholastic and conversational registers'. To do this would require a reworking of the curriculum and the production of decent materials for lessons – I found almost nothing useful to use on oracy. The result would be far more varied and engaging lessons for students, for whom lots and lots of writing, particularly mundane writing, switches them off. It would channel their natural propensity to chatter into learning.

My small contribution to an upsurge in oracy is to teach as many students as will listen – in small groups or large – how to write and then perform speeches.

I meet with Jane again before the lesson to go through the running order, so that she can fine tune the timings.

The night before my first lesson I don't sleep. This is the first time since leaving Number 10, that I have had a sleepless night because of work. I am panicking about losing control of the class, making a fool of myself, the students showing no interest, Jane thinking I'm hopeless. I get up early, go into school and start checking I have the right materials. My lesson is just after break.

I get to the classroom during break and write the objective on the board. Then I rearrange the chairs and tables into four sections because I want the class to work in groups. Jane comes in to give me a hand, and writes place names on Post-it notes, so that the students are sitting where she wants them. This is one of the keys: who is in control of the classroom? The teacher or the students? I put the first work-sheet on the table so they have something to do as soon as they get into the room. The piece of paper says: '*The thing that makes me most angry is* ........................ *Because* ......................................'

The students enter and I greet some of them at the door. One or two who are not in the class come into the room to shout at a friend. Jane tells them to leave. The students are looking for their places. One or two ask if they can swap with someone else, but most sit down in the right place. I see a few faces I know well from the exclusion room. One of them, Jamie, is a regular customer, but I get on well with him, even though he never does what I ask.

It seems that only a third of the class have their own pen, so only a few get going on the task in front of them. Jamie starts reading a comic book. I go round, individually trying to interest them. 'What makes you angry Jamie? When was the last time you shouted at someone?' I say, before taking the comic off him.

'I never get angry,' he says.

'Oh yeah,' says one of his friends. 'That's not the Jamie I know.'

The room is almost full and Jane is handing out a few pens. She whispers at me that I can start and, slightly hesitantly, I do. I give my introduction that I worked with Tony Blair and now I want to do this special lesson on speeches. 'So let's start with the page in front of you. What makes you angry? . . . Has everyone written something down? Right, who's going to come up and perform it in front of everyone?' I know a few of the class and so call one of them first: 'What about you Mickey?'

Mickey comes up and in a mumbling voice says: 'The thing that makes me most angry is my brother . . . because he gets on my nerves, because we fight.' He sits down to applause that Jane starts.

'Tom, how about you?'

Tom gets up and saunters to the front of the class. 'The thing that makes me angry is going to bed, because sometimes I am not tired but I still have to go to bed. When I'm playing computer, I have to turn it off and I'm really into the game. When a good film comes on late, I can't watch it if I have to go to bed.'

'Very good,' I say as he sits down. 'Right, that's good. Now I want you to think about what makes for good public speaking. What did people do best when they came up here? I've got a Post-it note for each of you. I want you to write one thing and come to the front with it and stick it on the board.'

They are excited by this, as Jane predicted. It's a bit different. They enjoy coming up and putting notes on the board. Jane comes up quietly and removes one of the notes. 'There's always one,' she mouths, 'Rude words.'

I can see to the right of the class a couple of boys talking to each other and not paying attention. Jane is now trying to get them to be quiet.

'There are some great ideas here,' I say. 'You've got your chart in front of you; I want you to write each of these down as I read them out . . . Someone has written "eye contact". That's good. Who wrote that? Yes, well done. "Talking loudly". That's good. "Confidence", that's good. "Don't put your head down when speaking", that's very good, well done Jessica. "Using interesting words". Very good – vocabulary is important. "Hand gestures keep people engaged", well done. "Passion", good, "relaxed", good. That is really excellent. Now we're going to break down into four groups and debate a question.'

There is quite a lot of low-level chit-chat by now. 'Please, listen for a second,' I say, a little feebly.

Jane backs me up. 'No talking without your hand up, please,' she says far more authoritatively.

I write on the board, 'Which causes more harm to society – domestic violence, alcohol abuse, smoking, or drug abuse?' I hand out work-sheets and give each of the four groups a different subject within the topic. 'I want one of you in each group to do the writing and one to make the speech. Now, let's have a vote at the beginning to see what you think before we start. Let's have a show of hands.'

Domestic violence wins, drugs are second, smoking is third and there are no votes at all for alcohol abuse. The sheets I've handed out show the extent of alcohol abuse and the harm it can cause. I am interested to see if this sways any votes.

They all get on with it. I have given some of them a gruesome anti-smoking advert that I found on the internet. It shows a girl about the same age as those in the class with all the ailments that are caused by smoking: blackened teeth, eyeballs popping out, heart destroyed, liver bulbous. 'They've got better sheets than us, I want to do smoking,' says one of the students dealing with drug abuse. I reassure him that he's got a hot topic.

The students spend fifteen minutes writing their speeches. It's clear in each group that some are working hard and some are not bothered and are letting one or two do all the work. It's hard to know how much effort to spend cajoling each of them. I go round each group, trying to stimulate debate and help them write their speeches.

Then, one by one, I ask them up. Jessica who has written the drug abuse speech also performs it. It is very powerful and the attention of the class is held. Jane tells me afterwards this is her best piece of work this year.

As each group's speech is read out, I look round the room and realise that one student, who was chatting a lot at the beginning of the lesson, is no longer here. I have not even noticed his departure. Jane must have spirited him away to help me. I feel embarrassed that, with all my talking at the front, I haven't even noticed that I've lost a child.

'Now, let's have a second vote,' I say. Hands shoot up, and alcohol abuse still gets no votes. Domestic violence and drugs are equal winners, drug abuse has gone up as a result of the debate.

I end the lesson, as Jane has advised me, asking one student from each group to tell me what they have learned. I don't make this clear enough, I am hoping they will talk about what makes for good speechwriting; instead one student says, 'Drugs are bad.' The next says, 'Domestic violence is bad.' I suppose in the end that is a better lesson for them to take away.

'Thanks a lot,' I say as they rummage for the bags and jackets. 'You've been great and I've enjoyed the lesson.'

Jane comes up to me to encourage me. 'You've done well,' she says.

'But I didn't even notice you'd got rid of one of them,' I said.

She smiles and says, 'The hard thing is how to deal with a mixed-ability class.' She shows me the register. 'The ones who misbehaved are all the ones down here with the lowest marks in English, the ones who are basically illiterate – that's why they are bored. I would far rather have a small class of those kids together, where I can give them the right work and help them get on, than mix them up in this class.' I can see her point.

We also discuss what sort of person makes a good teacher. There are some schemes that get the brightest graduates from the top universities and put them into schools. Islington Green is starting to use them, but Jane makes the strong case, particularly at a school like this, for the teacher with a real rapport with the students. 'You need someone with presence, someone who can understand them and deal with them.'

I'm pretty sure you need both: great subject specialists, as well as those who can deal properly with crowd control in the classroom.

I am exhausted. My first-ever lesson is over. I have got through it. Some of them even seem to have enjoyed it. The planning proved essential.

I collect up all the stray pieces of paper, and notice that on the first assignment one of the students who didn't come up to share his contribution with the class, has written:

> *The thing that makes me most angry is* . . . when some one is
> in the barth room when you need to go a poo! *Because* . . .
> you mite need to go a poo bad and it's poping out your
> bum check.

'Good use of apostrophe,' I say to Jane.

'You should do this again,' she says.

'How do teachers do that five times a day?' I ask.

'You'll get used to it.'

The big question for me is: could I do this day in day out? Do I have the skill or the stamina or the focus?

# POLITICAL STRATEGIST

I'm in a hurry, but not like the teachers around me who are rushing to a lesson, focused intently on making the next hour stimulating for thirty children. I have another mission. I'm looking for a television, looking for one that's not being used in one of the lessons. I finally alight on a flickering black-and-white TV in the room of the school printer, Sam, who is in charge of all the publications, prospectuses, newsletters. I ask him if he minds me sitting in his little office. He says no, so I make myself comfortable and tune in to a great annual political event: the Budget. However much I feel I have moved on from Number 10, there are certain things I feel compelled to soak up.

The jargon of politics is more jarring than usual. I am normally at home with the standard lexicon of spending reviews and White Papers, public service agreements and efficiency targets, but today it seems so elevated and pompous. But then my new world has its own jargon, the language of education: Key Stage 3 strategies and Year 11 Assemblies, SATs tests and fixed-term exclusions, BIPs (behaviour improvement plans) and EWOs (education welfare officers), G and Ts – gifted and talented students. If the public don't understand politicians, similarly parents can't possibly understand educationalists.

Halfway through the Budget it's lunch time at the school and I have to strain to hear Gordon Brown above the banter and shouting of students leaving their classrooms and hurtling down the corridors. 'And so our prudence has been for a purpose. Today I can announce that . . . Lisa is a bitch.'

No one at school is interested in the Budget. Even the big extra spending for education washes over people. I can see why. With growing distance from my previous job I can see both how irrelevant national politics is in the daily lives of most people, and how the politics played out in the media appears to be one elaborate, confusing, frustrating, excluding game.

But politics matters and nothing I am seeing at the school makes me alter that view. I am not a cynic who believes that there are no differences between the parties. It matters whether Britain is in or out of Europe, whether we put money into public services or give away tax cuts, whether we are tolerant or divisive. My opinion of politicians after working with them for ten years is higher rather than lower. Given the pressures, the long hours, the intrusion into their lives, the commute from often far-off constituencies, they are not the gargoyles portrayed in large parts of the media – or reflected in the comments of the teaching assistant who asked me in my first week: 'Why do politicians only tell the truth after they've left office?'

The politicians I know are decent, hardworking, committed to their ideas. They may have their little idiosyncrasies, but then don't we all? They may at times be self-centred, but then you need to look after yourself in politics: no one else will. The worst of them are not liars, or dishonest or up to no good, they are simply not very good at running a department or are simply uninspiring.

★

'What is politics?' A boy asked me in the exclusion room after I had told him I used to work in politics. He wasn't asking a philosophical question, he simply had no idea. Slightly surprised I gave him an answer about political parties, power, changing the country.

But what is the best definition of politics, or the 'project' as we liked to call it? The answer is different depending on whether you are a conservative or a radical. For conservatives politics is about navigating the ship of state across choppy waters while avoiding shipwreck. It is all about survival, maintaining the status quo. For a progressive or radical, political strategy is about affecting change.

My personal definition would be to leave all aspects of the country – its attitudes, its institutions, its culture – more progressive than when we started out; shifting the odds as far as possible away from the mighty to the underdog, while forging the widest possible support for that change. For me politics should never just be about survival.

Tony and Gordon have slightly different perspectives on this. For Tony, politics is about meeting the challenges the country faces and shaping them in a progressive way. His starting point is what he believes the country needs.

Gordon, on the other hand, starts with his progressive goals, which reflect the injustices and challenges people face, and for him political strategy is about shaping the landscape to achieve them.

For some conservatives the left will always be doomed to failure because it is too deterministic, too grandiose in its vision, too intent on moulding the character of a fiercely independent people.

For progressives the conservative vision merely preserves a status quo that is unjust and indefensible. For me the point about being progressive is to continually strive to make things better, never being satisfied with the current state of the world.

So New Labour, I believe, has to change again, because it has succeeded in changing the political landscape in the last few years. Policies like the Minimum Wage, devolution, a windfall tax on the privatised utilities were thought to be dangerous before 1997, yet very quickly became accepted as common sense. In turn, ideas that ten years ago would have been unacceptable, congestion charging for example, or paid paternity leave, even introducing a new top rate of tax for the very wealthy to pay for tax cuts for the poor or investment in education, are slowly becoming sensible mainstream policies. The more you change the landscape the more you have to move on to the next big challenges.

The substance of the project derives from three main inputs: what the country needs, what the public want, and what the party, or an individual politician, believes in. In government there were advocates and experts for each of these. The Strategy Unit, looking at long-term policy and based in the Cabinet Office, undertook a strategic audit which benchmarked Britain against competitor countries, trawled the latest research and data, interviewed ministers and civil servants about the key challenges in their area and came up with a view about what Britain needed. Labour Party polling and information from other social research gave us a detailed sense of what the public wanted. This could be segmented in a number of different ways. There was never just one 'public'. Finally there was the essential compass of the party's beliefs, and the burning question: what would it take to make Britain a more social democratic country?

The diagram below is a crude way of illustrating this. These overlapping circles are constantly shifting. The diagram would have looked different in 1997 and will change again as the agenda moves on. Political strategy is about ensuring your agenda firmly intersects all three circles. What goes in each of the segments is entirely subjective. The current agenda is: economy, public services, jobs. People will disagree with the choices. Other issues fit into either one or two of the segments. There are issues that I would argue are vital for the country but that the public do not have strong views on or are opposed to and Labour Party MPs and members don't get worked up over: freeing up universities to compete in the world, harnessing of genetics, even being pro-European, are all examples.

Constitutional issues are important for the country, and the party is passionate about some of them, but there has never been a clamour from the public. Some issues, like tough asylum rules, are certainly wanted by the public, but very few Labour Party

## The Shifting Circles of Politics

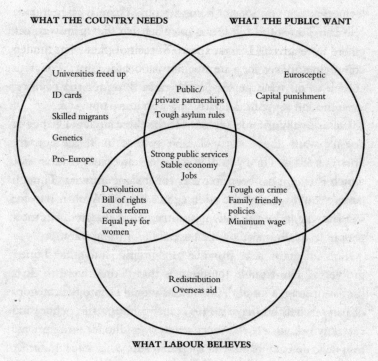

WHAT THE COUNTRY NEEDS · WHAT THE PUBLIC WANT

Universities freed up

ID cards

Skilled migrants

Genetics

Pro-Europe

Public/private partnerships
Tough asylum rules

Eurosceptic

Capital punishment

Strong public services
Stable economy
Jobs

Devolution
Bill of rights
Lords reform
Equal pay for women

Tough on crime
Family friendly policies
Minimum wage

Redistribution
Overseas aid

WHAT LABOUR BELIEVES

members join the party to curb asylum. Crime is an issue where the public wants government to act. Many Labour Party members believe 'tough on crime and its causes' helps create a strong community, but given that crime is falling and we are not a high-crime country, an audit of what Britain needs would not put tackling crime on top. Before the Asian tsunami disaster, I would have put overseas aid solely in the 'Labour believes' segment, but the public response shows how much they too want to support the most vulnerable in the world.

If you carry out too many issues in the 'what the country needs' category that have little public or party support, you get into trouble. Too many that the public want but the party doesn't and you look unprincipled. Do a lot of populist things the public wants and the country doesn't need and opinion formers attack you for not being serious. There is often a trade off. The Tories and Lib Dems calculate that they gain with the public by opposing Labour's plans for tuition fees even though commentators say they are not serious on the issue. Tony has chosen to do what he sees as the right thing for the country, even though some in the party and public are opposed.

Occasionally an issue falls outside the three circles. The public doesn't want it, the party doesn't believe in it, the country doesn't need it. Then you're in trouble. Iraq comes close to this, which is why it has been so tricky for the government. Though Tony would say that the country needed the War on Iraq for security, the lack of WMD means many now disagree. For most people Iraq falls outside what the public or party want.

This diagram also provides an insight into the Tories' problems. The trouble for them is that if they were to do a similar diagram a lot of their passions would fit into the category of party beliefs but have no resonance amongst the public, and certainly not what the country needs: subsidies for using private hospitals, defence of hereditary peers, support for fox hunting.

They are seduced by other issues simply because they have some resonance amongst the public – euro scepticism, for example. They are not, however, what the country needs and so cannot, in the end, seize the central agenda.

Political strategy consumed my life. At weekends I was mulling over a speech or thinking about chinks in the Tories' armour, or gossiping with Philip Gould about what Tony should be doing next. I spent my days working out how to improve the language of a White Paper, how to make a Prime Ministerial visit capture the imagination, how to get coverage for a technocratic environmental statement, how to convince the public Labour was delivering on public services. There were big decisions about public services strategy or how to play the euro. There were smaller decisions about each detail, where the detail counted: any mistake would be leapt upon by opponents. What should the backdrop say at Tony's press conference on education? Should Tony speak to a doctors' conference or a nurses' conference? Should he do an interview with *Saga* magazine or *Vanity Fair*?

Politics is part chess – you need to position politician and party in the most advantageous place in relation to the media, political opponents, interest groups, and ultimately the voter. It's part football, with the same tribal loyalties – there can only be one winner, one government, one Prime Minister. You are either up or down, either in government or in Opposition, and every twist and turn in between General Elections are the matches to see who wins the championship. It's also part religion. For some the ideology they are fighting for is all-consuming: the belief in equality, the desire to help the poorest in the world, a passion for peace.

Political strategy is a blend of policy, politics and communications. Great policy can be a political disaster if not communicated properly. Great communications fall apart if the substance is not there. Both policy and communications need a political component – a dividing line from opponents, an argument for supporters to carry. Tony is best at combining these skills. Politicians and advisers are usually good at some of it, but not all of it; they are often great policy people but clueless about how to communicate it; or good with the press but don't get the nuance of the policy; or good at both but have no understanding how it will play in the party or with sections of society.

I always straddled policy and communications. My task was to make sense of the many policies the government was producing, so that our project was coherent. I had to focus on the medium and long term while others were inevitably sucked into the day-to-day. That meant writing strategies with key objectives for the six months ahead, devising events and speech programmes to support those objectives, writing some of the speeches, working on themes and messages. From 2001 I was Head of the Strategic Communications Unit, which was set up in 1997 to think longer term than the press office. I restructured it so it focused on Tony's two second term priorities of public services and Europe, as well as dealing with the planning of regional media and articles and interviews in women's magazines. I was lucky to have a highly talented and professional group of civil servants and advisers working with me.

In the second term, at the same time each week at the end of the day, Alastair Campbell, Peter Mandelson, Philip Gould and I would meet to talk about strategy, Tony's personal position and the issues facing the government. The meeting would take place in Alastair's room.

Alastair used these meetings to let off steam about the media and to give acute insights into Tony's current thinking. Alastair's greatest skill was giving those around him the confidence to make things happen. No situation, no person cowed him. Philip would reflect the public mood and the longer term. He was the most strategic of Tony's advisors. He never lost sight of the big picture. More than that, he was always thinking of new approaches and new insights. Peter would treat us to his subtle and reflective monologues on the current political position and the required tactics. He was the master of political nuance, and would know instinctively how a media story would play and where it would go next. I attempted to focus the discussion on the project, the next few months, the big strategic decisions we faced. The meetings had no real agenda, though when we needed urgent decisions on big strategic issues I would draw one up.

The strategic issues were always similar. How does Tony show momentum? How do we make the Queen's Speech or the party conference take off and connect with the public? Is Tony appearing too out of touch, too technocratic, too preoccupied with foreign affairs?

These were intriguing meetings. The relationship between Alastair and Peter, following Peter's second resignation, veered from exaggeratedly pally to combative. Philip would interject by trying to bring them both back to the issues in hand. Alastair liked clarity and certainty and then drove the agenda through with huge commitment. Peter liked pre-planning and order, everything written down, professional, nothing left to chance.

Political advisers come in different guises. There are the *Policy Wonks* who are policy experts and usually get a thrill from the detail of policy, love thinking of new ideas to crack problems and are invaluable for the Prime Minister when a crisis arises on an issue of which he has little knowledge. Simon Stevens on health and Andrew Adonis on education were two of the best at Number 10 at combining policy detail with a sense of strategy and project. There are the *Spin Doctors* who range from the supremos like Alastair Campbell and David Hill to those who enjoy the furtive conversation in a pub, the surreptitious phone call, and the boozy lunch imparting tit bits of knowledge. Then there is the *Security Blanket*, the adviser who is there to sustain, promote, comfort and cajole the politician, and to make sure despondency is kept to a minimum and euphoric 'I can rule the world' phases are kept in check. Anji Hunter and Sally Morgan did this brilliantly for the Prime Minister, and Sue Nye performs this role for Gordon Brown. Then there are the *Fixers*: the people who do the deal with the unions and work out how to win votes in the Commons, the people for whom arm twisting and brinkmanship are all in a day's work. Pat McFadden was one of the best at this at Number 10. Finally, there are the *Strategists*. These are often the irritants, those who push the ministers the whole time to do better, think differently, change their approach, deal with issues. I loved performing this role.

The government's approach to communications was the result of three influences: first, the mauling that Neil Kinnock got when leader of the Labour party and the fear of the right-wing press; second, the sense we all had that John Major's government had been weak, lacking control, and therefore appearing to drift; and third, the demands of 24-hour media. We were the first government to be truly under 24-hour-a-day pressure. That meant extraordinary demands on us for information, for quick responses.

The Number 10 press office would get hundreds of calls a day – from Japanese TV to local radio, from *Woman's Own* to the *Telegraph* diary, wanting to know the Prime Minister's age; how much he paid for his hair-cuts; his favourite books, or jams, or pop singers, whether he would do five minutes on Turkish radio, speak to CNN about Bill Clinton, endorse the *Northern Echo*'s campaign for a Northern Assembly. The list went on and on. At the same time, columnists and political editors were keen to have a few precious moments with Alastair, on what Tony thought of the Northern Ireland peace process, or what his message was going to be at party conference.

The big question for us was: how in the age of 24-hour media, with many parts of the media hostile to the government and with less deferential voters, do we communicate successfully with the public so they understand what we are trying to do?

There were many overlapping layers to what we attempted:

## First, get expectations in the right place

The area that caused us most trouble, where we made errors, but where it was hardest to get it right was 'expectations'. We were accused frequently of hyping up expectations only to leave them unfulfilled. Expectations were sky high after 1997 because of the size of our majority and the sense of hope our campaign had generated. Despite our modest pledges, people expected rapid improvement. We compounded the issue by talking of huge sums of extra spending, of ambitious targets, or of policies that were only ideas but the public assumed would happen soon, rather than after a lengthy parliamentary process. There is a formula for expectations: satisfaction (or votes) = expectations+/- performance. We needed to ensure that we underpromised and overdelivered.

## Second, provide clear messages and policy definition

Bill Clinton had told us that 'definition was all in the media age'. By that he meant that it was up to government to provide the themes that would give shape to government initiatives. I asked him once about this and he said, to my surprise, given how much we agonised over the subject, that our messages were far better than he ever achieved. I'm not sure he was right – we never beat the simplicity of his mantra 'opportunity plus responsibility equals community' – but it was a pretty good endorsement.

Tony is obsessed with definition. During the seven years I was at Number 10 this consumed a lot of time, and a lot of my time in particular. We would devise high-level messages which were designed to demonstrate our values: 'a future fair for all', 'opportunity for all', 'rights and responsibilities'. Other messages defined where we were on a journey: 'a lot done, a lot to do', 'the work goes on'. But the trickiest area was policy definition. Tony believed that the Tories had managed to define their policy reforms in the eighties and, because they did so, civil servants and those on the ground knew what was intended and could start to develop and implement policy without always needing to check back that they were on the right lines.

The following extracts are from a 'definition' note I sent to Tony in October 2002. It was the best take of our message based on discussions between Number 10 and the key departmental ministers involved – after about a year of discussion of our key arguments. The whole note started with a general explanation of our public services approach, followed by a couple of pages each for education, health, crime and transport. I have only included education here. The note was then handed out at Cabinet. The aim was that every Cabinet member would be able to use these themes in interviews and speeches.

## *Public services message – greater definition*

*Moving from **big state** public services to **personalised** public services that are open to all.*

### *We have a compelling argument:*

The Labour Party is most successful when it has a reform-ing passion – at our best when at our boldest – unafraid to make the reforms necessary to meet new challenges. It is time to recognise that the 1945 settlement was a huge achievement but a product of that age and we should not be its prisoners. To deliver opportunity and security today public services must be radically recast from monolithic top down public services to personalised public services. Out goes the big state, in comes the enabling state.

This was a bold argument to make in the party.

***We have a clear New Labour approach that rejects old Left and Thatcherism:***

To combine universal (open to all) services with personal (tailor made) provision.

***Universal*** – an engine of equality so that we ensure equal chances for every child.

***Personal*** – so that they are responsive to the rising aspirations of the public.

In other words we reject the 1945 approach which emphasised the universal (minimum standards) but not the personal.

We reject the Tory approach that offers choice for a few but with no regard for the many.

This is classic triangulation, Tony's favourite formulation – not old Left, not new Right, but New Labour. The essence of our approach to public services was that we wanted universal services – everyone must have access to them – but that they must be increasingly personalised to each citizen's needs.

# Education

*From the **comprehensive era** to an **era of diversity***
*From the **old style comprehensive** to a new system of*
***specialist schools***

Over the years these lines on comprehensives were the most controversial of any area. David Blunkett, education secretary in the first term, would not say 'replace' the comprehensive or 'move beyond'. The formulation we agreed with him was the 'post-comprehensive' argument. Estelle Morris, his successor as education secretary, with a well-deserved reputation for getting on with teachers, would not, she said, unnecessarily antagonise the profession by talking about the end of the comprehensive. However, Tony thought this definition was crucial to an understanding of what we were about. What we couldn't decide was the branding of the new system we were creating. This too was important because the word used would clearly signal our intentions. A new system of specialist schools was the closest we got, but we had concerns that this would be confused with special needs schools that already existed.

## Public offer

***Reform of secondary schools to create higher standards, better***
***behaviour and more choice***

***Higher standards:*** strong leaders, better teaching
***Better behaviour:*** tough new measures on truancy and assaults
on teachers
***More choice:*** with new City Academies, more specialist
schools, advanced schools

There are always layers to message. Some are aimed at the public, some are aimed at professionals and opinion formers. All the discussion of post-comprehensives was really aimed at opinion formers. We needed in addition an offer to the public. David Blunkett had made 'standards' his own, with a successful focus on the 3Rs in primary schools, but when we moved on to secondary schools the message got harder. For secondary schools, standards didn't seem to be enough. Behaviour was a big concern. In the Department of Education polling, behaviour outscored everything including standards as the key issue for parents. At a meeting that I had organised on strategy and communications between Tony and Estelle, with Alastair and special advisers present, we tried to thrash out the key offer for parents. We wanted to boil down the mantra to three key words, so that initiatives would become part of a bigger picture rather than appearing random. 'Standards' and 'behaviour' made sense to everyone. We then toyed with the third word. Tony pushed 'choice' on the grounds that it was what we aspired to, even if there was not enough of it at the moment. The department reluctantly agreed. 'Standards, Behaviour, Choice' became our key public offer for secondary schools. The only trouble was, that ministers never liked using other ministers' words or phrases. When Estelle Morris resigned and Charles Clarke took over, this message, crafted over many months, was put on the backburner. Ruth Kelly, and future Secretaries of State, have the chance to create their own messages.

### What is the Post-comprehensive System?

A system where

- each school has a distinct ethos and specialism with a centre of excellence

- each school has more freedom in employing staff
- each school has state of the art facilities
- each school has a strong head, or he or she is removed
- each school has a range of professionals: teachers, classroom assistants, mentors
- each school has a curriculum tailored to individuals: different length of lessons, different settings, more vocational options
- each school has a strategy to deal with poor behaviour

The following type of table were an obsession of mine and several health and education White Papers contain them. They aim to encapsulate the 'before and after' of reform. They give people a clear sense of the ultimate goal and a sense of our radicalism. The second one also reassures, by showing that the values remain the same despite the upheaval.

**Third, keep in touch with the public**

From an early stage I was joining Philip Gould on regular focus group evenings. Normally there would be two one-hour sessions, one with men, the other with women, about eight or ten in each group.

Focus groups have often been derided, yet they are no more, nor less, than talking to members of the public. If a politician says he has spoken to some constituents there is no gasp of horror. This is what a focus group is, only a little more structured. Through these groups I got closer to understanding the way people voted, and the strange and complicated interplay for any leader of leading and listening.

What struck me first, besides Philip's ability to be rude to a certain type of garrulous middle-aged woman ('OK love, we've got the message' as she is half through the story of her redundancy), was how little people know of the detail of politics.

### The Shift from Old to New Model

|  | Old Model | New Model |
|---|---|---|
| **Values** | Every child of equal worth | Every child of equal worth |
| **Mission** | Opportunity | Opportunity and attainment |
| **School structure** | Uniformity and isolation | Specialism and collaboration |
| **Headteachers** | Following orders | Powerful and effective leaders |
| **School performance** | Failure unchallenged | Ladder of improvement |
| **Accountability** | Weak | Strong accountability framework and incentives for success |
| **Resources** | Boom and bust | Sustained investment |

Focus groups are always a corrective to the Westminster bubble. The basic truth, and politicians should never forget it, is that the public are going about their hardworking lives without much thought for the ins and outs of politics. For politicians the most humbling feedback from these groups is that, unless they are the Prime Minister or one of a tiny number of maverick politicians like Ken Livingstone in London, the public don't know their names and have very little idea what job they have. Few government announcements are noticed by the public and if you think about it that's not surprising. Most announcements last less than twenty-four hours in the media. They will make a TV headline, if you are lucky, and a few column inches in the following day's newspapers. Why would a busy family, that has probably missed the news that night and may not buy a newspaper, know anything about it? The Budget is an exception because it directly affects taxes and benefits, and it is in everyone's self-interest to find out the contents, but the rule of thumb is that unless something runs for several days it has no penetration. That is why 'scandals' lodge in the public's mind for longer than policy announcements. They almost invariably last days because the media, hunting in a pack, look for all the news angles to keep the story running.

In government we all tried hard to give announcements more penetration and 'breakthrough'. We were constantly asking, 'What will make this fly?' The problem was structural. Government departments produced chunks of policy. They were then sent to the press office who wrote press releases and sent them out. However, these were often bland announcements, and the political lobby who reported on them – and who have very little interest in policy – found them tedious. Their job was to track down political debate and argument. My solution was to get away from the traditional type of announcement: £50m for school toilets; five new hospitals; new dentistry strategy. Instead we should be creating 'talking points' by being clearer what problem the policy was meant to be addressing and raising issues and questions which would engage the public. The test for an effective government story was 'could you have a radio phone-in on this subject?'

So, the public may not be engaged in every twist and turn at Westminster – but the second thing these focus groups taught me is never underestimate the sixth sense of the public. They may not know who the politicians are but they have a strong sense of whether a party is fit to govern, or is doing well, or has lost the plot. Admittedly a lot of this is filtered through a media which they say they don't listen to, but which has a big influence.

**Fourth, bring order to government announcements**
If we had to make sense of all that incoming traffic, we had to make sense of the outgoing traffic too: twenty-two government departments with four or five ministers, each producing announcements, speeches, reports, surveys and events seemingly at random, all with different themes. What was the point in the

Chancellor and the PM inadvertently making big announcements on the same day? Wouldn't we look stupid if the Home Office announced a relaxation of cannabis laws on the same day that the Department of Health was warning about the danger of drugs?

We, at Number 10, believed that unless we had daily control over the news agenda, unless we fought for every headline, rebutted every lie or inaccuracy, we would sink under the media onslaught.

I came up with a solution to keeping an eye on government activities which was obvious, simple, but new: a grid. The grid was a simple A4 piece of paper for each week, divided at the top by days of the week and down the side by type of news. The top line was main news, then other news, then statistics. The point was to see the shape of the week, look at what clashed, ask ministers to move a particular event to a better day. The main news column was meant to indicate what in an ideal world would lead the news that day. The grid needed someone painstaking and with authority to gather the information day by day, week by week, and Paul Brown, a dedicated civil servant, was the man. He became a legend at Number 10 and soon impressed the Treasury too.

For a time we used to meet daily in Gordon's office at the Treasury at 8 a.m. to discuss the grid. Gordon would cast his eye over it and then look round the table at Alastair or me or Douglas Alexander and ask what the point of a particular event was. None of us had enough detail or enough rationale, so I suggested to Alastair we bring Paul across to the meetings. He was masterful. Gordon would say pointedly: 'Why is John Reid making two speeches on consecutive days on the same theme?' Paul would say, very calmly, that neither could be changed because they were preplanned and, in fact, on different topics. Paul's encyclopaedic knowledge made all of us round the table realise quite what a feat it was co-ordinating the hundreds of disparate government activities into one whole – but it did not stop Gordon rightly wanting more order to it.

**Fifth, find new routes to communicate with the public**

We were constantly looking for new ways of communicating with the public. Tony Blair was the first Prime Minister to do public town-hall meetings in front of cameras where people could ask whatever they liked. We did webcasts using the internet for the first time. We had regional strategies because we knew that people trusted their local media more than national media – and regional media was less cynical.

We also had what we called non-news media strategies, most of which were targeted at big-selling women's magazines. Our argument was that most people are not interested in politics, most don't read nationals – and if they do, it is not for the news pages – so we needed to find new ways of reaching them. This was often a struggle. A magazine whose features included fashion, diets, sexual exploits, horrific murders or tap dancing aliens, was hard for politicians, and in particular for the Prime Minister, to find their best way in, without making a complete fool of themselves. However, we had one device that often worked: readers of the magazine were invited to tea with the Prime Minister to ask him whatever questions they wanted and the results would be published in a feature in the magazine.

On one occasion, when the Prime Minister was about to make the most important decision of his political career, at a time when he was strutting the international stage and his day was chock full of security and intelligence meetings with a war on Iraq looming, we inserted an exciting event into his diary to maintain his domestic profile: tea with the readers of *Chat* magazine.

So the PM comes off a phone call to George Bush, he swats

up quickly on the childcare issues he is expecting from the readers and enters the pillared room at Number 10, the grandest of all the state rooms. Surging towards him is an elderly woman with her hand halfway up a furry dog glove puppet – Jingles, the ventriloquist dog, has been smuggled into the building past security and starts nipping the PM's hand. Tony manages to sidestep her, only to be confronted by a woman clothed head to toe in black who approaches him and asks the searching question: 'May I read your palm?' Joyce turns out to be an amateur but persistent palm reader and psychic and grabs Tony's hand.

Her prediction, that she could see the PM with Arabs in the desert was remarkable. What was not quite so remarkable was her forecast that both the PM and the Arabs would, at the time, be attending a racing pigeon meeting. As for her final and most confident assertion: the PM has not, to my knowledge, been involved in a major investigation into the production of white bread.

The PM's future, however, was nowhere near as exciting as that of Cherie. She was told she would take the helm of a boat, adopt an Indian child and be kidnapped. No wonder the PM was not always enthusiastic about our non-news media strategy.

**Sixth, deal effectively with the political lobby and national media**

The above six ways of being more strategic with communications went largely unseen. However, dealing with the political lobby was the area where battlelines were drawn and the relationship gradually broke down. Every story was fought out, every headline worried over. Sunday papers were bought on a Saturday evening from one of the big London stations, so that we knew in advance if there was any scandal running in the morning.

During the ten years of Tony's leadership of the Labour party, the relationship between politicians and the media could be divided into two halves.

The first half was Labour's almost unencumbered drive to power. We were picking up supporters like passengers on a busy commuter train – standing room only, the carriages were crammed with former Tories, business people, celebrities, all with a slightly different destination in mind, but all believing in the driver Tony Blair to get them there. The media were interested in us and people wanted us to succeed. We got the benefit of the doubt.

The second half built steadily: the chipping away by opponents, the Tory press cranking up the attacks, the charge of spin, the systematic attempts to erode the government's reputation, the actions we took – most notably on Iraq – that divided the country. Then came the breakdown of relations.

To a lot of us in government the media was an uncontrollable rampaging beast. It would look for the weakest prey and then hunt it remorselessly, finding every angle to bring it down and then devour it. The aim of government press relations was to tame this beast, keep it at bay as long as possible, and try and get on with governing. The techniques that were employed attempted to do this. So, it seemed to make sense to give stories to journalists who would do them straight and not distort them. It seemed to make sense to give excerpts from speeches in advance to the broadcasters, so that the story that ran on the morning headlines was as we wanted it, not as others did. It's nothing new and we did it to great effect. Journalists were desperate to speak to Alastair and get 'the line'. They wanted to speak to someone close to Tony so they could know what Tony was thinking. Where we made mistakes, it was out of sheer frustration at inaccuracies we believed had been told, or the fact that our side of a story was not getting across. We did over-react, worry about every daily headline, every story. We needed to move beyond the war-room mentality of a political campaign and be more patient.

Relations between media and government became increasingly bitter and, although I did not handle media relations myself, sharing an office with the Prime Minister's official spokesmen Godric Smith and Tom Kelly, I could see the toll it was taking on these highly professional civil servants. The fact that these non-political people were equally baffled by the ferocity of the mauling they received every day demonstrated that something was going badly wrong.

This would be my summary of what we felt, with differing degrees of intensity. This was our case against the media we had to deal with day in day out:

1. Labour has to seize the daily agenda, or hostile stories from the media dominate.

2. Given the number of departments and the amount of 24-hour media, government must make sense of its activities by planning them properly using grids, consistent themes, disciplined communication.

3. Many broadcasters are lazy and work too much off the newspapers' agenda, which is mostly hostile to the government.

4. The media love political soap opera – froth – not substance, which means that anyone entering public life has to put up with huge intrusion.

5. The media has power without responsibility; it seldom corrects error.

6. Many newspapers have stopped being newspapers and become campaigning papers. So, for example, those papers that opposed the war on Iraq would not put a good story about Iraq on the front page, however compelling or important it was.

7. So, government tries to control the agenda – keep ministers on message, brief favourable papers to get a good showing.

8. Media exaggerates splits and nuance, so it is impossible for ministers to highlight genuine complexity or be open on key issues.

9. Media reports bad news not good because it sells newspapers. Sensationalism rather than balance also sells papers.

10. Comment is more important than straight reporting. Broadcasters now rarely report political news or give proper extracts from speeches, but rather the reporters' often cynical interpretation of what has happened, normally focusing on the processes behind the speech not the speech itself.

In short we simply felt we were not operating in a rational world where the media cared about policy, where it treated politics as a worthwhile occupation rather than contemptible, where there was complexity not just black–and–white arguments.

That was our case, but I knew, because enough journalists had told us, that they saw things entirely differently.

Their case was this:

1. There is little difference between the parties, so politics is boring.

2. The spin doctors exercise too much control, so politicians never speak from the heart which makes current affairs dull.

3. New Labour is hypocritical. It loved the media when it was ripping the Tories apart; now it expects them to be pussy cats just because it is Labour in power.

4. In trying to get the best case across, the government often distorts information, hides it, only gives partial truths or downright lies, which has brought the government into disrepute.

5. Politicians don't treat the public as adults and give them the hard choices. They pretend everything is possible.

6. There is so little access to real information that newspaper journalists have to make the best attempt, with tight deadlines, to piece together nuggets of information to give their readers. Mistakes are genuine, and there would be fewer of them if government was more open.

7. Politics has become Americanised, taken over by PR and slick presentation rather than issues.

8. The government, by and large, gets an easy ride with no real Opposition, so someone, namely the media, has to step in and at least challenge it from time to time.

9. Tony Blair liked it when things were going well; he is

only complaining now that things are going less well.

10. The media only hunt as a pack when there is something to hunt. Most of the stories they have gone for have been genuine, and many of them self-inflicted wounds by the government itself – like the row over Formula One boss Bernie Ecclestone's donation to the Labour Party.

This battle between politicians and the media has contributed to what Philip Gould has called 'the empty stadium': a football match on a pitch where the spectators have gone home. The public were indeed tuning out.

More than that, trust was slowly being eroded with government and politicians, as well as the media, all suffering. In survey after survey, some of it gathered for an audit on 'Trust in Government' by the Prime Minister's Strategy Unit, individual professions – including teaching and medicine – came out top; politicians, parts of the media (broadcast media are more trusted than newspapers), trade union leaders and heads of large companies were trusted least. There seemed to be a big difference between those that the public have an individual relationship with and the big faraway institutions. 'My local MP' is always more trusted than 'Westminster politicians'. Local newspapers are trusted more than the nationals. The three key qualities for keeping or restoring trust seems to be: honesty and keeping promises, working for the common good, and personal contact and accessibility.

For politicians this means far more locally-based politics, tailored to each community, with real access to politicians rather than over stage-managed events. It means politicians explaining how they are driven by values – 'the common good' – and constantly avoiding situations that make them look as if they are in it for themselves. It also means – which is what the pledge card was all about – making limited promises but keeping them, exceeding expectations. Politicians need to speak in a more open and grown-up way about the choices the country faces – acknowledging complexity, and not pretending they have all the answers.

For the media, particularly newspapers, it is harder in a way than for politicians because they often have commercial considerations to put first. But if they wanted to follow the same prescription to restore trust they would redress mistakes more often and more prominently. They might acknowledge too that they are part of the reason why there is such a gap in perception between the favourable views of many users of public services and the more hostile views of those who don't. As a result, the media might do their bit for 'the common good' and their own standing by carping slightly less and giving those who are trying to achieve something – frontline staff for example – a bit more space to succeed.

Schools, I was now discovering, like other public services, are caught in the middle of the Westminster game between politicians and media. Because we wanted to show momentum, departments and Number 10 were constantly looking for things to announce. A quiet department, not showing evidence of reform, was a department that was adrift. A department that did not respond to a media campaign on a certain issue, however spurious, was also seen to be out of touch. Every time a Minister paid a visit or made a speech, he or she needed a story to accompany it, something 'new', something eye-catching, something that would make headlines. With twenty-four hour media there is never a chance just to say: 'I'm continuing to govern well, the plans are in place, I'm waiting for them to bed down.'

Policy was also made for party conference, for the Queen's speech, in the Budget and the spending review. This was true of all governments. It was made because a Minister was going on the BBC's *Breakfast with Frost* programme or speaking at an important conference. Its development followed the political calendar, not the timings of schools. It met the personal needs of the Minister to get out of a hole or change the agenda or respond to the media. It came in a sequence that often appeared random and sometimes contradictory.

So schools would face pronouncements on uniform, or healthy food, or homework, or drugs testing, and would not know how seriously to take them, not knowing if they would result in legislation or were merely Ministerial thoughts. No wonder schools just get on with their own plans and implement only what is strictly necessary.

Communicating with frontline staff was equally fraught. 'Pressure and support' was supposed to be our big strategy for teachers, indeed all public servants. We were on their side, yet we wanted them to raise their game. The trouble was, firstly, that 'support' gets little media coverage, and 'pressure' gets lots; and second, New Labour and Ofsted under Chris Woodhead, enjoyed the headlines that came from suggesting tough action on failure, pointing out that thousands of teachers were not up to it and many lessons were poor. It put us on the side of the anxious middle-class parent. It was part of our repositioning. It showed our reforming cutting edge. And to be fair, we thought that unless we identified the problems honestly then we would not get support for the solutions.

Very soon we gained a reputation for heaping the pressure on without giving enough support. Tony's 'scars on my back' speech, and references to 'wreckers' – aimed at particular unions, not frontline staff – were two notorious cases. I remember well the worst example. Following the 'forces of conservatism' speech at the 1999 Labour Party conference, Tony was determined to show that opponents of change were on the left as well as the right. We had an education speech to new headteachers coming up, and we believed it would show confidence to continue with the 'forces of conservatism' theme. Not only that, but there was a lot of frustration from Ministers aimed in particular at the unions, who we felt had got so used to complaining about Tory cuts and poor salaries, that they found it impossible to get out from that position when the Labour government started increasing resources. So we inserted a sentence in the speech that said: 'We must take on what I call the "culture of excuses", which still infects some parts of the teaching profession. A culture that tolerates low ambitions, rejects excellence and treats poverty as an excuse for failure.' The denunciation was swift from all quarters. It was too strong and, with hindsight, it was clear that our short-term goal of defending the 'forces of conservatism' speech was damaging the long-term goal of building a consensus for public service reform.

We tried to redress the balance over the years and I spent much time with departments developing strategies that would allow us to explain our policies and show our respect and warmth to frontline staff: new magazines aimed at teachers or doctors, and conferences where Ministers, including the Prime Minister, would speak to staff face to face, without the media present, to deliver the message.

But the tension remained between 'pressure' and 'support'. Indeed, policy advisers would often think the SCU had gone 'soft' when one or other of us would suggest an article in a staff magazine simply praising the efforts of staff, without the bite of a new reform message, which we knew always sounded like a criticism of their current efforts. One of the constant fears was that we would appear to be on the side of the producers and not the consumers. Yet the best businesses, however consumer friendly they want to be, recognise that by treating staff well, they in turn treat customers well. I was determined we should do the same thing.

Now in the staffroom at Islington Green School I was seeing the other side of the story. I was witnessing the tyranny of 'momentum' politics at first hand. The techniques I had been a great advocate of, 'talking points' that would start debates, constant reforming activity to show a department was serious about change, all conspired to make the lives of frontline staff more frustrating and more difficult.

There is definitely a weariness from teachers about government, but it extends beyond politicians to any 'busy-body' who is not getting their hands dirty but instead pontificates from the sidelines. That might mean an LEA consultant, an inspector or a departmental advisor. Top of the irritation list appears to be the examination boards that change the exam requirements mid-year or two weeks into term without warning. Anyone, in short, who can express views from a distance, without having to go and teach the 'bottom set' on a Friday afternoon.

Most teachers seem to treat measures on their merits, though some of the unions can appear to take a knee-jerk reaction against reform. Most teachers may be cynical about 'yet another initiative', but if it is practical, easy to apply and improves their teaching, they are likely to use it. What they hate is change at short notice, or huge volumes of reading material. The other great irritation is faddiness. To many, teaching is about having the authority and knowledge to enthuse and control a class, it's as simple and as hard as that. What they don't like are the wheezes, the suggestion that there is some easier or better way of doing the basic job. When I discussed the latest government idea – 'personalised learning', something I had been passionate about in government – the notion that every child should get an education tailored to their needs, based on regular assessment, one teacher looked at me blankly and said: 'What do you think a good teacher does? Don't you think I know which child needs help on a topic and which doesn't? The only obstacle is time.'

The government's response, I would expect, is that a really personalised, tailored education is not the norm, and with new technology there are now better ways of assessing children and challenging them in each subject.

So the balance for government is difficult. In future it should concern itself less with the need to prove its reforming zeal. Professions need challenge from outside, all organisations do – it sometimes takes an outsider to shift you out of a rut or give you a fresh insight. But the government should approach change with humility, give proper warning and consideration to timing, and if the challenge of the new is backed by real resources, training and support then long term change *and* the enthusiasm of staff may be possible.

Without the government and the media changing, the battle between the two, the Westminster game, has the potential not just to drag down the reputation of both, but also to sour the relations between politics and the people, politicians and the frontline, and in doing so make the improvements the country so badly needs much more difficult to achieve.

# WORDS, WORDS, WORDS

I am about to start one-to-one lessons with Jimmy.

I bump into him on the staircase at the beginning of break time. 'Sir, when do we meet?'

'I'll get you from the lesson, after break,' I say. Paul has told me not to assume he will turn up at the library. I should always go and collect him.

I go to the library to try to sort out where I might conduct the lesson. The library is a zoo. Flora is overwhelmed by numbers. It is a frosty day outside and the place is swarming with students. Flora is bellowing. There is no teacher helping her out and I am worried that my lesson is going to be disrupted. I head over to the Dance studios to get Jimmy, hoping that when I return the library will have cleared.

I have swotted up on Jimmy, read his school file. Attendance is a problem. He has had several internal exclusions, some for racist bullying including repeatedly calling a student in his class a 'Paki'. He has a low CAT score which is the IQ test done when children arrive aged eleven, but he's not bad at maths. He was tested last year and had a reading age of about eight. Paul says that corresponds to the *Mirror* or the *Sun*, so this may be a good place to start.

Jimmy is waiting for me and we walk together to the library. He walks with an odd arm movement. He's recently had an elbow operation and it's still not right. He says the doctor has told him that one arm is longer than the other.

Reading and writing, say the experts, is far harder than you might at first think. The feat of writing letters in the correct order with the right spelling, grammar and punctuation will always be a struggle for some. There are two basic approaches to literacy. One is based on phonics – the English language consists of forty-four phonetic sounds. The aim of this approach is to blend the different sounds together. The other approach is called 'whole language', or 'whole word', which is to recognise the whole word and not to break each word down. Most schools try to use both approaches.

Paul's book on teaching literacy in secondary schools, which he argues is a completely different skill from teaching reading in primary schools, sets out a warning for me:

> The young people you work with will have their own unique sets of strengths and weaknesses and a principal feature of your role will be finding a way of getting alongside them emotionally. Ultimately, no intervention can be successful if you are unable to form a positive rapport and bond of trust with these young people. The emotional angle is as important as any single specialist literacy strategy you attempt to introduce.

The library is quieter and we sit in a corner. I ask him what he wants from the sessions. He says his reading, spelling and writing are bad, and he would like to be able to write essays. 'My mum says it's about breaking words down and then putting them back together. That's what she did in school, but she says it's all different now.'

I reassure him that the same principles still apply, and ask him what he is interested in. I have been told by one of his teachers it is mopeds and motorbikes, so have a book ready on the subject.

'I quite like go-carting,' he says. 'I don't like motorbikes since a friend of mine crashed into a car and his brain swelled up and he was in a coma.'

So my first bit of reading material goes down the pan.

I look briefly for go-carting books, but can't find any so I start him on the sports pages of the *Mirror*. The headline is 'Chelsea swoop for Figo'. He struggles, not surprisingly, with the Portuguese name. The first paragraph is equally hard. I haven't thought about this enough. I should have known this would be difficult. He will be losing his confidence not gaining it. I have forgotten how much there is a tabloid language using phrases that someone like Jimmy would not have come across that often.

Jimmy talks about his eight-year-old brother who annoys him because he wants to watch cartoons on Saturday when Jimmy wants to play computer games. His father is a builder and his mother is a dinner lady in a primary school. He says he would like to get into carpentry which is what his uncle does.

He comes alive, however, when talking about a fireman's course that he did at the local fire station. He talks about rescuing dummies from burning buildings, using special equipment to cut through metal. He speaks quickly with an infectious excitement in his voice. He is a good storyteller. This is ideal. 'Tell me the story again,' I say, 'and we will write it down. This can be your first essay.'

I give him a brand new yellow A4 exercise book. He writes his name painstakingly on the front and turns to the first page.

'Why don't you give it a title?' I say. He decides on 'fire-fighting'. I help him with the 'gh'.

He tells me the story. I stop him after each sentence. We say the sentence together then he writes it down.

the whole course lasted a week. if you get there later than 7.45 then you are told off. if you do it twice you are not allowed back.

Jimmy has neat writing. He forms his letters well but doesn't use capitals at the beginning of sentences. He struggles over the words 'whole', 'course' and 'allowed'.

at 8.15 you go down to the yard and fix the hydrant to the fire engine. You then fill it up with water so we can use it all day. then we practise rolling the hose out.

'Hy . . . drant . . . break it down.'

'How do you spell the hy bit?'

'Yes it could be Hi but in this case it's Hy. Drant is dr at the beginning, like draw or drain, and ant is like the insect.'

Any word Jimmy struggles with we turn to the back of the exercise book and practise it before returning to the essay page. That way he writes it correctly in the essay without the need to cross anything out.

on one day we tried to climb a ladder, and put the ladder against a wall and make sure it is safe. on another day we might try out the breathing apparatus.

As Paul's book keeps warning, if you can read it's very hard to get into the head of someone who can't. 'Might, now that's a hard word. The gh in the middle is silent. Let's go to the back of the book and do a few words like this for you to remember. What rhymes with might? Yes, fright, sight, tight, light. All of them have this same gh in the middle.' I have read somewhere that using rhymes is helpful, but have no idea whether it will work for Jimmy.

> on Wednesday we learnt how to rescue someone from a car accident. first we put a dummy in the car then we had to break the roof in. so the doors would not open. then we had to smash the window without the glass cutting the dummy. then we used the 'jaws of life' to cut the roof so the dummy can be taken out.

Jimmy writes 'rescue', 'accident' and 'break' at the back of his book. He is excited by the 'jaws of life', a specialist piece of equipment used for cutting through car wrecks. He is delighted to have seen it work and tells me about it in great detail.

> the best thing I did was the passing out on the last day. we made a pretend fire and my part was to bring the dummy out.

'Let's stop there. You've written a whole page. Your first essay. That's really fantastic. You must be proud of yourself.'

Jimmy *is* proud. 'Yeah it's good.'

'Do you want to read the whole thing through for me now?'

He reads it with only a couple of mistakes. He's done well, and his confidence seems high.

'Next lesson we will see what else we can do on fire-fighting. I'll try and find a book so we can read about it. Shall I keep your exercise book or do you want to?'

'You better,' he says.

I escort Jimmy to the library door. 'Do you know what you've got next?'

'Maths I think.' He leaves and I return to my room with a sense of satisfaction. I start reading a note that Paul has written for me.

## What is dyslexia?

Dyslexia is most simply defined as a difficulty with processing written language. It has nothing to do with natural intelligence levels and generally affects up to 10 per cent of the population – 4 per cent very severely. 40 per cent of the school's population has problems associated with it.

## Why is there such a high frequency of dyslexia at this school?

Some pupils had delayed speech in their first five years. They failed to grasp the link between letter and sound and fell behind, never to catch up.

Some pupils will have experienced emotional trauma for a period of time.

Some come from families where there have been persistent problems with literacy and numeracy from one generation to another.

Some pupils experience dyslexic problems for no apparent reason. They are the only one in their family.

The note then provides some solutions: 'Dyslexics often need to understand how and why in order to learn. Show the whole picture first before breaking down into steps and details.'

Next lesson Jimmy appears, this time without his bag or a pen. I lend him a pen. We start reading a book on fire-fighting that I have found, but it is difficult and he is struggling. I don't want to dent his confidence, or the relationship I am building up, so I cut it short. I decide to build on the fire-fighting essay with another trick I have read about – writing a play.

'Do you know what a play is?' I ask Jimmy.

'Yes, it's with actors and that.'

'Exactly. We're going to write one about fire-fighting.'

So that Wednesday in January at Islington Green School, two budding playwrights, one fourteen, the other thirty-five, embark on what might prove to be an award-winning collaboration. Jimmy is up and running. Hunched over his exercise book he writes:

### Jimmy and Mr Hyman play

He leaves two lines of spacing.

### The car crash

'Right,' I say, 'you be one fireman. I will be the other.'

'How shall I do it?'

'Why not put Jimmy in the margin with a colon – that's two dots – and then leave a space and then I will write my part with a colon.'

Jimmy:          look, the patient is trapped.

Mr Hyman:     Is he still breathing?

| | |
|---|---|
| Jimmy: | we've got to cut the door open to find out. |
| Mr Hyman: | We're not going fast enough. Shall I smash the window? |
| Jimmy: | no, i'm using the jaws of life. |

'Put speech marks before and after jaws of life. Yes, that's right. Let's use initials instead of our names. It's easier.'

| | |
|---|---|
| H: | How did the accident happen? |

'I don't know,' Jimmy says.
'What do you think?' I ask.
'He might have been drunk.'
'Well put that then, that's good.' There is chatter from other students in a different part of the library. Jimmy turns to look at them, momentarily distracted, but goes on.

| | |
|---|---|
| J: | he drank 5 pints of beer, lost control and hit the tree. |
| H: | When will people learn you shouldn't drink and drive? |
| J: | nearly done, get the stretcher ready. |
| H: | Yes, we haven't got long. His breathing is getting slower. |
| J: | i'm still trying to get him out. you give him gas and air. |

| | |
|---|---|
| H: | Well done, you've got in. Let's get him out quickly. |
| J: | you hold that end. i'll take his feet. |
| H: | The paramedics are here, put him on the stretcher. |
| Paramedic: | Well done boys, you've saved his life. |

'That's great,' I say. 'We've written a play.' I don't know who's more pleased, him or me. 'Right, let's read the whole thing through. You read Jimmy, I'll read Mr Hyman. You play the paramedic as well, Jimmy,' I say generously. We read the parts with feeling. We are no longer teacher and pupil but two fire-fighters saving the life of a drunk driver after a horrendous accident. If the National Theatre won't have us, this will make a good radio play at the very least.

Many teachers mention the difference between good one-to-one behaviour compared with naughtiness and disruption in big groups. Jimmy is nothing like the description of him in the school reports. To me he seems keen and motivated. He just finds reading a big struggle.

After the lesson I ask Paul why he thinks Jimmy isn't a better reader. Paul says that once thirteen, it is very hard for them to catch up because they have tried so many times and failed. Getting children to read in secondary school, he says, is an agonising and difficult task. If they were going to get it, they would have got it before now. This seems such a terrible waste. Jimmy is not stupid. There is no reason why he can't learn to read. Yet it hasn't clicked and Paul's view seems to be that it's unlikely to click now. My concern is that Jimmy needs more than just one-to-one help or lots of practice. He needs a literacy expert, someone trained with proper techniques to give him the basic tools of reading which he hasn't got.

According to Paul's book, 'Secondary pupils respond well to games around phonological processing. The most popular game I've used gives them letter sounds from the alphabet and is called a Boggle diagram.'

I need to make the lessons varied, so next lesson I give this a go. I write out six letter sounds, and say to Jimmy that the aim is to find as many words as he can, using as many different combinations of these letters as possible.

| g | r | t |
|---|---|---|
| e | ch | a |

Jimmy starts slowly but then gets the hang of it:

|       |     |     |     |
|-------|-----|-----|-----|
| eat   | get | tar | art |
| chat  | tea | rag |     |

'What about a five letter word?' I suggest.

'Cheat.'

'Very good.'

'Great.'

'You're motoring now.'

'Chart.'

'Well done.'

I then ask him to write five words beginning with certain common sounds. 'Try c h, that's ch. What starts with ch?'

'Cheat, cheering, chart, church . . . What else Jimmy, come on Jimmy what else,' he says to himself, egging himself on. I let him ponder. '. . . Chair.'

'Very good.'

For Tr words he suddenly surprises me, and himself. Long words cascade from his mouth as if another part of his brain is being engaged. He looks at me, shocked, as if someone else has come up with them. 'Treacherous . . . that's a word isn't it?'

'It's a fantastic word,' I say. 'Do you know what it means?'

'Not really.'

'Well, it can mean dangerous or betraying.'

Jimmy is bounding on. 'Trigonometry.'

'Brilliant.'

He is on a high, so I try him out on one of the good factual books for low-age readers. There is a series on famous actors, sportsmen, pop singers, world leaders. I start him on a footballing one.

'He is six foot four inches tall. He . . . what's that word?'

'Weighs. That's difficult because of the ei in the middle.'

'He weighs fifteen and a half stone . . . He seems to fill the goal . . . like a human wall . . . He looks like a g . . .' 'No it's a j, as in jug.' 'He looks like a giant . . . but he is fast, very fast . . . He is brave . . . He can jump . . . He can dive . . . His . . . r . . .'

'Break it down.'

'Re . . . ac . . .'

'Yes, how do you say t i o n?'

'Tea-on.'

'No, it's shun.'

'His reactions are quick . . . They call him Mr Re . . .'

'Break it down.' I cover one half of the word.

'Re . . . li . . . able. Reliable.'

'That's it, well done.'

'When he signs autographs . . . he signs himself Safe Hands . . . His name is David Seaman.'

Paul has advised me that you know a book is the correct reading age if the reader gets about eight words out of ten. The book about David Seaman is at the right level. Jimmy's confidence grows as he speeds through the pages. He also seems interested in the subject. These books seem exactly right for him. The lesson ends and he saunters off to his next one.

I feel I am bonding with Jimmy. He has not missed a lesson yet. He works well for the whole hour. I'm not sure whether I am doing much good, but he seems pleased with the attention. I am told by one teacher that he is more polite and attentive in lessons, and Karen, one of the PAs who logs bad behaviour, encourages me by saying he has been in the exclusion room less. On the other hand, I keep hearing about odd incidents he might have been involved in. There's some very unpleasant graffiti with his name on, round the corner from the school.

At the next lesson I ask him, subtly, why he has not learnt to read before: 'Jimmy, why do you think you have had difficulty with your reading?'

'The primary school I went to were more interested in us sitting in church than reading,' he says bitterly. 'What my mother says anyway.'

'What about here. Have you had help before?'

'Yes, I had some in Year 7 but then it stopped in Year 8. Dunno why. My mum got me someone to help at home, but she didn't last long. She went off somewhere.' This seemed to be a family that knew the problem and wanted it addressed, but it was never quite cracked.

Next lesson, Jimmy forgets his bag again. This is about the eighth time. How does a child turn up so frequently without his bag? 'I was in a rush this morning and I forgot it'; 'It was by the door, I just forgot it'; 'My mum didn't remind me'; 'Sorry, sir, left my bag and my book at home.'

I don't want to ruin my relationship with Jimmy so I don't have a go at him. I ask Paul. 'What is it about Jimmy that makes it so difficult to bring in his bag?'

'It's cultural. He's part of a group that thinks it's cool to swan into school, arms free, not holding anything.'

'But he's not one of the hard kids, and a lot of the cool ones bring in Nike bags,' I say.

'Yes, but he's on the periphery and wants to get in with them, so he doesn't bring in his bag.'

Jimmy is becoming a frustrating mixture. On some days he makes great progress. On other days he seems bafflingly clueless. I sometimes want to shout at him: 'Couple. It's not "coo plea". I've told you this about thirty times. I've broken it down for you. We've written it out. Just remember it.' This job requires great patience and it's not something I am good at.

This is the chasm between Downing Street and the frontline, between a job where we demand quick delivery and one where there is no quick delivery. In government it was all big picture and big targets: literacy targets, numeracy targets, GCSE targets. We demanded that schools and teachers delivered. Can Labour deliver? Will Labour deliver? We had set ourselves up to achieve delivery. No other government in history had been so precise about what it intended to do, and as the media and in turn the public urged us to deliver more and deliver it faster we in turn put more pressure on frontline staff to raise their game. However, there are no 'quick wins'. Jimmy will learn nothing quickly. He *can* get there, and with support and effort *will* get there, but it has to be eked out. Here I am now in the library. I am frontline staff. And I have to deliver.

My task is to get Jimmy to read. That is delivery for me. That is what delivery means in practice. It is about the small human interactions. Will Jimmy bring his book into school? Will he be in the mood to learn? Will he understand today what he didn't understand yesterday? Will he suddenly recognise vowel sounds?

Delivery in education for the Labour government of which I was recently a part depends on thousands of teenagers in haphazard families, some with drunken mothers or abusive fathers, with brothers and sisters to look after and cook for, in grimy housing and shabby bedsits, getting out of bed the right side, turning up to school on time, opening their books at the right page, not getting into a fight with the child sitting next to them, doing their homework instead of playing on the estate, resisting the urge to have sex or go shopping or take drugs or nick something or run away, and turning up on time today, the next day and the next day, and the next day, to the rhythmic drumbeat of a school they don't like and lessons they find boring, so that they can systematically and conscientiously acquire the knowledge they need to regurgitate for an exam so they can get to college and get a job.

All those who have spent the last few years berating the government for not being ambitious enough or radical enough or delivering enough should see for themselves just how hard it is in reality.

For the next lesson, I decide to do something different. I have just been teaching my politics group about speeches, so I have a photocopy with me of Churchill's 'We shall fight on the beaches' speech. Why not raise the tone a bit, why not challenge Jimmy with some different material. I produce it and before showing it to him ask him casually, 'Do you know who Churchill is?'

'Churchill, he's that dog on the advert,' Jimmy answers with absolute certainty.

'Sorry?'

'The one in the back window of the car – you must know the ad.' Jimmy thinks I'm having him on. I must know that Churchill is a nodding dog.

'So who do you think Churchill is?'

'A dog.'

'He was Prime Minister during the war,' I say.

'No he's not, you're being silly now, sir.'

'He was Prime Minister.'

'You do know he's a dog, sir, don't you? Everyone knows that.'

'Winston Churchill, a dog?' I look bemused.

'Well I don't know the dog's first name, sir.' He looks at me as if I am a fool.

'He was Prime Minister of Britain,' I say definitively, hoping to end this bizarre argument.

'OK, which war was it then?' Jimmy thinks he can catch me out with this probing question.

'The Second World War.'

There is a long pause. It's as if there is a small attic room in the recesses of Jimmy's mind and he is climbing up a long ladder to get there and retrieve something. Slowly he pulls out what he's been searching for, a fragment of memory.

'He's the man with the cigar, ain't he?' he says with a smile.

'That's right. Well done.'

'Fight them on the beaches and all that. Yeah, my dad told me about him.'

I'm impressed. I look at some of the words in the speech to check he knows them. 'Have you heard of the Nazis?'

He looks blank.

'Do you know what they did?'

'No.'

'They killed people like the Jews and invaded countries.'

'What did they use in the war, cannons like olden days? Bows and arrows?' We have had a lesson reading about gladiators and this must have stuck in the mind.

'Bombs and guns,' I say. 'Have you heard of the blitz? When bombs rained down on London every night.'

'Yes, like the films where they had to hide.'

Jimmy reads the speech very slowly and in a monotone: 'We shall fight on the beaches . . .' It passes through my mind that the outcome of the Second World War might have been very different if Jimmy and not Churchill had been on the radio every night, attempting to rouse the nation to action.

In the staff room I mention Jimmy to Ted, his maths teacher.

'He's intuitive,' says Ted. 'If he gets it, he motors along and he's almost the best in the class. If he doesn't, he gets fed up and starts making mischief. By the way, he mentioned he did reading with someone. I asked him who and he said. "That posh guy, the new one." I assumed that was you.' Ted sniggers.

'That's how he sees me then,' I say. It's odd because I feel I have connected with him, despite our different backgrounds.

Next day, Neville Chamberlain-like, Jimmy comes to the lesson brandishing a piece of paper. He unfolds it and it is headed 'Surrealism'.

'I've got a test coming up in art,' he says, 'and 'I've got to learn this.'

I scan the page. It's very hard: lots of foreign names, lots of long words, lots of hard concepts. 'This will be a challenge,' I say out loud.

'Yeah, but it's all about melting clocks. I like those pictures.'

I find a book in the library on Surrealism and another on Salvador Dali. We go through the pictures and Jimmy loves it.

'Let's read this page now,' I say.

'Surrealism is a style of art that began in Paris in the early 1920s.'

'Well done, Jimmy,' I encourage; a faultless line of reading.

'It was a re . . .'

'Break it down.'

'Reac . . .'

'What's the t i o n sound? We've had it before.' Jimmy never gets tion endings, and I'm not sure how to drum them into his head. 'Rea*ction*.' I lose patience and tell him the word.

'It was a reaction against World War One. A group of artists led by the poet and artist And . . .'

'Break it down, this is hard because it's a foreign name.'

'And . . . ray . . . Bree . . . ton.'

'That's it, André Breton.'

'André Breton wrote a m . . . a ma . . .'

'Man . . . i . . . fest . . . o.'

'What's a manifesto?'

'A manifesto is something that sets out your aims. Like if you decide you are going to work at school in a particular way, you might set out your approach in a manifesto.' Poor explanation, I think. I read the next bit for him as it has a lot of big words.

> Surreal artworks have a lot of strange things happening in them. Objects that were solid become liquid, like Salvador Dali's melting clocks. Events happen in surreal art that don't happen in real life, like men in bowler hats raining from the sky. Surrealist artists also mix up the textures of objects. An example of this is a teacup that is made from fur. The process of metamorphosis is shown quite a lot. Artists also juxtapose objects in strange ways. They will show objects in bizarre places.

'How am I going to spell that big word?' he says, pointing at metamorphosis.

'You will,' I say, 'and then you'll be one of the only ones in your class who can. 'Break it up like this: 'Met . . . a . . . mor . . . pho . . . sis. You'll find it easier than you think.'

He does. He finds the ph instead of an f difficult, but soon gets it. He is chuffed.

We read on and look at all the big words: metamorphosis,

rational, texture, juxtapose, object, dreams, imagination. 'We're going to break these down and learn them,' I say.

'The teacher says I've also got to know these names.' He points at a list at the bottom of the page: André Breton, Salvador Dali, René Magritte, Joan Miró, Yves Tanguy.

'Right,' I say, suddenly inspired. 'We're going to make a mnemonic out of this. That means learn a word and then use each letter in the word to be one of these names. SAYJR. That's it. SAYJR. S for Salvador Dali, A for André Breton, Y for Yves Tanguy, J for Joan Miró, R for René Magritte.'

He quickly gets the hang of Sayjr and spells out the names. 'It's Yes with a v in the middle,' he says for Yves, pleased to have found his own way of spelling it. I then given him ten questions to answer as a mock test: 'When did Surrealism begin? Where did it begin? Name five Surrealist artists.' He does really well.

I suddenly look at the clock and realise an hour has gone without either us taking a breather – all on that single piece of paper. Jimmy is certainly motivated. 'Good luck in your test,' I say to him. 'You are going to be the best prepared.'

Jimmy leaves the library. I am exhausted but happy. Jimmy is now an expert on Surrealism, and he can spell metamorphosis perfectly. Not bad for one day. However, it's a hard slog and I worry that we're never going to get him good enough to pass exams properly.

The next time I hear Jimmy's name, he is in trouble. He has thrown a glass beaker down the stairwell and it hit someone on the shoulder. If it had hit him on the head it might have badly injured him. 'If you can talk to him and find out what happened I would be grateful,' Emma says.

I speak to Jimmy next lesson.

'I didn't know anyone was down there,' he says with a 'who-me-guv?' expression.

'But why did you throw it down there in the first place?'

'It was down the stairwell. I had no idea anyone was at the bottom. It was just to see how far it could go down. I wasn't trying to hurt anyone, honest.'

'But it was stupid throwing it at all,' I say. It is not for me to take it further, so I move on to the rest of the lesson. We plough on with a book on Vinnie Jones. Jimmy and his dad are enjoying this one.

'Did you know,' Jimmy says to me suddenly, 'that all words have vowels in them? My dad told me that last night.'

'Yes,' I say, 'though some just have Ys in them and no vowels.'

'Really,' says Jimmy excited.

'My, cry, fly. See they all have Ys and no vowels.'

'I'm going to tell my dad, he'll be impressed,' Jimmy says.

'You can impress him with this, too,' I say and write down the word 'rhythm', a six-letter word with no vowel.

'Great,' says Jimmy.

I try to imagine what words must be like for Jimmy. Imagine not being able to read an advert on a hoarding, or a medicine bottle when you're ill, or the sports page of a newspaper. Imagine not being able to read a football match programme, or a menu in a restaurant. Imagine a whole life never reading a novel cover to cover. Imagine surfing the internet but never being sure you have arrived, or looking at an *A–Z*, but never being sure you're in the right street. Imagine knowing only three hundred words and needing your fist to win an argument instead – words on a page, just words on a page – no rhythm or pleasure or poetry in them.

The world I have inhabited for the last ten years has been based on words, endless amounts of words: words for speeches, words for Parliamentary statements, words for White Papers, words in interviews, words in newspapers. Often the dissection of those words is what matters more than the actions they describe. The nuanced differences between ministers on the euro, a row on Iraq policy – all are based on words: words spun, words sexed up, words sneaked out. I spent hours of my life deciding whether 'opportunity and responsibility' was better than 'opportunity and security', whether the 'Age of Achievement' was a better phrase than the 'Age of Fulfilment'.

But now I am confronted with someone for whom words are a mystery. Each time he sees a word he seems to be seeing it for the first time. This is an inequality as big as any: those who can read and those who can't; those who can use language to express their opinions and feelings and hopes and those who cannot. This is what the education debate between the 'basics' lobby and the 'enrichment' lobby misses out. You've got to have the basic tools. Everything else flows from that. Learning a musical instrument is great, but Jimmy needs, more than anything else on earth, to be able to read. Only then can everything else be unlocked. Only then will he be able to do well in science which he likes, to do GCSEs which I am sure he could pass.

I pursue the literacy issue with Trevor. This I am sure is the key to everything. There is a direct correlation between bad behaviour and illiteracy at the school. Those with the worst behaviour are, in 90 per cent of the cases, the ones who can't do the work, who get bored and then mess about.

The government and schools have achieved a lot on literacy in primary schools. Yet still one in four leaves at eleven with a low reading age – and in Islington, because many of the good students leave the borough, 40 per cent of the secondary school intake are below standard. This is surely the priority for national and school policy.

I have seen how hard it is getting Jimmy to read, but that's partly because it is so late in the day. What on earth have these kids been doing in primary school? I know that students like

Jimmy may have been badly behaved or not bothered to turn up every day, but they had six years of schooling with the sole aim of giving them the basic tools. It really isn't the job of a secondary school to start from scratch on the basics. They are not geared up for it. However, as I keep saying to Trevor, given where we are we have to make literacy a priority in the first year of secondary school. There is no point in a student coming into secondary school to suddenly be given a wide curriculum – French, Spanish, science, RE – without the skills to read and write properly. This year of transition is hard anyway, with children going from the cosseted disciplined primary school to this enormous secondary school of one thousand students and lots of temptations and bad influences. It is essential that by the end of their first year they have the tools to succeed in the following four years.

I bump into Jimmy in the playground the next day. 'How did the art test go?' I ask him. 'I got twelve out of twenty, sir. It was one of the best. The teacher said I done good.'

'Well done.' I am slightly surprised he hasn't done even better, but this is a pretty good score. Our hard work has paid off.

Now it's time to meet the parents. Student review day at Islington Green School is a chance for form tutors to go through marks with parents and pupils and set targets for the coming term. It is also a chance to raise any problems. On this occasion I am meant to get involved, going through the option choices for some of the Year 9 kids, of which Jimmy is one. This means they are going to choose which subjects to do for GCSE. I go and find Jimmy's form tutor and ask if I can join her for the interview with Jimmy's parents. Miss Wild is a quietly spoken woman and one who knows her form very well. She agrees.

It happens on a Friday. There are no lessons that day; the school day is taken up with interviews with parents. I go to the fourth floor and sit in the classroom. Miss Wild has had Jimmy since Year 7. She says he has improved. 'He was a bit of a bully at the beginning, he did pick on kids in the class, but I agree he's got a bit better. Though I did have to write to his parents just last week for kicking a door in.'

Jimmy arrives with his parents. I am impressed that both have arrived. Most students come with one. Some don't come at all. He is quite pleased to see me. He smiles and says, 'Hello, sir, didn't know you would be here.' I'm pleased that he's pleased. His parents are both thin and tall with silvery hair. The father looks tough. The mother looks friendly but formidable. They sit down and Miss Wild begins to go through Jimmy's marks in each subject. Anything 5 or above is good and Jimmy has a 5 in art and a 5 in technology. His maths is a 4. I have been given Jimmy's mock SATs results this morning. I tell Jimmy he has a 4 for maths, a 3 for science and an unclassified for English. He looks disappointed.

I say to his parents, 'Jimmy has been working very well with me, but his English needs a lot of catching up. In terms of the SATs, the key is to make sure he gets up to 5s, certainly in maths and hopefully in science, and then we will get the English higher over the next year – but it won't come immediately.' I want to aim high with Jimmy, but I don't want his parents to think I can work miracles.

'But he's got all this old English rubbish for his SATs. How the hell's he going to get that?' Jimmy's mother asks. 'That *Macbeth* mullarkey. He's shown me them words. I've never seen anything like it. Why does he have to do that?'

'I will help with it,' I promise, 'but it's only a small part of the SATs. All the other reading and writing is important, and Jimmy *is* improving.'

'He's behaving well now, our Jimmy,' his mother says with pride.

'Well, not all the time,' says Miss Wild, interjecting in a calm but steely voice. 'I did have to write to you last week about the classroom door.'

'Well, I'm sure he just banged it on the way down the corridor.'

'We caught him on CCTV trying to kick the door in, actually,' Miss Wild persists.

'What you do that for?' Jimmy's mum rounds on him.

Jimmy splutters: 'There were a few of us, and they didn't get in trouble like me.'

'I don't give a shit about the others. You shouldn't have done it,' she glares at him.

Jimmy's dad sits nervously.

'And his attendance is still patchy.' Miss Wild is really on a roll.

'That can't be right. You show me then,' Jimmy's mum challenges the teacher. 'He goes to school every day, I make sure of that. He missed one day because of the doctor, but that's it.'

'But he's not showing up on the register every day,' says Miss Wild.

'You're not bunking when you get here, are you?' Mum says to Jimmy.

'No, Mum,' says Jimmy, no longer a teenager but a pathetic six-year-old. 'I'm always in lessons.'

'Well, let's make that a target shall we?' Miss Wild says, trying to gain a bit of momentum. 'That can be one of our targets. Right Jimmy, why don't you write this down on your sheet – "I will come to school every day and attend all lessons."'

Jimmy writes this down slowly.

'Come on, Jimmy,' says Mum. 'We haven't got all day.'

'Mum, why do you always speak to me like that?' says Jimmy, embarrassed.

I chip in with an addition. 'Jimmy regularly turns up without his bag. Can you make sure he brings it every day, please?'

'I will do. It's by the door. Don't know why he forgets it.'

'The other target,' I suggest, 'should be an academic one. Jimmy should aim for at least two 5s in his SATs.' Miss Wild agrees this is a good target. Jimmy writes it down, and Miss Wild gives him a third target about good behaviour.

'Good, well that's it,' says Miss Wild.

The next student is waiting to come in. Jimmy and his parents stand up to leave. 'I'll follow you out,' I say. 'I've got something to show you.'

I show Jimmy's parents his exercise book with the essays and the play in it. 'He has been doing really well,' I say.

'I can see his writing is a lot better. Anyway, he says he likes lessons with you and it seems to be doing the trick,' says Mum.

Jimmy and his parents leave. It's good to have met them.

I'm in the library at break time, looking for some books for the next lesson, when I come across a freak. At least he's seen as a freak at Islington Green School. He is otherwise known as a reader. He is the same age as Jimmy, but he reads voraciously. He has a huge paperback wedged into his school blazer, and I discover he is the talk of the English department because he reads a giant novel a night. He is a small, neatly-dressed Nigerian boy. I ask him how he got into reading.

'I was nine and I went on a journey to visit my relatives and I took some novels and I discovered I liked them better than watching television because you use your imagination so much more.'

'What do you like reading?'

'Oh everything – but I like fantasy books. I've read all of *Lord of the Rings*, all the Pullman books. He points to a shelf. Read all of them.'

'We can't find any books he hasn't read,' chips in Flora.

'Have you read *The Curious Incident of the Dog in the Night-Time*?' I ask him. I think he will like it and I can see it has just arrived in the library.

'Yes, it's good, read it a while ago. I'm on to the classics now.'

A teacher tells me that this kid might soon leave the school. His parents want a more academic environment for him.

I now have to gear up for Jimmy's SATs.

I get hold of the mock English paper from his English teacher and immediately get depressed. Jimmy has a very long way to go to be able to read and understand a paper like this. The eye-opener for me has been the sophistication needed to get to level 5 in English – the expected level at age fourteen. This goes way beyond basic literacy. It requires, as the government literature points out, 'a greater degree of analytical, conceptual and interpretative thinking from the pupils':

- to show understanding of a range of texts, selecting essential points and using inference and deduction where appropriate
- to retrieve and collate information from a range of sources, convey meaning clearly in a range of different forms for different readers and purposes using a formal style where appropriate
- to organise simple and complex sentences into paragraphs, use a range of punctuation accurately and write with clear and cursive handwriting

– to use vocabulary precisely and imaginatively as
  appropriate and spell words accurately

All of this is a tall order for many students.

I wait for Jimmy on the second floor as I always do, ready to take him from his French lesson to the library. He is a bit late, as he usually is first period. The lesson should start at 8.45. It's now 8.52 and I have the pleasure of watching students arrive for their lessons: a fat skinhead with an earring and a can of coke; two girls with baby dummies on chains; a girl with a bunch of keys round her neck, and bright striped tights – can't be school uniform. There is a sign on the wall by the stairs saying 'Keep left.' Another says: 'No hats inside the building.' A girl gets out of the lift beside me. She has asthma and has a lift pass. At least half the children are arriving with a chocolate bar or bag of crisps in their hand. That's breakfast.

Jimmy arrives, rubbing his elbow. He has got his bag with him. His mother is obviously on the case, at least for the time being. We go to the library and I get out the mock English SATs paper.

'I couldn't do it. It took me too long reading. You're meant to have fifteen minutes, so I didn't get to the end, and I don't know half these words.'

I look at the text. There are five dense pages, including sentences like: 'There is the mystique of the treasure, often based on the stories that go with its original discovery or concealment – for example the history of those whose burial chambers were filled with valuables, such as the young Egyptian king Tutankhamun or the Chinese Emperor Shi Huangdi, who was buried with life-sized models of his complete army.'

Jimmy has got 3 out of 32 for this paper, and there is no point us learning this vocabulary together, because the real SATs will be on a totally different topic. The best we can do, I tell him, is to focus on the reading and get better at that. 'The one area we can do extra work in is *Macbeth*, where we know there will be a question.'

For those who think Shakespeare is being left out of schools these days, they should come to Islington Green. You can't move for students struggling with Shakespeare. I had vaguely remembered the plot of *Romeo and Juliet* for the GCSE students. Now I need a lot more refreshing on *Macbeth*.

I say to Jimmy that, even if he doesn't understand the question, if he attempts to answer it and then writes out the plot he will get some marks. Jimmy has obviously been paying attention in class because he seems to know what's going on.

I get hold of a short version of the story from the library. It is a four-page cartoon of the whole play, and is more confusing than I remember: Thane of this and Thane of that; Malcolm and Macduff; Duncan, Glamis, witches. My head is spinning, but Jimmy sorts me out.

'He is going to be killed by someone who has not had a natural birth, the witches said it.'

'You're right, Jimmy,' I say enthusiastically.

He writes the plot sentence by sentence. He is confident he can remember it. I think I should test him on the spelling.

'Right, I'm not going to help you, this is a proper test, let me give you some words to spell,' I say. 'Macbeth.'

Jimmy writes it down.

'Malcolm.'

Jimmy writes 'Malcom'. That silent l is always difficult.

'Guards.'

Jimmy writes gurds

'Ghosts.'

Jimmy writes gosts. It's the silent letters, they just creep up on you.

'Castle.'

Jimmy writes casall.

'Feels.'

Jimmy writes fills.

'Now, the hardest of all,' I say, 'and I bet no one in your class will get this right: caesarean. I'll spell that for you – C a e s a r i a n.' I look at the word. 'No that's not right,' I say. I go and find a dictionary. 'No, you spell it C a e s a r e a n. Told you it was hard.'

Jimmy is pleased I've made a mistake. We practise the words again and Jimmy feels confident for the SATs. I give him a final pep talk. 'Remember, whatever you do, write as much as you can, even if you're not answering the precise question. Make sure on *Macbeth* that whatever you do, you get down the plot. You get no marks if you've written nothing. Good luck next week,' I say as he leaves the library. I am nervous on Jimmy's behalf. I am also nervous for myself. I hope my help is going to make a difference.

I see him the following week and ask him how things are going. He says the maths was easier than he thought and the science a bit harder.

At our normal lesson the week after the SATs have finished, I ask Jimmy how the last paper, the *Macbeth*, went. He says: 'Oh, I didn't write nothing. I asked the teacher if I didn't understand the question should I write what I know, and she said no you must answer the question. So I wrote nothing.'

'Jimmy,' I shout, 'what did I tell you?'

I am exasperated and angry by this nonsense. What had I spent hours drumming into him? How could he be so stupid? Why get a second opinion when I had told him to write what he knew? I calm myself down. Jimmy is looking alarmed at my reaction. 'Never mind,' I say, 'we will wait for the results.'

Jimmy has worked hard on his SATs, so I think this is a good time to talk about the future, rather than having a heavy lesson of reading.

'How many GCSEs do you need for college?' Jimmy asks me.

'At least five good ones,' I say. I ask him what he has chosen. They are business, technology, art, plus the double English, double science and maths

'That means you're doing eight GCSEs and you need to get five of them A–C. I believe you can do that,' I say to him, 'but we must continue to get your reading up. A subject like business studies needs a lot of reading and writing. Afterwards there are two routes. You can do a vocational route and learn a trade, or an academic route and go to university.'

'University,' he ponders. 'Yes, that's where you get that bit of paper tied up with a ribbon, isn't it?'

'Yes,' I say, 'a degree. If you do well at college, you could go to university. Otherwise, you could use what you have learnt at college to get a job.'

I produce a purple and gold pen, a school pen, that is normally only given as a prize to those with lots of merits. 'I want to give you something to mark how well you have done in my lessons and how hard you have worked.' I hand it over to him. He likes it.

'You will stick with me next term, sir, won't you? This is my favourite lesson, you know.'

'I will, Jimmy,' I say.

'You know something,' he says. 'I like books. If I could read better, I would read all the time.'

At the start of my journey I could never have imagined that I would have been so touched by someone like Jimmy. I now care deeply about the boy, who to many in the school is just another thug going nowhere, but to me is someone desperate to pull himself up and make something of his life – someone who could go either way: succumb to the temptations of his more unsavoury friends, or plough his own course and fulfil his potential. Soon I will know whether I have had any practical effect. The SATs results will be in, and I will test his reading age again to see how much he has improved. For Jimmy this is nearly last chance time. If his reading doesn't take off soon, he is going to find GCSEs impossible.

# THE END OF A BOG-STANDARD
# COMPREHENSIVE?

The first time that my new and old lives came into direct conflict was over the rebuilding of the school. The school was falling apart. Trevor had pledged to staff that he would rebuild it. David Miliband, than Schools Minister, had put forward an ambitious school rebuilding programme – Building Schools for the Future – promising that all secondary schools would be refurbished or replaced in the next ten to fifteen years. A bid by CEA, the private company that had taken over Islington LEA, had been submitted to the government to rebuild all of Islington's secondary schools. CEA were confident the bid would be accepted. Trevor was equally sure.

I shared their optimism for an additional reason: the London Challenge. This was a new government programme focused on the problems of London schools, with intense help to turn them round. I had been one of those arguing in government for a London strategy on schools. I believed that the problems of London schools were so long-lasting and so intractable that something major needed doing over and above what was happening in the rest of the country. Tim Brighouse, the education guru and former head of Birmingham LEA, was in charge of this project.

The London Challenge focused on five boroughs with deep-seated problems: Islington, Haringey, Hackney, Southwark and Lambeth. Fifty-seven schools had been pinpointed as needing special attention because they had a record of failure in the past, and Islington Green was one of them. Islington was also the borough with the most political baggage, the borough with the schools that Tony Blair rejected for his own children, the borough that many opinion formers and Labour figures believed had schools just too bad to send their children to. Islington was surely the borough to rebuild in the first wave, proof that decent schools were possible in this area.

For all these reasons, we thought money would be coming our way – but I soon got wind of the probable outcome of the bid. The department had not given the go-ahead for Islington in the first wave. Other boroughs in London and the rest of the country had been chosen instead.

I was outraged. I couldn't understand why the key criterion was not 'need'. I knew the government logic that a bidding process made LEAs think strategically and get their act together. It would ensure that money was not thrown at weak projects. However, I was convinced that the two bits of the department – the capital division and the London Challenge section – were not speaking to each other. I was now on the receiving end of government decision-making. It was painful. It was also bewildering. There was no clear explanation from the LEA or national government as to why we had not got the money in the first round of bidding. I felt, and I knew Trevor felt the same, that we were letting down the kids at Islington Green who desperately needed modern facilities.

When the official news came through Trevor was disappointed. He had not seen the final submission of the bid. To his knowledge it had not included actual plans for the buildings. Indeed, when the department gave feedback as to why the LEA had failed, lack of vision was cited as a main reason.

Trevor was frustrated. We might win the bid second time round, but he wanted to get a move on. He wrote in the newsletter to parents:

> You may have heard the PM and Secretary of State announce on Tuesday their plans for the rebuilding of a number of schools in different authorities but excluding Islington. This is very sad news although Islington was invited to resubmit its bid for next year. In the meantime I make a pledge to all members of the Islington Green School community that I will strive to bring about the earliest confirmation of a rebuild. It is my view that our main building is in need of complete refurbishment or rebuild urgently. It is a weekly, sometimes daily, event that a major repair is required, drawing on much needed funds and also disrupting the smooth running of the school.

Trevor believed that the best option, one that he had explored tentatively a year earlier, was Academy status. He asked me to find out more about what was possible.

Academies are one of Tony Blair's pet projects. They symbolise many of his aims for public services. They are state schools, independent from the LEA, with the freedom to innovate, with £2m sponsorship from an outside organisation – private, voluntary, foundation – matched by £25 to £30m from government. The best of them are spectacular new buildings, built by top architects. They are, to quote Tony, about 'excellence not mediocrity'. However, they highlighted a tension in a lot of our reforms: how to reconcile diversity and equity.

Michael Barber had once written eloquently about this. The

Right, he explained, championed diversity, but it usually came at the expense of equity: people paying to go private, or given vouchers. The danger for the Left was that it ended up with high equity but greater uniformity and lower standards. The ideal that was difficult to come by was diversity leading to higher standards for all.

That was the theory, but would Academies in practice be beacons of excellence, driving up the standards of all, or would their success necessarily be at the expense of other schools?

Academies were launched in 2000 by David Blunkett who said that their aim was to 'provide real energy in the comprehensive system', to create innovation in schooling for the most deprived children by giving free rein to educational and organisational ideas about how to create a successful school.

At the opening two years later of Bexley City Academy in south London, an extraordinary Norman Foster building replacing a rundown, failing secondary school, Tony Blair spoke effusively of its potential:

> All the radical things about this Academy – the inde-pendent sponsor, the business and enterprise specialism; the state of the art facilities and use of IT; the reformed curriculum and ways of teaching and learning – none of these are ends in themselves. They are all means to an end. The goal of developing each individual pupil in a tailored way, whatever their background.
>
> This isn't just about new buildings and fresh paint. It's about a fresh way of doing things. It's about keeping the ideal of equality of opportunity that gave rise to comprehensive schooling, but changing radically the traditional comprehensive model to achieve that ideal.
>
> It's about being honest that for too long we tolerated failure, when every failure to educate a child properly is a

blight on that child's life. Good education shouldn't depend on your class, colour, background or birth. It should be each child's start in life. Their chance to make the most of themselves.

The academies now opening are just one part of a fundamental change in Britain's comprehensive system. Taken together with greater flexibility in staffing and the greater freedom for headteachers and governors to run their schools to deliver the best education they can, they are ending the 'one size fits all' comprehensive system.

There is nothing standardised about this academy. Not its design; not its governing board; not its method of teaching; not its curriculum; not its facilities. It teaches children of all abilities but recognises that those abilities are different. It doesn't focus on children; it focuses on each child. That is where Britain's education system has to go.

Throughout my time at Number 10 the big debate on schools was about how much diversity and how much choice. At its core was a heated debate about comprehensives. Had they succeeded or failed? Had they been a vast improvement on the 11-plus? Or had they levelled standards down, giving no one a good education?

Comprehensives were set up as a reaction to the inequity of the 1944 Butler Act which had divided children between those worthy of grammar schools and the 80 per cent confined to secondary moderns. For the Labour party this was an inequality that had to be remedied. The answer was to get rid of the two-tier system and introduce comprehensives instead.

There were always at least two comprehensive ideals. One was that children should go to their local school. The other was that all schools should be truly 'comprehensive' in that they took children from all classes and all abilities. The first and second ideal did not always amount to the same thing. In some parts of London, for example, if every child went to their local school, then the school would be filled with those from poor backgrounds only. This would not be a comprehensive school in the sense of being all backgrounds and all abilities.

We sat in Tony's office once, discussing this, with Alastair going up the wall. 'You've got to understand not everyone wants all this choice,' he said to Tony. 'Most people want a decent local school – and what is more they think comprehensives, by and large, have worked. What is the point of condemning all comprehensives?'

Tony's view was that to attract the middle class back to state schools, we had to replace the comprehensive system. This did not mean returning to the 11-plus, but it did mean providing a range of different state schools for parents to choose from.

We worked hard to refine these ideas in a Fabian pamphlet that Tony used to explain his philosophy.

The answer is to move beyond the 1945 settlement because the world has moved beyond the conditions of the immediate post-war era. The 1945 settlement was the social equivalent of mass production, when uniformity after decades of the 'welfare lottery' was an entirely worthy ambition. For good reasons, it was largely state directed and managed building a paternalistic relationship between state and individual; one of donor and recipient. Its aim was to provide a universal, largely basic and standardised service. Individual aspirations were often weak, and personal preferences were a low or nonexistent priority. It was why there was some justification in the Whitehall knows best attitude of the time.

I sided with Tony at the time. Whatever it was meant to mean, the word 'comprehensive' was contaminated. People, particularly in London and other major cities, associated it with failing inner-city schools.

I walked into Alastair's office just before the launch of our secondary school strategy in 1999. It was a huge office with a large round maple desk, too big for the room but a present to a former Prime Minister from some potentate and rejected from other offices. On the wall were photos of Alastair's children and pictures of Burnley players holding trophies aloft. The Burnley photos had turned yellow at the corners. Either the sun had been dazzling or Burnley had not won a trophy for decades. It was 10.50 a.m., and lobby, the gathering of political journalists, was in ten minutes, down in the basement of Number 10. Alastair was doing his usual swotting up on lines to take. Press officers surrounded his desk, talking through what they had gleaned from departments. As they filed out, Alastair asked me how we were going to get this launch to fly. 'There is no one line that sums it all up.'

I had been discussing this with Andrew Adonis, the Policy Unit education adviser. Andrew is driven, academic but practical, and worked tirelessly to get the Academies programme off the ground. 'It's about the end of the bog-standard comprehensive,' we agreed 'moving beyond uniformity to a system of schools each of which have their own distinct ethos.'

I told Alastair that 'Today marks the end of the bog-standard comprehensive.' He liked it. So, whilst David Blunkett and Tony Blair were launching the White Paper upstairs in the white room, Alastair went into the lobby and used the phrase. All hell broke loose.

Conor Ryan, Blunkett's special adviser, was apoplectic. He knew this was too far for Blunkett and would annoy many teachers and unions. Andrew got on the phone to calm him down. Alastair got on the phone to calm Blunkett down. They were good mates, so Alastair blamed it on me. He complained that I used the phrase in speaking to him at the last moment, so he couldn't help but use it.

Ironically, this was the most distinct definition we ever got on schools, and was a phrase that stuck and was regurgitated in many guises over the next few years. In public, Tony condemned the phrase as being a bit over the top, and would not use it himself. In private, he thought it gave us some definition. There would be no doubting what we meant now.

Since being at Islington Green School, I had got a new perspective on all this. Whilst there has been complacency in comprehensive education, and in many cases low expectations of what can be achieved, to say it is the comprehensive as an ideal that has failed is plainly nonsense. Islington Green School is not a comprehensive in the true meaning of the word. It is not, as comprehensives are meant to be, a mix of all backgrounds and abilities. Nor is it a school to which all those in the catchment area go. Not much of the middle class is prepared to touch it with a barge pole. It is 95 per cent working class, and the vast majority are in the bottom third of ability. If Islington Green School had a real mix of children, 25 per cent most able, 50 per cent in the middle, 25 per cent from the lowest ability range, it would have a different learning environment and be able to pull up the majority. It is equally absurd to say that grammar schools, or for that matter private schools, are necessarily better schools than comprehensives. There are people still perpetuating this notion today. A school that selects children by virtue of their wealth, or intelligence, or both, is never going to get anything other than good results. The point about value-added scoring, which is finally being used more, is that you can test the true value of a school – what it achieves with its intake. A grammar school may end up adding nothing to the existing abilities of the children it takes in, yet get pretty good results based on their innate talent. This would make it an average, or conceivably a bad school, but one that can coast along, propped up by the one-dimensional reporting of results.

I looked at this in more detail. The London Challenge programme has produced a document that compares achievement against the numbers of students on free school meals. As you would expect, there is an almost exact correlation between wealth or class and achievement. The schools with 1 per cent free school meals are at the top of the list. Those with more than fifty at the bottom. Some schools are working hard to buck the trend and are succeeding. But it's a very difficult task and to condemn the schools with more than 50 per cent free school meals as failed comprehensives misses the point. I have seen few examples, looking round the country, of a school that has shown a huge jump in results whilst preserving the same intake, and not using GNVQs to boost results. Very few mixed secondary schools (girls schools are slightly easier to improve) that have more than 50 per cent of students on free school meals have results above 70 per cent five A–Cs. That is the scale of the challenge: how to create provision that really does deliver for the poorest. It is why we were wrong to ignore admissions policies altogether, however controversial they may be. It is why, in the long run, if social housing is more integrated, and the poorest don't live in housing estate ghettos, the local catchment areas will be more varied, as will school intakes. However, no one should underestimate the extra struggle needed to create a 'learning culture of high expectations' if there is not a critical mass of students – from working class or middle class – who buy into that goal. Academies, far from marking the end of the comprehensive, as I was intent on describing it in government, could in fact be their saviour. For if they have a truly comprehensive intake and attract a genuine mix of students, then they could prove that the comprehensive ideal – in other words, not selecting children at eleven – can produce first rate twenty-first-century schools.

If I was to pursue Academy status, I needed to find out who would sponsor the school and how fast we could move. The two people who were driving the process were Andrew Adonis in the Number 10 Policy Unit and Sir Bruce Liddington, a successful ex-headteacher who was now heading up the Academies division in the Department of Education.

Sir Bruce's view was that Islington in general was a hard place to crack, because of the levels of deprivation. Academies, he said, were aimed at schools well under 25 per cent five A–Cs: those on their last legs. Our school was in a different position, as it had a good head and was on the way up.

He said that sponsors usually fell into three categories: rich men who had made their money and now wanted to put something back and wrote out a cheque; grant-giving bodies like the Mercer Foundation that was sponsoring schools in the Midlands; and corporate sponsors, who wanted to set up schools because it was good for them and their employees.

Andrew told me there was a possible sponsor – a mixture of the first and second category, a rich man wanting to set up a Foundation – and so we arranged to meet at Number 10 with the sponsor to see if there was any potential.

It felt strange going back to Number 10 as a visitor: not being allowed in at the gate because I no longer had a pass, queuing up to go through the metal detector, entering the door at Number 10, wondering whether I would be allowed to go round the building unaccompanied, something no guest is normally permitted to do.

On entering, I was told Ben, our potential sponsor, was already there. Ben spun round. Casually dressed in jacket with open shirt, he looked to be in his late thirties. He was an American, had made a lot of money in hedge funds at Goldman Sachs, and was now setting up a charity, ARK education, as part of a bigger charity, to sponsor a network of Academies in London.

Andrew arrived and led us to the terracotta room. This is the middle grand state room at Number 10, and is, as the name suggests, painted throughout in a dark terracotta colour. Tea was laid out, as it always is for guests at Number 10, on a silver salver on a coffee table.

Ben started talking about his experience of New York schools, where he had spent a year trying to help the Mayor reform them. Now that he lived in London, he said his aim was to set up schools in this country. 'We've got limitless money; we can raise as much as we like. We now need to find the right projects. I want to meet Trevor and see what vision he's got. We've got the money. We now need educationalists to carry out the vision.'

Ben explained how he had looked at many sites already and they hadn't been suitable. Islington Green was potentially a better bet. I said defensively, on behalf of Trevor, that we did not have a worked out plan yet, but that he had some ideas that might be of interest. I didn't want the first meeting to be a disappointment for Ben.

Ben spoke in clipped, aggressive no-nonsense tones. He was a business man in a hurry. I was used to pushiness – I had worked with Alastair Campbell for ten years – but this was quite disconcerting. Every sentence was laden with frustration that people weren't moving fast enough to satisfy his needs.

The meeting ended with an agreement that I would set up a meeting at Islington Green, so that Ben could meet Trevor and see if he liked the site. However, I wasn't at all sure what Trevor would make of him. Trevor is used to getting his own way. He is confident of his own position and has his own ideas for the school. If he agreed to Ben as sponsor, he would have his own ideas challenged, and in some cases overruled.

Before leaving Number 10, I went to see some of my old colleagues in the Strategic Communications Unit. To my relief I was allowed to do this unaccompanied. My desk was still empty: less a sign of my irreplaceability than that no one had got round to occupying it yet. However, I had psychologically moved on. My mind was now full of the excitement of the school. If this Academy idea was to be pursued, I needed to find out why the school had not succeeded in the past and what would help it succeed in the future. New buildings alone were not going to be the answer. I decided to do some more research into the school's past.

Brendon, a teacher whose great authority I admired, had been at the school longest – almost thirty years – and I discovered he had a copy of the brochure for the opening of the school:

## Islington Green School

### Ceremonial Opening
### By
### The Right Hon. Frank Cousins MP
### Minister of Technology
### On Thursday 30th June 1966 at 3pm

There was an opening ceremony, and:

The school Creative Art Group will present:

Opera: A scene from Act 11 of *Madame Butterfly* by Puccini
Dance-Drama: 'Once upon a time'

Under a gleaming picture of the new seven-storey building, the brochure proclaimed:

> The school has accommodation for 1,250 pupils and is fully equipped to meet the educational needs of boys and girls of all abilities between the ages of eleven and eighteen.
>
> There is a separate, specially designed house block for house assemblies, dining and extra curricular activities. There is no streaming of pupils in their first two years and for the first three years all pupils have a basic curriculum in which there is no attempt to specialise or follow a particular course.
>
> Older pupils are encouraged to enrol as members of the youth centre. In the evenings extensive use of the school premises, including the floodlit playground, is made by Islington Green youth centre, which caters for young people aged 14–21. The centre has its own common room with a coffee bar and a warden's office and store. The youth centre is open five nights a week.
>
> The construction is of in situ reinforced concrete frame, floors and staircases, with brick or brick and mosaic infill panels and timber window frames. A special feature is the reinforced concrete roof of the assembly hall which has been constructed as a butterfly shaped folded plate, insulated with expanded polystyrene sheets and finished with bitumen and glass fibre composition. A games hall, one of the first of its size to be provided at a London school consists of a composite wall structure of cavity brickwork, blue and black externally and white internally.

The cost of the scheme was £590,000 and cost of furniture and equipment £38,000.

This was the brave new world of 1966: state of the art facilities, brand new capital programme. Less than thirty years later the school buildings were thought to be a disaster, about to be knocked down and replaced. I remember an audit of school buildings we did in government when we first came in that showed that schools built at the turn of the previous century had a life span of ninety years, those built in the Thirties had a lifespan of sixty years and those, like Islington Green, built in the Sixties had a lifespan of thirty years. The result was that almost every school was falling apart at the same time – the late 1990s. The previous government should have begun to plan for this but preferred tax cuts. To the credit of this government we were investing huge sums into school capital.

The following week Ben turned up at Islington Green School with a large entourage. This was not some private tête-à-tête with Trevor but a gathering of millionaires. Never has so much money walked into one inner-city school on the same day. Ben had brought with him other members of ARK and the culture clash was immediate. Ben was loudly finishing a conversation on his mobile as he entered Trevor's office. Janice and Robyn, Trevor's PAs, found this rude and disconcerting.

Ben and the other sponsors walked round the school with Trevor and me. They were not really interested in the school, more the size of the land and the amount of potential for building a brand new school. On a stairwell overlooking one of the playgrounds, Ben took me to one side and said, 'We move fast in business. We can do the deal. This is exactly what we are looking for. Far better than other sites I have seen. More space, good location. Let's go for it.'

This was quick and encouraging. Back in Trevor's office, he said the same thing. 'We'll go for it.'

Ben and his team left, leaving Trevor and myself shell-shocked. In the space of half an hour we seemed to have a deal to rebuild the school.

It was clear from subsequent meetings with Ben that, though not an educationalist, he had a clear idea from the United States about what sort of school he wanted. He asked to come and see us with a pioneering educationalist from America called Norman Atkins, who had successfully produced a school that had superb results for poor inner-city students. Ben sent ahead some chapters from a book called *No excuses: closing the racial gap in learning* by Abigail and Stephen Thernstrom. It describes how some successful Charter schools in America have managed to raise achievement in the poorest communities.

> No excuses. That is the message that superb schools deliver to their students. And that is the message that schools need to hear. Sure, some kids are easier to teach than others. But dysfunctional families and poverty are no excuse for widespread, chronic educational failure.

> Kids need to work much harder than they've been working, much longer than they've been working, and with much more discipline than they have been working.

On the wall in one school is the message: 'There are no shortcuts. Be Nice!!! Work Hard!!!! No Excuses.'

> Visit any classroom in any school, and it's immediately clear whether or not students are engaged in learning. In schools with a culture of work, no-one is slouching in a

seat, staring into space doodling, eating, whispering to classmates, fixing a friend's hair, wandering around the classroom or coming and going in the middle of the class.

Each of these successful schools 'engage in a national search for terrific teachers who will buy into their education vision' and whose commitment is staggering, from working long hours to giving their mobile phone numbers to students so they can be rung at any time of the day or night if help is needed. This is in contrast, the book says, to other urban schools:

One excellent teacher we encountered noted that many teachers look at teaching as just a job and are frequently absent. Whilst another spoke of how few applied for teaching positions that required extra hours and extra effort. Moreover, those who come in early, stay late, go the extra miles with students who need their help, find themselves ostracised by others in the staff and are the subject of ugly retaliation.

At the Charter schools, according to the book, team work is important: 'isolation is deeply ingrained in the teaching culture, you shut the door and you are on your own.'

First-rate principals are great instructional leaders – often in the classrooms, directing a continuous process of professional development, turning promising teachers into members of a superb team. The principals themselves are both teachers and instructional leaders.

The book quotes from some Japanese examples of 'lesson study' in which the minute detail of every lesson is planned, with great debate about framing the exact question at the beginning of the lesson and refining the best way of making students learn a particular topic. Eventually a planned lesson emerges and one teacher tests it with students before refining it again.

The authors mock some 'progressive' methods, which they believe have resulted in underachievement. Those who believe 'the teacher to be a facilitator – "a guide on the side, not a sage on the stage" – that the acquisition of skills occurs naturally through discussion, collaboration and discovery.' The result, they believe, is that children don't have the basics and end up as 'maths cripples' and poor writers. They describe schools where spelling is not corrected because teachers 'do not want to limit the youngsters' ability to express themselves.' So that work is displayed around the school with many errors in it. It's the poorest, they say, that need the basics most, that need teachers to correct bad spelling because there won't always be someone at home who is able to.

Some of these schools adopt a zero tolerance regime to tackle bad behaviour. Coming down hard on the small things so that the bigger things don't get out of hand. 'To ignore one piece of trash on the floor, one shirt improperly tucked in, one fight between kids, one bit of foul language, would send a disastrous no-one cares message.' A real connection is made between action and consequences. In some of the schools, anyone who has done something wrong, been late or misbehaved, has to apologise to the rest of the class or the entire school at assembly time.

Most of these schools have chants like: 'People, people, can't you see? Education is the key. People, people, don't you know? College is where we will go.' The students at these schools are taught 'small habits that make a big difference.' They learn to use their left hand for tracking where they are in a book while their right hand is raised to ask a question.

The book stresses that it is not just the basics these kids need.

The more difficult job is to teach 'desire, discipline and dedication,' the belief that they can go 'some place better'. What they call 'breaking the cycle of who starts behind stays behind.'

The authors ask the relevant question, the question that applies equally to Academies in Britain: 'Would these schools have the same success if their staffs weren't, as it were, running for sainthood? And if the schools require this level of idealism and energy – this sense of the job as in effect a religious calling – how many can there be?' Are academies likely to be pockets of excellence, having searched for the teachers who are willing to put their whole life into it, without the ability to replicate themselves across the board?

Sitting around the table in Trevor's office, Norman described the schools he had set up: '"Negative sell" is what they are all about. We go around telling local parents in the poorest areas that they should not come to the school if they can't stand long hours, if they won't help their children with homework, if they don't want strict discipline. The result is that parents are queuing up. We then have a lottery system. A town hall meeting and all the tickets from all the parents are put in a hat and pulled out. The only selection involved is that the parents have chosen to go to the school if they can. Choice entails commitment. For most schools, students are stuck with the schools and the schools are stuck with the students.'

The Americans in front of us, just like the authors of the book, had an intensity and a drive that was infectious. This in itself, I thought, was what Academies at their best should be about: the challenging of the status quo. Trevor felt uncomfortable experiencing this wave of 'can-do' enthusiasm. Norman and Ben were brutal about the CAT scores: 'They lower expectations. Teachers then think they've got dumb kids in their class. Why have CAT scores, why not start from the assumption that every child will go to college? Aim high for every child.'

Trevor was sceptical: you could never get away with this system over here, the negative sell would be hard to implement. Trevor did not believe that longer hours in itself cracked the problem – it is all about quality teaching, not quantity, he believed. And he was unconvinced that the regime that Norman and Ben were advocating was so different from the ethos he, Trevor, was trying over here. The other big differences were that the American Charter schools were far smaller and so the ethos far easier to create. Plus they were all schools started from scratch and not a continuation of an existing one. What he was in no doubt about was the enthusiasm and determination of our potential sponsors.

I had tried to warn Trevor at the beginning that if he went down the Academy route, instead of Building Schools for the Future, he would have less control. This was not just another way of getting cash in his hands. It was a partnership with an outside body that had to work if the whole project was going to be a success. What I was realising too, in a way that had not struck me in government, was just what immense power a sponsor has, simply by contributing £2m out of £30m. For £2m, small change for some very wealthy individuals, the sponsor was effectively buying the school.

This went to the heart of the government's public service reforms, and in the end it came down not just to the practicalities but a belief system. Was it against the 'public service ethos' that I and millions of people valued so much, to get private and voluntary sectors involved in schools? Or was it a welcome injection of different ideas? It was easy to ask: what does a businessman know about running a school? But what was striking about most Academies was that the sponsor, who often had a connection to the area, was determined to make the project work and would put great effort into finding the best educationalists and ideas to make it a success. Already I could see a head, as good as Trevor, being stimulated and challenged by Ben and Norman in a way he had not been by Ofsted or any other outside body. Trevor came away commenting that he had never been asked to articulate his education philosophy and plan in such a rigorous way, and I was surprised by how willing some of the deputy heads – like Emma, Eileen and Angela – were to go down this route. They were open-minded with no hang-ups about trying new things. 'If you always do what you've always done, you'll always get what you've always got,' Angela was fond of saying. Neither felt their huge commitment to public service and comprehensives was in any way undermined by getting outsiders involved.

Nevertheless, Trevor's scepticism remained and I thought it was time to inspire him, so I arranged for us to visit the most exciting public building I had ever been to, Bexley Academy.

Trevor likes cars. Except for the Mazda I used to own before having children, which had pop-up lights, I do not have the same passion. So he was proud to be driving me to Bexley in his Chrysler special edition something or other. The kids who saw him drive off from the school were suitably impressed. To me it looked like a glamorous Beetle, but I didn't risk telling him that.

We got to Bexley late. I got lost because I thought I knew the route and made a wrong turning at the end. Trevor, half jokingly, said he would never trust me with map reading or time keeping again. I had offended Trevor's desire for control and order.

Trevor was wowed by what he saw. Bexley has open-plan classrooms – no classroom has a door – large open-plan court-yards for art and technology, walkways taking you to the three floors, an atrium with a podium where assemblies for the whole school take place and a plush, modern canteen. It is a fantastic environment in which to teach, and changes your way of thinking about a school.

One teacher told us how she now loved the open-plan classrooms. 'I said to a student the other day, "I can see you behaving well in science, why can't you behave in my lesson?" The child was amazed that I had been watching him from my classroom and could see right into another of his lessons.'

The great facilities and stunning architecture were only part of the revolution. The curriculum had been changed, with five terms a year, two weeks holiday between each and four weeks over the summer. Every Friday, students would go off the curriculum and do projects with outside organisations. Lunch and break time were organised on a rolling programme with teachers taking their forms down to the canteen at different times between 10 a.m. and 2 p.m. The Head was proving an impressive innovator.

The teachers we spoke to told us how it was hard to get used to having no doors on the classroom; others found that not having a lunch time with other teachers was a problem; some had left because they did not like the new organisation; others joined because it was an exciting place to work – but what seemed to impress Trevor most was one small innovation: the cloakroom.

Like all teachers and headteachers who had wrestled with the nitty-gritty of organising a school, he was attracted to a neat solution to an enduring irritation. At Islington Green School, as at most schools, coats and bags are an issue. Lockers often get smashed and the durable ones are too expensive. So you end up with children lugging their coats to each lesson. Teachers spend huge amounts of time telling students to take their coats off and put their bags down. However, here at Bexley was the solution: a cloakroom, like in a theatre, where students could check in their coats with an attendant, get a ticket in exchange and collect their coats again at the end of the day. 'We're going to have one of those in our new school,' he said.

Bexley was impressive, but I wanted to learn from other Academies too, so we made a visit to a second Academy to get a different perspective. It was good that we did so. We were shown round by one of the managers, handpicked from business. She was perfectly polite and informative, but I would imagine a complete wind-up to the staff.

We entered the huge and impressive atrium. In front of us was what the designers – Fosters, as at Bexley – had called 'the street', a large corridor with two floors of classrooms up either side – but where Bexley had been spacious and had played around with the size of classrooms, this Academy had small box-like classrooms off the main walkway.

It wasn't just the design that we felt was wrong, there was something else not quite right. We found out what it was in the first classroom we were taken to. Trevor, Eileen, Emma and I entered the room and were introduced to a teacher. She had never met us before in her life, yet within a couple of minutes was attacking the Academy: 'Don't go down this route. It's a nightmare,' she said. She took us aside and told us that a lot of the staff were unhappy and the whole project had been handled in the wrong way. Trevor was flabbergasted. When anyone visited Islington Green he was incredibly upbeat, whatever the problems. He was shocked that complete strangers were given such a negative impression.

We left the room and went up the street. All the classrooms seemed the same: modern but poky. Trevor put his finger on it: 'It looks like a prison.' Eileen had a different take: 'It looks like a modern version of Islington Green. In other words there is no new vision.'

When we went back to see the headteacher, Trevor began with a leading question, hinting at the anxiety we had encountered. The head picked up on it immediately and began to open up. It had been a difficult process. The school that the Academy had replaced had been heavily unionised. The headteacher had not wanted to include the unions in the new school plans, so he had been the only one involved in the design, a big responsibility. This had also, he said, been what the DfES (department for education) had wanted. A real sense of a fresh start. The result was that the staff who transferred to the new school were disillusioned – so much so that they were going to strike, until the high court ruled it illegal to strike against a future employer.

'Culturally, politically and philosophically it was very difficult, particularly with changes to terms and conditions,' the head said. 'In retrospect I would have kept their terms and conditions, removed that spectre and then made future changes.'

We went away feeling sorry about the situation, but with a bitter taste in the mouth at the friction we had seen. Trevor, Eileen and Emma seemed to share a professional sadness about a school which was not a happy place to work in. I found out later that the head had agreed, just that week, that he would retire at the end of the year. This served as a warning for us, about bringing people with us on a project of this scale and about making sure the educational vision and design was really imaginative.

So, our next task was to decide what we wanted for our school. Ben had also given us the strong impression that he required a worked-out vision within a week.

This was the exciting part for me; I loved the idea of designing a school. For Trevor, for any headteacher, this must be their dream: to be able to construct a school from scratch.

In response to Ben's probing at the first meeting, Trevor had come up with an idea that chimed with the sponsors and was met enthusiastically by the department: schools within schools.

This was Trevor's big idea. His belief was that the key thing wrong with secondary schools, what drove bad behaviour, what mitigated against personalised learning, was the size of the school.

Size is one of the drawbacks of the comprehensive model. Before comprehensives schools were broadly either grammar or secondary modern. Both were smaller because they were not trying to do everything. Grammars focused on academic subjects, secondary moderns on more vocational subjects. The point about comprehensives was that they had to do everything and so, to get a critical mass of teaching staff and make the timetable work, you needed a lot of students. Some secondary schools ended up with well over 2,000 children.

Trevor's view, which he said was backed up by psychology – as well as the popular book – *The Tipping Point* by Brian Gladwell – suggested that units of around 200 were the maximum size for creating a meaningful community. The idea would be to have smaller schools each with their own head, all reporting to an overarching Principal. That way teachers would get to know students in a more intimate atmosphere.

The other problem we were trying to crack was common to a lot of boroughs in London and other cities, and that was the transition from primary to secondary school. This causes great headaches. It is a strange problem into which a lot of government effort has gone. In Islington the problem is two-fold. First, middle-class parents commit themselves to Islington primary schools, but when it comes to secondary schools, choose to go outside the borough to another state school or send them private. Tony Blair himself is a good example of this. All his children went to Islington state primaries, then they all went to state schools outside the borough. The big question is how to hold on to such children. The second problem of transition, familiar in most areas, is that many children leave the cosseted, disciplined environment of the primary schools, where they are based in one room with one teacher, and are suddenly thrust into a secondary school with hundreds of older children, many new subjects, many new teachers, much travelling around the school to lessons and many new temptations. Rules and discipline go out of the window, and very soon a number of those children are not learning but messing around or, worse, being put off secondary school altogether.

The solution favoured by Trevor and the sponsors was to have an all-age Academy – from age four to eighteen. That way, children who liked the primary school would be less likely to leave at secondary because the secondary would be a natural extension to what they had already been part of. We would also be able to shape the ethos of the primary school children rather than inheriting children from other schools and then trying to mould them.

So Trevor crystallised his vision of the school into:

When your child joins our Academy he or she will see a breathtaking modern school that is open-planned. A school that provides secure and open spaces to learn. A school organised with smaller schools inside it, so that every child is known to all their teachers.

Our aim is that each child joining the school has a sense of awe and wonder while they are at the school. They will not only enjoy their learning but love their school – feel it is part of their community but one that challenges them with exciting new and inspiring experiences. A school that pledges to make learning active, personalised and demanding so that they progress as academics but also as people.

I then set out, in a vision paper, the key elements of this new school: the 'schools within schools'; the implications for teachers, including more flexible hours, a longer school day, and possibly five or six terms instead of three.

Staff were now getting wind of our plans for an Academy, and John the NUT rep, was not happy. His preferred method of attack was the photocopy in teachers' pigeon holes. He knew what he was doing. Teachers read what is in their pigeon holes, in case it is about a child in their class or some duty they have to do.

John's first strike was a document with the front page:

### Why the NUT, the TES and professor Alan Smithers are all against (city) academies

Inside the dossier was the NUT resolution.

> At its April annual conference the National Union of Teachers voted to adopt the following policy:
>
> Conference notes with concern the Government's intention to establish City Academies as a further way of increasing private sector influence in education and a further attack on comprehensive education.
> Conference instructs the Executive to oppose the establishment of City academies on the grounds that:
> a. the school will not be under the democratic control of the LEAs but under the control of private sponsors including businesses
> b. they will deny students access to a broad and balanced curriculum
> c. they pose a threat to teachers' pay and conditions

The *Times Educational Supplement*'s contribution was an editorial that John had photocopied, saying:

> Quite why it is assumed that property developers, holiday companies and car traders are able to govern schools better than representatives of the local community is hard to fathom. Their academies are the educational equivalent of the private housing estates gated and walled to keep out the riff-raff. Ministers will say they are in favour of a decent education for all, and continue to call on schools to collaborate to raise the game of the weakest. But academies are likely to have precisely the opposite effect. With better funding they are able to attract the best staff and more able or better-behaved and motivated pupils, leaving other schools less well equipped for an even tougher job.

Alan Smithers's contribution was to accuse the government of a secondary school policy that 'defies comprehension', is 'woefully lacking on coherence', and is 'economic lunacy'.

These documents were the prelude to a big NUT meeting, called for after school, to debate the issue. John had announced at the staff briefing, that Fred, regional NUT rep, would be coming. This was the chance for staff to get up to speed and give their views. I had decided to go as an observer. This was allowed, though it was stressed I would have no voting rights. Eileen and Angela from the SMT decided to go too. This would be my first ever NUT meeting. I was quite excited.

The meeting was to be held in John's classroom. At 3.30 the classroom was empty, so I hovered outside. Then John appeared with Fred, and other staff arrived in dribs and drabs. Soon the classroom was full of about twenty-five teachers – out of a potential eighty – who all sat at desks, students listening to their NUT teacher. Fred sat at the front of the classroom next to

David, a science teacher, who was in the chair.

Fred began by saying how sad it was that a school like Islington Green, that he knew and loved, was choosing to go down this route. However, he said, he would begin with a balanced view of the issue: 'Yes, there could be advantages. The school would get new facilities. It could be well resourced and well managed. It would be free to develop an expertise. You are right on the edge of the city. The school may well end up with some of these advantages.'

John, perched on a desk in the corner of the room, was looking worried. He had not dragged the NUT regional rep across London only to hear him bang on about the advantages of the Academy. His disappointment was not to last.

'Other things would happen as well,' said Fred. 'It would be an independent school, separate from the state; instead of LEA governors there would be business governors. It would be a self-governing body open to no one.

'In Haringey the city academy was a failure. The teachers were run down, the only way back from the abyss was to become a more normal school again.

'Now staff will get guarantees through employment regulations. There may be advantages in terms of money, but disadvantages in terms of hours. The school day may be longer, there may be compulsory homework clubs. It may sound fine, but, at an Academy across London, instead of 1,265 hours a year it went up to 1,450 – but they did get a laptop.

'On balance, for teachers it involves little benefit, less certainty, and more abrasive management.

'The bigger picture is that the Labour government should be ashamed of itself. We thought it believed in comprehensives not one school getting advantage at the expense of another. Take this area. Holloway Boys will find it more difficult. Academies' success depends on there only being one or two of them. Think of yourself if you don't stay here; you may want to work in another school in the area but it will be worse if this school is hogging the resources and the limelight. The union is opposed to privatisation and profit. That is the dogma bit. But we are also opposed for a more fundamental reason – inequality. Ultimately this will improve education for a few at the expense of the majority.'

This had been a calm summing up of the issues. His reasonable tone and semblance of balance were going down well with the audience. The questions and comments came quickly.

'There are already inequalities in the system,' said one surprising defender of Academies.

'We'll be shafted if we don't do it, so we can't win,' said another.

'Is there any other way of getting a new building without selling our soul?'

'This is an ethical issue of sponsorship. The doors are open to all sorts of things. Why shouldn't Coca-Cola sponsor us? Like motor sport or football. Where will it end?'

Even Fred thought this was going a bit far. 'There is protection,' he said. 'Coca-Cola couldn't put logos round the school.'

He went on to admit that most union members were not opposed to Academies but wanted the union to sort out the best deal on terms and conditions for the staff.

John had been waiting a long time to intervene. Fred had been too reasonable. 'Our task is to help the underprivileged, not to become gated and walled. You don't need to tell me it would be nice to have a new school. I've been in the same classroom with one coat of paint and a new carpet since 1988.'

This was indeed a chilling thought. Sixteen years in this classroom; sixteen years of lessons in the same room, trying to control disruptive kids, trying to get them to understand Cabinet government or the benefits of the European Union.

'But we can win a new school anyway,' he continued. 'I don't want to get a new school a year or two earlier but sell out on equal opportunities.'

'And, of course, let's be clear – it weakens trade unions. Other teachers won't be able to strike on our behalf. We will be in a weaker position. Forget it if you need support.'

David then made it clear that his position was far less militant than John's. Having said he was opposed to PFI, which he saw as worse than Academies, he then supported those who suggested this was the only show in town and urged staff to try to get the best deal. 'This can be different from other Academies,' he said. 'We can be in the vanguard of getting a deal that protects teachers and is a non-selective school.'

The teacher next to me, young and recently graduated, had had enough pussy-footing around the subject and started to let rip. 'It's so obvious what this is about. Tony Blair is modernising the country for the future.' She said this with a sneer, as if by definition modernising was an evil thing to do. I sat there, delighted that anyone had remembered one of our slogans. 'If it means knocking down every school and building them in the fashion he wants, he will do it, be warned. The war on Iraq was a classic example of him not listening to the people. Well, *we* have to listen; when Tony Blair speaks he means it. We don't want our school to change. We've got to make our stand. We don't want it.'

John purred with delight – though there must have been a little envy. With this outburst and the direct link between Iraq and the Academies, John's position as the most left-wing teacher in the school was facing a head-on challenge.

'Sorry for the passion,' she said, 'but it had to be said.'

The debate moved from high principle to more mundane matters. John had been asked by Trevor to be on the project board, overseeing the Academy scheme if it went ahead. John wanted to go as an observer rather than a proper member. Some in the room thought he would have more clout as a formal member of the group. John was adamant he should just be an observer. 'I am against it in principle. We must tell the governors and get the school to consult parents. My job, with Fred, is to protect the pay of staff, but that is difficult if I am part of the body designed to implement the change.'

It was resolved that John should just observe.

John wanted more out of the meeting. He wanted to put his strongly-worded motion condemning the Academy to a vote. Others wanted to defer the vote, but John said, 'I want a vote. This is a matter of principle.' Others thought it was premature to have a vote. 'No, let's do it. If I lose, I lose,' John said.

This was tense. If he won this vote he would have the ammunition he needed to put before the governors.

The vote was taken by a show of hands. Four voted in favour of the motion, five voted against. There were sixteen abstentions. The vote against the academy was lost. I was relieved. I told Trevor who was both surprised and relieved that staff were going along with his plans.

For Trevor the Academy process was causing a lot of anxiety. He was beginning to realise quite how much the sponsor called the shots and was finding Ben's style off-putting. Ben would challenge everything Trevor said, implying it was not nearly heroic or bold enough. He began conversations as if Trevor could and should get rid of most of the staff and start again. Trevor explained that building a team was important, and he wanted to keep them because they were good – and, legally of course, the staff had to be allowed to transfer to the new school if they wanted to.

I was realising that the Academy model had a flaw when applied to improving schools with good heads. The original point of Academies was to replace failed schools where the head and most of the staff were leaving. This suited sponsors who, by and large, wanted a clean slate to start afresh. In our case the chemistry between the sponsor and the current headteacher was key to making the relationship work. Yet from the beginning the school and the headteacher were on the backfoot. Despite government policy wanting to put more power in the hands of heads, the Academy documentation involved DfES, sponsor and LEA rather than the school. The sponsor would have total power over the process from the moment the deal was signed. I was brought face-to-face with the reality of the policy. What looked exciting and creative from Westminster seemed like a lot bigger gamble at school level. For just £2m anyone, subject to government approval, could get control over a school. This was certainly a bold policy, but for Trevor it was becoming particularly galling to see non-educationalists driving the educational vision for the school, even though he agreed with much of the philosophy himself. The Academy process was also putting me in a vulnerable position: rather than being an unthreatening and naïve outsider, my role up until then, I was starting to look like a man with an agenda. It almost seemed as if I had come to the school with a deliberate plan to turn it into an Academy. This wasn't in fact the case, it had been pure chance; but I was becoming a controversial figure at the school. When one of my staff-room friends said, only half jokingly, 'You're the enemy now', I knew things were getting more serious. However, I was still convinced it was worth pursuing.

It was now on to the next hurdle, getting the governors to agree.

By the time the governors met, John had got the school's NUT members to reverse their previous decision and support a watered-down motion opposing the Academy. This he had sent to Cec, chair of governors, along with a long letter condemning Academies.

I could see Trevor was tense about this meeting. Normally the governors would agree to his plans, but this was a big decision and the Lib Dem councillors on the governing body were highly unpredictable.

Following a sceptical staff meeting, Trevor had written out a series of pledges to staff about the Academy. Tony had used the personal pledge on many occasions. The question, as it was for Tony, was whether there was enough trust in the bank for people to go along with it. Though I was worried he had conceded too much from the beginning, Trevor insisted it was necessary. These he now circulated to governors, along with our vision statement and the NUT's opposing view. Trevor's pledges included:

> I want to take the team of staff that we currently have into this project. We have worked well over the last two years and there is no sense in which I want to break that up.
>
> So there will be no wholesale change of staff – no reapplying for jobs. I have found IGS an exciting and welcoming place to work. There is good team work. I want this to continue.
>
> I do not believe that more is better, so there need not be an increase in the 1,265 hours we currently work to.
>
> We will not be working for Goldman Sachs. One of their directors has set up an educational foundation which will donate the money. They will have two or three places on the Governing Body and will not become the owners of the school. There will remain DfES governors, LEA governors, parents, teachers and staff governors. The governing body will become the owners and the employers.

I have no intention of changing the Conditions of Employment and will stick with the national pay and conditions as agreed and as colleagues work to now.

We will not divert to a commercial curriculum. We shall follow the national curriculum.

We will not select by ability. I am committed to a full comprehensive intake.

As I said in the meeting, this is all about getting resources. It is pragmatic not political. We all have our own views of political policy – but we must work together in the best interests of the school and students' education.

This was it. The most important governors' meeting since Islington Green School had been built in 1966. This was the meeting to decide whether to go ahead with the Academy. The governors began to gather in the only meeting room in the school – known to all staff as room 008, it had always had a notice on the door saying 007.

Five minutes before the meeting began Trevor asked me: 'What is the exact number of governors the sponsors are allowed?'

I wasn't certain, and in truth Trevor and I had both been skirting round this issue. I phoned DfES and couldn't get hold of anyone, so I tried Sir Bruce on his mobile. The ringtone sounded as if he was abroad somewhere. Should I disturb him on his holiday? He didn't sound put out. I asked him the question.

'Yes,' he said, 'in all cases the sponsors have the majority. Those are the rules. They also have a slimmed-down board usually, but there are guarantees of one place for the LEA, one for parents and one for staff. I'm in Milan and I'm now off to *Carmen*.' The next couple of hours was going to be very different for Bruce and me.

It was clear that we were asking the governors to vote for their own abolition. In Cec's case she would definitely lose her job as chair to the sponsors of the new school, but Trevor would also lose control as the sponsors would have a majority. I returned to 008. The meeting had just begun. I scribbled a note to Trevor with the answer and waited for a moment to pass it round the table to him.

The room was now full. Angela, Eileen, Paul, three of the deputy heads, were there, as was Bob from CEA, the private company running the LEA. Trevor was cross about this and thought the LEA, who had blown hot and cold, might still want to pull the plug on the scheme. Brian, the Lib Dem councillor, was ready for action. When would he make his intervention? Which part of the fence would he be sitting on this time? The parent governor looked as if she would speak her mind. Would she think this was a good idea? Tom, a city accountant, who specialised in getting to the point, was there, as was Alex, the young research director of ARK, a posh-sounding, articulate, city man with floppy hair and a polite cheery manner.

Trevor was by now reporting back to governors on progress at the school: 'The canteen has been refurbished over half term. A competition has come up with a new name, "Izzy on the Green". I think we might have done better, but we asked the kids and that's what we got.'

'Now the main item,' said Cec. 'Academy status. Trevor, do you want to take us through these papers?'

'In the last two years I have confirmed my view that the problem with this school and those like it is its size. That is why the big idea here is "schools within schools". So instead of 1000 kids in an unstructured way we would have, for example, one floor just for Year 7, with specific teachers who the students get to know. That model could be applied across the school. We also think it would be helpful to have a primary school and to have an active partnership with the sixth-form college with an aim of all going to college and university. The DfES came to us with a couple of sponsors. ARK was well funded by people from the city. The Robin Hood trust in the States had done similar things. They seemed like a group of people we could work with. What we are agreeing today is to go ahead with the feasibility study. The DfES will give us £250,000 to explore Academy status. That is the proposal. We will report back, and if things don't go the way we want, we will pull out.'

Tom got straight to the point. 'Who will run the school?'

Trevor replied: 'There are no fixed numbers. Governing bodies of Academies vary from thirty to eight. It allows for sponsors to have 50 per cent plus one.'

Tom: 'That would be quite a change.'

Cec: 'The sponsor governors could pick you and me,' she said, ever the optimist.

William, an architect who had joined the governors, asked: 'So if they do have more than 50 per cent, they could control decisions of the governors?'

Tom: 'By putting up a small amount of money they have control.'

William: 'And the governing body can then appoint the headmaster.'

The penny was dropping.

Brian, the Lib Dem councillor, asked: 'Could the sponsors push their own curriculum choice?'

Trevor: 'No, I don't think so.'

Bob from CEA: 'The simple answer is that the sponsors can determine the curriculum, but from what we know of ARK and

339

what they have tried in New York, what they are proposing will be a good thing, and the kids will be given something more relevant. The school will be independent, but the council is building in safeguards so it doesn't go its own way. It will be part of the community of schools.'

Norman, a teacher governor, asked: 'Can we enshrine into the trust document, when the time comes, our key principles?'

Trevor was beginning to get exasperated.

'What motives are we frightened about? Do we think the children will be tied up and taken as slaves to America? There will be Ofsted, the law, the framework for all schools, and we will be funded as a state school. I am quite certain the sponsors are trying to do the right thing or why would they put the money in?'

Bob weighed in. 'We think this is a forward-looking way of doing education in the twenty-first century.'

'Perhaps we should hear from the sponsor now,' said Cec.

'Hello there, OK, my name is Alex. I am director of research at ARK. Let me tell you about ourselves and hopefully shoot a few bears.

'My role is to spend money. I research what to spend money on. Our aim is to help deprived children. We seek trans-formational change, to invest serious money rather than give small cheques which are a small drop in a large bucket. "Strategic philanthropy" is what we are about. We evaluate and develop projects we think will work. So our previous projects include the biggest anti-retro-virus, anti-Aids drugs programme, in Cape Town which the South African government is going to use as their model and scale up.

'And orphanages in Romania. We didn't just help bring a few children over. We closed three whole orphanages and made a significant difference, including setting up proper child protection arrangements.

'And on Academies our aim is to use our skills to have leverage on the governing body. We believe in "schools within schools" for children in deprived areas because we think that works best. We plan five in the centre of London with teacher recruitment and teacher training. We won't change the teachers here, but some of our schools we will build from scratch. We will be ruthlessly pragmatic. We are not medical people when we do the Aids project, or educationalists for this project, but we want the best people and the best solutions. We are about researching interventions that really work. We are non-religious, we want to help deprived kids and reject selection which would defeat the purpose. And as for the land transfer, it is entirely marked for education, not something else, so we are not going to sell it off and build something nasty.'

Norman: 'Who is responsible for delivering the building on time and on budget?'

Bob: 'Department for Education will pay the full costs, apart from the £2m from the sponsors.'

Tom: 'Can we have a written agreement on issues like selection? What guarantee will there be that these won't change after control is handed over to a self-electing body? We are passing over control of this state school to this organisation, but need to be sure that the key policies of this community school will not change.'

Alex: 'Yes we need to be clear we are non-selective and non-religious.'

Bob intervened. 'There is a watching brief from government. That is the absolute safeguard.'

Tom: 'So central government rather than local government. It would still be nice to get a series of pledges out of ARK. These pledges of yours are important I think.' Tom pointed to Trevor's list in the pack of papers. 'We need to make sure these are written into the deeds of the new school. I think these are good.'

Trevor nodded.

The room went silent, and then out of the blue came an electrifying moment. Mavis, the parent governor seated next to me, said 'I listened to all this as a parent. I'm just a parent. Trevor was wonderful. He seemed fine.' She pointed at Trevor. 'But listening to that other guy Alex,' she pointed at Alex, 'I'm not sure. I've just got a feeling we need something in writing. When he spoke, I'm just not sure. As a parent that is. Just not sure I trust him.'

Alex looked crest-fallen; he had obviously tried not to sound too businessy, too off-putting, but the one school parent in the room simply had not bought it.

There were shuffles of slight embarrassment at her brutal frankness, but she had clearly spoken for a lot of them.

'Go with Trevor,' I whispered to her, hoping things hadn't run away from us.

'Don't get me wrong,' she whispered back, 'I want a new school building.'

Bob from CEA, it turned out, had come to praise the project not to bury it – a relief to Trevor who still thought sabotage was on the cards. 'I have spoken to many sponsors in the last eighteen months,' he said magisterially. 'Some I have been sceptical about, but in dealing with ARK there is no question about their motives or commitment. Their intention is not to bring in middle-class children but to support local children. I am keen that the Academy is linked with the rest of the education community – that the other nine secondaries are not upset. We have worked well together and there is scepticism amongst the other heads. They just don't want to see this becoming a flagship and leaving the others behind. As for the sixth form, we have one of the best colleges in London at City and Islington, and this school needs to work as partners with them. So my bottom line is partnership.'

Brian, the Lib Dem councillor, had been quite quiet up until then. 'I think it may be time for a few ill-chosen words from the council,' he said whimsically. 'This government has set the agenda for a lot of Academies and that's their privilege. One Academy, the Church of England, is already underway in Islington. These sort of things become a negotiation. It's not good practice to express wild enthusiasm for the sponsor. It's not a done deal until it's resolved. It weakens our hand to express a view. It's really not right to express wild enthusiasm.'

The governors were obeying orders. Wild enthusiasm was in check.

Brian was not to be deterred. If you're not going to express an opinion it's just as well to do so at length. 'What sort of experience will ARK governors have? The LEA will have a maximum of one governor. That means one of the current two must go. So I am not opposed but wild enthusiasm is not right. I will continue to express an interest in flexibility at this stage.'

Cec came in quickly as Brian wound up. 'All we are asking now is to go to the next stage. We are getting very woolly, a sledgehammer to crack a nut. Let's have a vote. Do we want to at least go to the next level with no cost to ourselves and the ability to pull out at a later date?'

Alex left the room and the vote began. Hands went up.

To my surprise the vote was passed unanimously.

Buoyed up by this victory, Trevor agreed to go to the States with ARK to visit some of the schools that Ben and Norman had talked about. Over the Easter holidays he spent a week looking at Charter schools and came back totally energised. He said he had seen the best organised, best disciplined learning environment he had ever been to. He was a convert to Ben's ideas and wanted to begin implementing some of them immediately.

He thought the key was to ring-fence the Year 7s (eleven-year-olds) from the rest of the school: to start the idea of schools within schools even before the Academy was up and running. His plan was to create what he called a Charter 7 school – to use the American title – and ensure that students new to the school had one corridor with classrooms together. Teachers would come to their classroom rather than students traipsing round the school. There would be different lunch hours and break times. Their school day would start fifteen minutes earlier at 8.30, and there would be an hour's compulsory homework after school. The curriculum would be drastically reduced to ensure a real focus on the core areas of literacy and numeracy. This would require some building works in the old technology building. It would mean moving a food technology classroom down a floor. Most controversially, for Paul at least, it would mean turning his office into toilets to be used by the Year 7 students. Emma would then be the head of this project and make sure it ran smoothly. Though there would only be three months to get it ready for September, Trevor believed it was possible.

At a senior management team meeting Trevor put forward these plans. The reactions to them were interesting. Angela and Emma, who had been on the trip to America with Trevor, were enthused and thought it was a great idea. Eileen who had spent months on the September timetable was less enthusiastic about changing it again, but up for the plan. Paul was the most sceptical. He didn't see the need to rush it, and he was very worried about losing his room. It brought home to me one of the key and often ignored points about change. People go along with change when it is generalised, or means little work for them. When it means physically moving themselves or genuinely doing things differently it becomes harder. I was keen that we were clear about what these sensible changes were for: that the aim was for every child to be able to read and write properly by the end of Year 7.

Trevor announced these changes almost in passing at a staff meeting in which the main focus was the Academy. The Academy seemed to meet with general approval, but the Charter 7 idea clearly set hares running. Trevor's instincts were right, after the meeting, when he said to me, 'I'm worried there were no questions.'

The first time I got wind of real trouble was when a head of department came up to me and said: 'Does Trevor listen to you? You know, he's getting like Tony, floating off, the only person he now communicates with is his maker.' She pointed to the heavens. 'He shouldn't run too far ahead of the rest of the staff.' It was clear that she and others were concerned with the squeezing of their subjects in Year 7, and teachers, who I knew were usually up for change, told me it was all being rushed.

A staff association meeting was called to discuss the plans, but Sanchez, head of the staff association, came up to me in the staff room and asked me not to come. He said I had intimidated the staff by coming to the NUT meeting on the Academy and they would be freer to speak if I wasn't there. I agreed to his request, not wanting to cause any friction. I shouldn't have done so, for this meeting was to be explosive. Speaking to people afterwards, I pieced together what had happened.

One after another the accusations flew: for a start Trevor had misrepresented the governors' decision of voting in favour of the Academy, they had in fact only voted in favour of investigating it. Most of the flak, however, was for Trevor's plans for Year 7: 'Non-core subjects are being marginalised'; 'Staff professionalism is being eroded'; 'No consultation has taken place'; 'Parents are not all in favour of the new Charter 7'; 'What is the rush? Why do we have to do this for September?'; 'Teachers' conditions of service are being eroded'; 'There should be three months' consultation to change the school day'; 'Education is about more than reading and writing.'

A motion was suggested: 'We, the staff of Islington Green School, feel that the Charter 7 idea should not be introduced in September 2004.' It was carried overwhelmingly by 26 votes to 2 with 5 abstentions.

Trevor wrote an angry note to all staff, saying that there would be a special briefing meeting on Friday. Then, after a sleepless night, he decided that he would back down on the Charter 7 idea, because it would strengthen him in the upcoming battle for the Academy.

At the staff meeting the following morning he said with great passion: 'Let's clear up what the governors did vote for – they voted for the expression of interest. There have been no cover ups, half-truths or deceptions. I spoke to you only last Wednesday about Charter 7. The only thing I apologise for, in that sense, is our enthusiasm for a fantastic idea. I believe that Charter 7 is a fantastic idea. We saw some of the best schools I have ever seen in the US. We are failing about 70 per cent of our kids and we must not allow ourselves to excuse this. Being able to read is the key to all subjects. The parents I spoke to all thought it was an excellent idea. However, I read your motion and you know, I agree with you . . . it is a rush. So we will put off the plans until September 2005 – but then we will make it happen and it will be a fantastic success. Unlike Peter Hyman's old boss, I can say, "Sorry, I got this a bit wrong." So, let's have a calm end of term, look forward to your summer and return in the autumn ready for a serious professional debate.'

There was applause for the Head for the first time ever at a morning briefing. Some who were committed to the idea were in tears. Those who had scuppered it were clearly sheepish. They had wanted to flex their muscles. No one had thought Trevor might actually listen. It was clear he had gained from listening on one level, but in future days, I thought he might regret giving in. It might be a bad precedent to set.

★

The last three months and the appearance of our sponsors on the scene had caused great excitement, but resulted in a lot of tension with staff and had made Trevor anxious. He was used to being in control. He had entered the Academy process, I believe, without really understanding quite how much control he would be handing over to the sponsors. What was becoming clearer by the day was quite what a bold personal decision Trevor was taking. He could sit tight, see the school improve and probably get the Building Schools for the Future money in the next round. Instead he was getting into bed with sponsors who were hard to deal with, who constantly seemed to be testing Trevor's views and commitment, and, though forced by law to guarantee the jobs of the teaching staff, were required to do no such thing for the headteacher. If they went off Trevor, if he wasn't implementing their vision in the way they wanted, they could get rid of him.

I felt guilty. I had put Ben and Trevor together. I had speeded the process along. I had believed it was a great way of injecting both money and dynamism into the school. Now, however, it seemed as if the person who had trusted me, offered me a job, taught me so much in the last few months, was now vulnerable to the whim of a few businessmen.

Trevor's job was on the line and I was to blame.

# WORLDS APART

A year ago, almost to the day, I was at the Labour Party Conference in Bournemouth, helping Tony on what was being billed as the most important speech of his career. Now I am sitting in a classroom on the third floor of Islington Green School's tower block, helping two sixteen-year-old girls on one of the most important speeches of their lives. Tessa and Aisha, headgirls of the school, are going to deliver a speech at the presentation evening at Sadler's Wells in October 2004 in front of 1,000 students, parents, and local bigwigs.

It's going to be a tense few weeks for me. I have been asked by Trevor to organise the event. I am expecting the decision on the Academy any day. I am nervously awaiting Jimmy's SATs results, as well as the GCSE scores of my 'marginal' students. Most importantly of all, the whole school is going to find out whether this year's efforts have been rewarded by a step-change in GCSE results.

I know Tessa and Aisha well, as they have been taking my political debating class. Both are smart and attractive, with the talent and potential to do whatever they want with their lives, given half a chance. Tessa, tall and striking, has a rebellious streak. She likes wearing badges on her tie. The one I like best is green and says 'thimble-headed gherkin' on it – a phrase that has a certain ring to it. Another badge sports an anarchist symbol. A third is an American flag with a smiling face.

'I thought you were anti-America and anti the war,' I say to her.

'I am,' she says, 'but we have a lot of family friends in America so I like Americans.'

Aisha is self-effacing but very talented. She has long brown hair, too, and a full smile; she has charm and intelligence, but is dreading the speech. 'It's your chance to say what you want about the school,' I say.

'It's a lot better than it was,' Aisha says. 'When we first came here, we were really scared. We were scared to go to the toilet because the Year 11 bitches, as they were called, would look over the toilet at you.'

Tessa agrees: 'It's definitely got better in the last couple of years.'

Aisha chips in: 'Trevor's too good for this place – sorry, Mr Averre-Beeson. We shouldn't call him Trevor. I'm sure he wants to be more than just a headteacher. He has the charisma. He should be a politician. I'm sure that's what he wants to be.'

'Let's start on the speech,' I say. 'The Head is keen that you thank people for coming and then say a bit about the school.' They sit at the computer together and write out the speech that they will take turns to deliver. Neither of them has asked me 'What's the big argument?' or 'How shall we do policy?' as Tony would have by now. This seems an altogether less painful process.

Tessa reads out her words. 'Our new headteacher recently said: "This school is no longer a lack of success school," and we believe that this is due hugely to him and the turning round of Islington Green. We also think this is partly thanks to last year's

Year 11 who succeeded in getting the school's highest GCSE results ever.'

'Let's practise it,' I say. 'Remember to speak more slowly than you think and project your voice.'

In my previous job I couldn't stop thinking about strategy, political positioning, upcoming speeches. In this job I couldn't stop thinking about the students. They have an ability to get under your skin, for good and bad. They touch you with their neediness, their reliance, their resourcefulness, their humour. Trevor told me his first years in teaching had been the same. You feel depressed in the holidays because you are missing the students and the intense atmosphere of the classroom. 'It's like having a fan base,' said this ex-pop singer. 'They need you, they look up to you.' Being a teacher is a position of profound power and responsibility. I feel this more intensely than I ever felt the power of being at Number 10. When a twelve-year-old student recently called me 'Dad' in a lesson and got all embarrassed, I was proud that he felt comfortable enough with me to make the mistake, but also realised that teachers at a school like this are not social workers, as some claim, but surrogate parents; they are literally socialising children, teaching them the values that their dislocated families have been unable to give them.

In the time I have been at Islington Green School I have read media pieces on the young generation I have been working with: at one and the same time the children are supposed to be more interested in sex, less interested in sex, obsessed with shopping and fast food, obsessed with money and celebrity, more caring, harder working, lazier, less respectful. Teenagers get attacked by the media and attacked by government for a series of sins: being teenage thugs, for teenage pregnancy, for teenage smoking.

I cannot possibly claim that the students of Islington Green School speak for a generation, but what I find is a culture dominated by TV and DVDs, with many students staying up late, watching scary movies, and coming to school tired the next day. They have a love of music, mainly hip-hop and garage; an enjoyment of bikes, scooters and mopeds; a terrible diet, with a large number of children coming to school with a chocolate bar or bag of crisps for their breakfast, and then having chips and pizza every day for lunch. There is a racial tolerance, with White, Black and Turkish children often making most friends within their own groups but mixing in the main harmoniously and respectfully. There is a lack of respect for authority – even when they crave the praise and support from authority figures – with no qualms about shouting at a teacher, interrupting her in mid-conversation. From what I have seen, drug, sex and violence are not the problems some want us to believe.

I am not optimistic about all the students at my school. I love the company of some, love their optimism and naïvety, their sense of possibility. There are twenty or thirty students out of a year of 180, who, like Tessa and Aisha, join the clubs, hoover up every opportunity the school puts their way, do their work and brighten your life every time you talk to them. The majority, however, are more challenging, and a minority have horrible behaviour. Rudeness is starting to get me down, and I can see that the low-level niggling all day, every day, as well as the wandering about, lateness to lessons, failure to remove hats and coats, not turning up with a pen, chatting all lesson, scribbling on the desk in Biro, would drive even the calmest teacher up the wall.

Yet every time I sit down with the most challenging students, I listen to a story that almost at once explains why they refuse to behave: an alcoholic abusive mother; a father who says he hates his son and never wants to see him again; a twelve-year-old boy, with tears running down his face, who says with disbelief: 'Is it really too much to expect my dad to remember my birthday?'

In many cases it doesn't make the child more lovable – their behaviour is still bullying, insulting, victimising – but it does explain a lot. The stories leave me sad and dent my belief in progress. I realise that for some of these children their life will not necessarily be better than their parents'.

Their futures are held in a fragile balance. School is trying to right the wrongs of their past, yet the powerful family history is pulling them back in the opposite direction. The famous adage, that we are slowly being poured into the mould of our parents, applies to these students. It will be a Herculean task to break free. Each one of hundreds of children is in this fragile state. One lucky break when they leave school can take them on the path to a decent job and life. A setback, the temptations of the wrong person, can lead them to crime and eventually prison. All those years of frustration in school, never acquiring the tools needed to get on, being told you're not clever, laughed at, life stretching out ahead of you with only the prospect of a string of boring tasks for not much pay – what a contrast, particularly in trendy Islington, to the super-rich lifestyles of the resident advertisers, editors, architects and writers, eating out at expensive restaurants, frequenting shops that sell overpriced kitchen accessories or designer T-shirts. The thrill, the self-esteem, the buzz of stealing, doing scams, living on the fringes of society becomes, for some, too much to resist.

I can't help thinking that it is as much personality – tenacity and optimism – as it is any government support that will lead students on the right path. I am convinced that one thing can make a real difference – every child should have a strong relationship with at least one adult at the school. Research from educationalist John Gray and others backs this up. That means more than just having a conscientious form tutor. Government should fund the idea of every child in secondary school being guaranteed a one-to-one tutorial – as in many universities – on academic and pastoral issues, preferably two or three times a term. In the case of the most needy, once a week. The knock on effect for behaviour and for commitment to learning can be immense, as I found with Jimmy.

New Labour's rhetoric has been about 'the many not the few'. We singled out the privileged few, the very wealthy right at the top, as outside our big tent. Yet from where I am looking now, it is clear who the few are. The few are those right at the bottom. The privileged few are part of the many – the 80 per cent – above them. The few are those who poverty and illiteracy over generations, or recent immigration, have left squarely at the bottom of the heap. It is those few who the rest want little to do with; those who no middle-class parents want their children to be educated alongside; those few who are just too rough – too beyond the pale – to be part of the many. Some, who are jobless, do not even fit the other New Labour slogan of 'hard working family'. And for harsher advocates of our 'rights and responsibilities' rhetoric, many of these students have been given opportunity after opportunity but have refused or been unable to take them.

Yet, despite being at the bottom, they have not been ignored by this government, unlike the last. Money has been made available and policies have been devised for their benefit: action zones and excellence in cities, behaviour programmes and referral units. The most challenging students get support from social workers, psychologists, specialist units – in short, ten to twenty times more resources than the quiet average student. The trouble is that money alone, support alone, is not enough. The challenge for teachers is to make the money and the policies connect in a meaningful way to the student, so it results in high expectations.

I can't help falling into the judgemental, occasionally patronising, trap that a lot of teachers find themselves in: of wanting to 'civilise the barbaric masses'. It is easy to identify bad parenting, bad manners, the inability to follow social norms, a lack of aspiration. One teacher says: 'Never underestimate the English working-class aversion to education.' Another says: 'Give me an ethnic minority any day; at least they have aspirations.'

It is tempting to advocate paternalistic solutions. What I want is for the working-class parents to start becoming more like the pushy middle class, demanding the best for their child. I want them all to value education, to want their child to get to university, to have opportunities and be stretched, to see that education is the gateway to fulfilment.

It was this attitudinal, cultural angle that proved so elusive. I remember Tony's first major speech as Prime Minister. It was on a London housing estate, and under the heading of 'The Will to Win', a not very good phrase we came up with at the last moment to give a good speech a simple message. Tony said: 'For eighteen years, the poorest people in this country have been forgotten by government. I want that to change. There will be no forgotten people in the Britain I want to build. We need to act in a new way because fatalism, and not just poverty, is the problem we face, the dead weight of low expectations, the crushing belief that things cannot get better. I want to give people back the will to win again.'

Seven years on, despite all the benefits of the new deal for the unemployed, the minimum wage, the regeneration money for housing estates, what many of the children and parents I met lacked was not material goods, though some did, and was not just literacy skills, though too many did. As a result of all those things and more, they lacked self-belief. Self-belief is the essence of what makes a middle-class person middle class; the belief you will get on, go to university, get a job, own your own home, start a family, have decent holidays; the belief that you can achieve what you set your mind to. The belief may never have been present in some or was snuffed out in the first months of life: belief in themselves; belief in their surroundings; belief that people cared for them, that they had a future. For all the money that was being thrown at them, for all the help that the government was providing, this is the thing you can't legislate for, you can't make happen: belief in the power of education to give them a chance in life. They simply didn't realise that the hours they spent at school, even at one they didn't think much of, was the best chance they had to succeed. As one teacher put it, 'they are not used to deferred gratification and they can't grasp the immediate win from education.' Some do have a warped kind of self-belief. It is a cockiness that school doesn't matter because they will duck and dive as adults and do well without needing qualifications. And some of the parents of the poorest children, particularly many of those from immigrant families, aspire to a better life for their children. But I'm not sure how much they really believe it will happen.

Schools like Islington Green need to do far more to cultivate that confidence, to give children the public speaking skills, the links to universities, the mentoring that will build their confidence, but in truth it needs to start far earlier. The research showing that the under-5s matter most, is right. That is when the basics of language and sentence formation begin. It is also the time when the socialising needs to begin, when expectations need to be fostered. Secondary schools can't do it all. It's like a man who has smoked sixty cigarettes a day and has lung cancer turning up at his GP's and expecting an instant cure. Early intervention should be the key to policy going forward. Building on Sure Start and other policies, we need to give the most disadvantaged the most support in the first couple of years of their child's life.

*

Aisha and Tessa are by now happy with their speech. I am on track for the presentation evening.

It was in June that Trevor made it clear that he wanted me to be in charge of the Sadler's Wells event in October: 'We need to start planning early.' The aim of the event is to celebrate the school's success, to award GCSE certificates to those leaving the school, and to award prizes to the best students in other years. Trevor likes big statements that show the school is on the way up. Confidence matters to Trevor. Painting the school purple, providing glossy brochures, a lovely calendar with photos of school children, all might seem like a waste of money, but Trevor believes they help parents, students, and teachers feel better about the school, giving it a sense that nothing but the best will do. Hiring one of London's foremost arts venues is the most dramatic of these statements.

Trevor assumes because of my experience of Labour conference this will be a doddle for me, the only flaw in the logic being that at conference I sit and write. Here, I am meant to be stage-managing a show, making sure students and parents turn up on time and coping with the 1,001 problems thrown up by unpredictable students. There is always a first for everything, but I'm certainly feeling the pressure.

My first task is to ask teachers to nominate students for prizes. I have suggested that there are academic prizes for each subject, rather than just prizes for attendance, behaviour and doing homework. Trevor agrees. I ask each head of department to nominate two students from each year.

Trevor also assumes I will be able to land a heavyweight guest speaker. He is hoping for Tony Blair but party conference and foreign trips will make that impossible. In any case, I am not sure that Tony will want to make an appearance at a school that is not yet riding high and is connected to his own decision to send his children out of Islington.

'How about Alastair Campbell?' Trevor asks. This would certainly be a controversial choice for those, like John the NUT rep, who are vehemently opposed to the war on Iraq, but I know Alastair has a strong commitment to comprehensive education and will do it if he can.

There are other more pressing events before I can concentrate fully on Sadler's Wells. The summer term has a disjointed feel to it, but the teachers clearly like it because there is less teaching. Year 10s go away for two weeks on work experience. Year 11s are off studying for their GCSEs. Year 9s have their SATs. For two weeks the school is a lot smaller, with less aggro and greater calm. However, the SATs results for the fourteen-year-olds are about to arrive, and I wait nervously for Jimmy's. Unlike with GCSEs you don't have to hang on until August. They dribble out subject by subject before the end of the summer term. A score of 5 means you are on track for a good GCSE. Below 4 means you have little chance. Jimmy believes he can get a 5 in maths and with luck a 4 in science. His maths is out first. It is a 4. I then get the list from Paul and discover that he has only managed a 3 in science. I wait for his English but it doesn't arrive, part of a nationwide marking cock-up.

I need to know whether I have made any progress with Jimmy. We both need the confidence of knowing that, late in the day though this is, he can crack reading and writing, so I decide to test his reading again for myself. The last time this was done was in March 2003, more than a year ago. His reading age then was between 7.7 and 8.8 years. Although I have only been with Jimmy twice a week for six months, I hope I have started to make a difference.

The library is too noisy so I take Jimmy down to a meeting room. I want him to have the best possible conditions to perform in. The reading test is a series of passages that get progressively harder, with pictures next to them to help provide a context. Each passage tests accuracy, then there is a series of questions about the passage to test comprehension.

I say to Jimmy, 'I can't help you with any of this. You just have to read it the best you can; break down words if you don't get them immediately. Then there will be a series of questions. You've done this kind of test before.'

Jimmy nods.

The first passage he reads faultlessly:

> Ted went up to the box.
> Then he took off the lid.
> He soon put the lid back on.
> The box held a big black rat.

'Great Jimmy.' I ask him the series of questions, the first of which is: 'What is in the box?' Jimmy answers all the questions correctly. He is fine on the first and by far the easiest passage, which corresponds to a reading age of about seven.

The fifth passage includes, 'The explosion occurred in the early hours of a cold December morning. The entire eighteen-storey block of flats fell down as if it had been made of matchsticks.' Jimmy makes more than the allowed sixteen mistakes and so scores nought for this passage, which means there is no point trying him on the next one. I ask him the questions, but he doesn't understand them. Overall he has read four passages well and I am confident his reading age must have gone up. It is the end of the lesson, so I leave him and tot up the scores in my own room and look at the mark scheme. Jimmy is now at a reading age of between 8 and 9.2. I do a recount. I want it to be higher. It's not. Jimmy has made a slight improvement but nothing dramatic. I am disappointed. I can see him improving in lessons. I can see his confidence rising. I have been encouraged by other teachers telling me he is doing better in lessons. Yet, on this test, there is little to shout about. Jimmy though is remarkably upbeat about his performance. He is keen on getting on with his GCSEs, even though some of them will require a lot of reading and writing. I hope that his optimism and the school's support can get him through.

The thing that strikes me more than any other at this school is that, despite the huge improvements in primary school test results, we have not yet won the battle of the basics. Let's be clear about one thing: if you enter secondary school unable to read and write properly you will have a dreadful, boring, frustrating, often humiliating time. There is a stunning and depressing correlation in the statistics between results at eleven and GCSE results. If you haven't got the basics at eleven you don't get good GCSEs five years later. It's as simple as that.

There needs to be a new and more intensive basics strategy. Secondary school teachers need government to realise that patting primary teachers on the back for 75 per cent literacy and numeracy results is only OK if they really stick at it and go on to get 85 per cent and then 95 per cent, because, frankly, the 60,000 to 100,000 kids who still represent that difference are going to find life difficult in a secondary school and make the job of teachers that much harder. In Islington it is 40 per cent, not 25 per cent, who leave primary school with a reading age well below eleven. We need to build on the effective literacy and numeracy strategies, with well-funded recovery courses that start from scratch with those who do not learn the basics the first time, or with students new to the country. Then there is a strong argument for children not to leave primary school until they have got Level 4 in English, with some exceptions for those with particular special needs. This happens in other countries. I believe it would act as a spur to a lot of children, not wanting to stay down while their friends moved on. I would provide basics summer schools for all those just below Level 4, between leaving primary school and getting to secondary school. These could be held in the secondary school the children are going to – to get an early feel for the school – using skilled literacy professionals.

At secondary school Key Stage 3 for eleven to fourteen-year-olds, in challenging inner-city schools in particular, there needs to be focus on basics and behaviour. We are wrong to give the entire national curriculum to students who are not up to speed on the basics. It is, for example, absurd for some of the eleven-year-olds at our school to be doing Spanish, given that they can't read English. Yet each subject area, within a school and nationally, rightly has a vociferous lobby defending its place in the curriculum. Government policy is too prescriptive on this, too rigid in forcing schools to stick to the national curriculum. And head teachers juggling members of staff, and dealing with unions, seem too scared to be very imaginative with timetables. Students should have fewer teachers in Year 7, and have most lessons conducted by one basics-trained form tutor who can ensure that by the end of Year 7 students have settled into the new school, have strict codes of behaviour, and are literate. The form tutor should be up to speed on study skills, so that children start to learn the techniques necessary to succeed throughout the school – memory skills, mind mapping, information gathering, note taking, essay writing, team work.

Throughout primary and secondary school, there should be a greater emphasis on two areas that have been neglected. The first is grammar, spelling and punctuation. This is the generation of teachers and adults, and I include myself, who were not drilled in grammar and spelling at school. The result seems to be that many teachers are neither confident enough nor interested enough in teaching it themselves. At a school like Islington Green there is a real sense that it should have been learnt already, or else it is boring to learn and will lead to a less fun and therefore more disruptive lesson. Basic grammar and spelling amongst even the brightest students is poor. Second, there should be far greater emphasis on speaking. Our students, all students, need to learn how to communicate persuasively, using standard English not street slang, with eye contact and projection. There is little systematic teaching of this in primary or secondary schools.

All this will only happen successfully in secondary schools if we are more serious about training and then employing teachers who are skilled literacy practitioners. A school like ours, and some already have this, needs a literacy department of up to ten specialist teachers. We have three, and they often have to act as classroom assistants, shadowing one or two children per class, rather than doing tailored work.

We need to use teachers' time far more imaginatively, too. We know that 'challenging' students often respond better in small groups or one-to-one. Teachers simply don't have the time to do what I did with Jimmy; sit down one-to-one and talk, building a deeper relationship, understanding exactly where they are coming from. A teacher with a full timetable will have five or six classes of up to thirty students; that's 150 or 180 students to get to know, and to give personal assistance to.

I would cut classes in inner-city schools – one teacher told me that just having two or three fewer would help – and divide up a teacher's timetable more flexibly. This has been tried in a few schools, but is not common practice. If a teacher is teaching nineteen hours a week, then why shouldn't ten hours be whole-class teaching, five hours be with groups of five to eight students – either gifted and talented students or those who need extra help – and four hours be one-to-one work. The teacher would probably enjoy their working week more because it is more varied, and students would get the benefit of the best classroom teachers in different settings.

In terms of behaviour, the consensus of every teacher I've

met, however delicately or indelicately they put it, is that there are two or three children per class who make life hell for the teacher and for other students. In the words of one blunt teacher: 'No one has cracked what to do with the underclass, the nutters. Whatever school or institution they are at, they are the problem.' On this I tend to agree with Paul: difficult children need to be off-site and given proper catch-up work. It is right that pupil referral units are properly funded and places expanded – but the moral questions still remain. How many chances does a child deserve? Is it fair to keep a child out of the mainstream permanently? Won't he benefit from the good influences of well-behaved children to get him back on the right track? And isn't the key to behaviour in many cases better literacy? The link between poor behaviour and illiteracy at our school is striking. Those able to do their work well usually behave better. Cracking literacy, giving every child in secondary school a fighting chance of grasping what is going on, would, I am certain, lead to better behaviour.

Trevor is right that for the majority the key is consistency, fairness and reliability. That is what many of the students miss at home, where shifting patterns of insensitivity and inconsistency provide little basis for secure relationships. One of the most difficult, but important tasks of school is to provide that certainty.

I speak to Paul about Jimmy's results. We have talked endlessly over the last few months and I have enjoyed arguing with him over the best way of improving the school. He is the ultimate realist, some would say pessimist, about what can be achieved. I resent the fact that he thinks Jimmy is not a priority. 'You see,' he says 'it's slippery, slippery, slippery. You have tried your best but it's hard, as you've seen, to make great progress with someone like Jimmy. I wouldn't start with him, I would start with those who get Level 4, who you can push up to Level 5. Jimmy is well below that and there is not a lot we can do with him now.'

'But,' I say, 'it cannot be beyond us to help Jimmy get five A–Cs. He's keen, he's not stupid. We've failed if someone like him can't get GCSEs.'

'You've got to target those who have a chance,' Paul insists. Just as in government there is always a choice between targeting Middle England and targeting the poor, so at the school it's the same choice: target the middle, the nearly-made-it students, or target the really difficult cases? Both government and the school are better at providing a safety net for those at the bottom; it's far trickier to put a ladder of opportunity within their grasp.

Michael Barber said to me at the outset: 'Do they really have high expectations?' But the answer is complicated. I believe that the teachers are trying incredibly hard to make a difference, in stressful conditions. Yet the expectation, in the literal sense of the word, is that many students will, as they always have done, leave school with few qualifications and few prospects. The most difficult thing of all when teaching some of these students, as I now know for myself, is giving them one more chance, never giving up hope; trying to light that spark that changes the dynamic, that makes them see even one subject or one lesson in a different way. The hardest job in teaching is being big enough, patient enough, resourceful enough to give the child who's made your life a misery lesson after lesson one more chance to make it work.

Angela comes up to me. 'Just spoken to Jimmy,' she says. 'He's really coming on, had a proper conversation with him for the first time. You must be doing a good job.' I tell her that progress has not shown up much in the test results. 'It will,' she says reassuringly.

★

It is now time to make more plans for the presentation evening. Trevor wants as much control over this event as Tony Blair does at Labour party conference – for recalcitrant union leaders read wild Year 9 students. Trevor is going to be strict on invitees turning up in neat school uniform and behaving properly, or they will be sent home. I have a chat with Martin, a music teacher, to see what barnstorming numbers he has in mind for the show. We agree to some break-dancers, two solo singers at a piano and my suggestion of a Year 7 showstopping song. In addition the school has some great steel pan players who can perform in the foyer and an accomplished jazz pianist who can play the guests in and out of the theatre.

However, the evening will only work if the school has something it can genuinely celebrate. The GCSE results in August are crucial. There's more at stake for Trevor than something to say at Sadler's Wells. He needs a big leap in results this year if he is to show potential Academy sponsors that he is a transformational leader, and if he is to show the school and the community that Islington Green really is on the way up. Unlike other public services, secondary schools have one point in the year when judgement comes. There is no way of knowing what the outcome will be. Predictions can be made and mock results taken into account, but in the end it is about how the students perform on the day. This is Trevor's big exam. In the middle of August, whilst most staff are away on exotic holidays – I am amazed at the destinations, far more glamorous than where most Number 10 staff go: Thailand, climbing in the Himalayas – the GCSE results appear. The schools have to add up the totals themselves and calculate how many five A–Cs before the LEA and then the DfES confirm the score.

I phone Trevor the evening before the students come in to collect them. He has just got the results. 'I started to hyper-ventilate,' he says. 'I was sure they were 44 per cent. Then I realised I had been given two sheets of identical names. We think we are on 34 per cent up from 28 per cent last year. Not bad, but not quite the breakthrough I wanted.'

I brood on the 34 per cent overnight. I, like Trevor, am disappointed. This is good but not very good. I get in early the next day and find Trevor counting at his desk. It's the first time I have seen him in casual clothes: a short-sleeve blue shirt and dark blue trousers. 'This is complicated,' he says, 'but I think we have got 37 per cent. That would be really good.'

He explains that there are several exam boards, each of whom send in results. Then there are some GCSEs taken early that need to be added. Some students have taken GCSEs in languages, often their home language, which we need to make sure we include. Then there are some students who can be taken off the roll because they have not turned up since the beginning of the year and it would be unfair to count them as they have taken no exams. Then there are some who, if they have arrived in the country after the start of GCSEs, can be removed; or if they have come from another school but have not yet got a unique pupil number, they too can be taken off. All of these decisions make a big difference to the overall total, because instead of dividing the sixty or so who have five A–Cs by 177, Trevor can divide them by 170 or less and get a higher percentage.

He asks me to look down the list of names and verify his count that there are 61 with five A–Cs. What becomes clear immediately is how many have got their five A–Cs thanks to GNVQs which now count as the equivalent of a GCSE. One particular subject, IT, counts for four A–Cs. One girl has got ten Cs at GCSE. Sixteen students have got at least five As and Bs. Twenty-three students scored an A grade in at least one subject. Sixty-one per cent of students got one C or above which Trevor believes is proof they could have done better.

We soon find out that other schools in Islington have done

well too. Two are now in the 60 per cent range and others are in the fifties and forties. In three years the borough has climbed from an average in the mid-twenties to one in the mid-forties. Across London inner-city schools are improving faster than the rest of the country. Nationally there are fewer than 100 schools getting under 20 per cent five A–Cs, compared to more than 300 in 1997. We are one of the many schools that have broken through the 30 per cent barrier. In 1997, 896 schools got less than five A–C grades. In 2004 only 258 did.

I was eager to find out what had happened to my 'marginals'. Had I succeeded in getting any of them up from a D to a C? Perhaps not surprisingly, as I scanned down the scores in front of me, the students had lived up to my expectations. For Vanessa, clever but refusing to apply herself, she stayed at a D and didn't get five A–Cs. Humeyra, who needed little help, got her five A–Cs. Abdul got his five A–Cs but only with the help of four IT GNVQs. Monica, who obviously had something going on at home, had got close. For all of them, even those with the lower grades, the chance of going to City and Islington College, a rebuilt, sixth-form college, was still a distinct possibility. The lesson for me, and for the school, was that this kind of intervention had to start earlier in the year and the students chosen carefully, focusing on those who were likely to take advantage of extra help.

Trevor is pleased with his 37 per cent result, though he had hoped it would creep over 40. He now thinks we can get to the mid-forties next year and he would effectively have doubled results in just over three years. This school started out with as many disadvantages as were possible: poverty, transient population, many different languages, broken families, a ratio of boys to girls of two to one, crumbling buildings. Yet the teachers are beginning to turn it round – and it should be a big enough leap, from 23 per cent to 37 per cent under Trevor, for the sponsors to be impressed. I have confidence that the school will continue to improve. His target of 50 per cent is reachable in two or three years. The question is, how high can a school like this go without radically changing its intake?

I would attribute the school's improvements, and those of other Islington schools, in the last three years to four things: government investment, a group of first-rate headteachers, high quality and better-paid staff, and an accountability framework which intervenes quickly on poor performance. As yet the structural changes – Academies, specialist schools – have not been significant in Islington and have not been the driver of these changes. One of the big debates in government was between those who thought structures needed changing and those who focused on the classroom. Both strategies are obviously needed; the question is: which drives up standards more? I am now completely convinced it is what goes on in the school. It is about the head, the ethos, the teachers.

In the first term the government's approach to education was 'standards not structures'. This in part was a way of getting off the grant-maintained debate that we had inherited. It also led to the improvements in standards in primary schools. However, Tony soon thought this was a mistake and that structures did matter. Ever since, he has been focused on diversity and choice, moving beyond the old-style comprehensive. Diversity and choice obviously only apply to the cities where there is more than one local school in each area. Part of that vision is attractive, though if it is going to be done, it should be done properly. Giving schools the chance to take pride in one particular area – by becoming specialist schools – helps galvanise some, but as Trevor, who is not convinced by the policy, says, good heads will give their schools a strong ethos anyway. No, what should drive diversity is two things: first, a push for smaller schools because comprehensives, particularly in inner-city areas, are too big – they are not conducive to good discipline or the building of a strong sense of belonging – and second, an injection of some necessary innovation into education, the school day, the use of the curriculum, teaching methods. A borough such as Islington, currently with nine secondary schools, would benefit from having fifteen or twenty smaller ones. Assuming adequate funding, there should be less concern from the LEA and DfES about excess places: given how fluid London borough boundaries are, good schools will be filled. However, at the moment government policy is not encouraging this. The schools being built are reproducing the size and current provision of existing secondary schools.

The single biggest structural change I would make would be one in which the intake of schools like Islington Green changes. A school with more middle-class children and a better spread of ability – in other words a comprehensive – would immediately make it easier to create a learning culture. At the moment there are obvious absurdities in our system and there is a clear pecking order of schools. Nationally 5 per cent of children, or nearer 20 per cent in Islington, are educated privately; then there are grammar schools, ex-grammars which heavily select, girls' schools and church schools which tend to have it easier, then at the bottom are mixed comprehensives that were formerly secondary moderns. In London and the other major cities, primary schools are comprehensive in that they take all abilities, then at eleven the division begins. The 11-plus still exists in all but name, but the issue of admissions is ignored – partly because no one wants to go back to a heavy-handed allocation system, but also because it threatens some of the privileges of the selective schools. A banding system that, where possible, allows schools, particularly those that are oversubscribed, to pick a mixed-ability intake, would do more than any other structural change to help drive up standards across the board.

So, diversity can spark creativity and more balanced admissions should be a goal of policy. I would make one further structural change. Heads and teachers are right to complain about LEAs. They employ too many staff – several hundred – doing jobs that are often marginal to the task of raising standards. Most heads would far rather have an extra teacher. In government we skirted round the future of LEAs on more than a dozen occasions. The solution should be for money to go directly to heads. The new three-year ring-fenced budgets for heads will make a big difference. But the money that the LEA gets should be tied to specific objectives and outcomes, ensuring that as much money as possible goes directly to projects that have an impact on schools.

None of these changes matter as much as what goes on in the school. So I would do everything to continue to attract the best heads and teachers into the profession and direct as many as possible to the inner-city areas that need the most support.

It is noticeable that our school is isolated from other schools and from best practice. One of the primary roles of government should be to bring the best practice from around the country to the attention of all schools. That way standards will rise quicker. Our senior management team, like others across the country, sit down to brainstorm problems, without any clue as to which schools have cracked exactly the same problems already. Healthy eating, the best lunch queuing system, literacy in Year 7, calm corridors, stimulating assemblies, personalised learning – every school should have access to a website and resources that give the best practice.

All the changes I have suggested, including more literacy support, require money. The amount of money provided has undoubtedly increased in education – teachers are paid better; there is a huge capital building programme, which should transform the school environment over the next decade – but more is needed, particularly in inner-city schools, if every child is to be given the attention they need. One of the successes of New Labour has been to cut 'the bills of failure' like unemployment, and put the money into public services. However, that alone is not enough. If education is to be the number-one priority, as it should be, if it is seen as the best chance for someone to escape their background as it is, then the amount spent on education needs to increase further in the coming years. Money, of course, is never the only issue, and it's easy to waste it on projects that have little effect. But I know how much the students I am working with would benefit from extra resources. The debate between spending and tax cuts is a clash of distinct ideologies. In government we discussed whether the increase in spending so far had been a one-off catch-up, or whether it needed to be sustained over a longer period. I would argue strongly for another step-change in spending in education: 5.4 per cent of GDP, the current level, is in my view not yet enough; it is less than Britain spent as a nation in the Seventies. If we are serious about the future, the success of our country, the success of our children, that needs to increase substantially with all the tough and imaginative decisions on tax that must accompany it.

As I congratulate Trevor on his success, he shows me the work he has had done over the summer holiday. The playground has grass, trees and a walkway put in, designed with the help of students. The hall has been redone and looks a lot smarter. Trevor is slowly but surely refurbishing the school, whilst, as students regularly point out, waiting for the go-ahead to tear the lot down in under a year's time, should the Academy get the go-ahead.

As the new term begins, the plans for Sadler's Wells hot up. The invitations have gone out, the names of prize winners are in. We have a big debate about what prize should be given. Normally it's a voucher, but I think it would be nicer to give the subject prize winners a book, a symbol that we value books and they should do so too. I have found a beautiful one called *Human* by Robert Winston, which shows every aspect of human experience across the world with stunning illustrations, and there is a book club that will sell them to us a lot cheaper.

I go to the hall where Martin, the music teacher, is drilling his Year 7s for the performance. They seem a particularly lively group, and are chatting and talking when they are meant to be walking silently on stage.

'I said quiet. Right, we'll do it all again. We have spent fifteen minutes now not singing a note, merely getting on stage without talking. We'll soon be into your lunch break.' There are groans. 'Every time you make a noise we will start again.'

Finally, they are quiet. Martin gets behind a battered upright piano and thumps out Lulu's 'Shout'. Within about five seconds it is clear that this is an ambitious number for this particular group. They are neither singing nor shouting but mumbling. The trouble with 'Shout' is that the high notes are very high and the music is very fast. The sound is horrible. Martin sees me wincing. 'Don't expect the King's College Choir,' he says. I don't, but I expect the song to be completed without them falling apart. 'They'll be fine on the night,' he says. I suggest to Trevor that he might want to come and hear for himself, to judge whether he wants to pull the plug on them. At the moment, I say, it's going to be a travesty. Trevor wishes they had chosen a simple middle-range musical number like something from *Oliver*. This is my fault. I thought a pop song would be less naff than one from a musical.

I haven't begun to master all the secrets of teaching yet, but I'm now picking up on what gives one teacher authority and another less of it. The key ingredient is certainty: the absolute certainty in the tone of voice that what is being said is going to happen; certainty that you know your subject and have planned meticulously for the hour ahead; certainty, if you say: 'You will stay behind if you do not sit in silence,' that you will carry out your threat. I know that my voice wavers too often. They know that I'm not really going to keep them behind. In one lesson that I was having with a particularly difficult Year 7 group, I was asked frequently by one child, humiliatingly in front of the rest of the class: 'Sir, why aren't you strict like the other teachers?' That child and many like him respond to shouting. They're used to it at home, and often respond to it in school. I can't shout. One teacher has told me that occasionally you need to shout as an act: it is not that you are at breaking point and the only thing you can do is shout, it is that you turn on a quick shout for effect, when other things have failed – but the kids have to know you are capable of it. My approach is respect: I show the students I care about what they do, what they say, what they write. This works only some of the time. It needs greater authority and steeliness to back it up when the more challenging students mistake respect for weakness. Too often I still find myself making the fatal mistake of wanting to be their friend. Though one of my proudest moments was overhearing Jimmy tell a friend: 'that Mr Hyman – he's *nang*.' This is a word, unique to our school I think, meaning 'all right'. I spent the rest of the day saying to myself 'I'm nang'.

There is no feeling quite as exhilarating as teaching a lesson that works: where the kids are excited and stimulated and the time flies by. There is no feeling that I have had which is as desperately lonely and demoralising as a lesson where control has gone, and the students are deliberately testing you to breaking point, as a kind of sport. Then the hands on the classroom clock never move. The lesson is the longest hour of your life, and you leave emotionally drained.

There seem to be two types of teaching and they seem worlds apart. Teaching at Islington Green is all about the banter, the cajoling, the pastoral support for needy students, the crowd control. Teaching in a girls' grammar in the Home Counties, or teaching in a private school, is, I am sure, about the subject, about being intensely interested in science or maths. A number of the teachers are at our school because, as one put it, they would get little satisfaction out of teaching A level to A grade candidates who hardly need any help from the teacher.

It is from a teacher that I get the most important sign of government success on my journey. A teacher who said to me, a little grudgingly as she opposed the government on many things including the war, that it was hearing Tony's 'education, education, education' speech and him talking of life-long learning and the chance for everyone to retrain, that had inspired her to do something different with her life and become a teacher. It was, she said, the best thing she had ever done. Creating a climate, changing attitudes, is without doubt the best route to long term change.

Trevor goes to the hall and the eleven-year-olds don't change their antics; they are still larking about on stage. Martin asks them to start from the beginning, and they do their best-ever version, a tribute to Martin's skills. If they are like that tonight we will be fine. Trevor, a connoisseur of classic pop songs, nods with approval and leaves.

It's now time for the run-through of the prize-giving ceremony in the hall. We have asked all the prize winners to be there at 11.30. Angela has drawn-up a seating plan. Purple badge winners have got their prizes for 100 per cent attendance. Those with 100 merits get gold certificates. The subject prizes are for the best two students in each year for each subject.

Trevor stands at the front of the hall. 'Right, I will read out names and people should sit in this order tonight.' As he reads out the names there are titters at his pronunciation. He says forcefully that no one has ever spelled or said his name correctly, and if one of the students is called out wrongly on the night, they shouldn't make a fuss.

Emma is worried because last year the students and their parents didn't know how to get down to Sadler's Wells, so I quickly leave the hall and hand-draw a map of how to get there. I do three hundred photocopies and return to the hall just in time for Trevor to announce that I will be handing out maps.

We find out at the last moment that Joe Swash, who plays Mickey Miller in *EastEnders*, will hand out some of the performing arts prizes. His sister is at the school and has just joined the *EastEnders* cast. Alastair Campbell has agreed to be the guest speaker; a couple of members of staff, including John the NUT rep, are boycotting the evening as a result. A walkout that reminds me of Derek Hatton storming out during Neil Kinnock's conference speech in 1985.

All of us make our way down to Sadler's Wells where the rehearsal begins at 4 p.m.; the concert is at 7 p.m. The programmes are put on chairs. The piano is tuned. The steel pans are set up in the foyer. The prefects, looking smarter than ever, are briefed on their roles as ushers. The performers are geed up by the teachers. Angela, Eileen and Emma go and change into their posh frocks. Trevor, Paul and I stay in our boring suits. The flowers arrive to decorate the stage. Angela has chosen purple to go with the school colours. I look over the stage directions and talk to the stage manager. Karen, who works in Trevor's office, has the most difficult job of all – ticking everybody off a list as they turn up and then rushing the amended list to the Heads of Year in time for them to read out the names on stage. I am worried we won't get it done in time. 'This isn't Labour Party conference,' she says, 'We do things properly here.' That's as may be but I am as nervous as I was

for Tony's first major speech when accepting the party
leadership in 1994. This is all unpredictable for me.

It is not like most West End performances. I can tell that the
teachers, Trevor in particular, are less worried about what
happens on stage and more worried about the audience. I see
our potential sponsors in the front row of the stalls. They have
been invited to the extravaganza to get a feel for the school. The
DfES has now given approval for the Academy to go into its
feasibility stage. The future remains precarious for Trevor,
though he is more relaxed about it – 'there are plenty of other
schools or LEAs I could work at' – and my hunch is that, in the

long run, he will want to try something new. But for now he is getting on better with the sponsors and the potential is there to make the project work.

If the Academy comes to fruition, for all my reservations about handing over the school to someone putting in £2m out of a total cost of £30m, there is the potential for real innovation, for piloting new ways of delivering education. I would hope that the environment will not just be very different – open–plan and modern – but we will think imaginatively about the way we go about teaching our teenagers.

My experiences have made it clearer to me that School should focus on three things: culture, character and skills. By culture, I mean, the Matthew Arnold definition. In his great book *Culture and Anarchy*, Arnold, headteacher and thinker talked of 'those who have a passion for diffusing, for making prevail, for carrying from one end of society to the other, the best knowledge, the best ideas of their time; who have laboured to divest knowledge of all that was harsh, uncouth, difficult, abstract, professional, exclusive; to humanise it, to make it efficient outside the clique of the cultivated and learned, yet still remaining the *best* knowledge and thought of the time, and a true source, therefore, of sweetness and light.' Our aim should be that all students are exposed to the best music, arts, history and literature. Some students attending Islington Green School hardly ever leave the square mile they are living in. They have no exposure to the museums, palaces and parks of London. Jimmy has not been out of the school on a trip in the last year. I can understand why the school does not want the hassle of organising outings, particularly with the more challenging students, But all Jimmy and his like are getting are the voices of their teachers, the sights of the concrete jungle of the school, and the endless banter of their friends. Their world is small when the job of education is to make it big.

By character, I mean that part of the role of a good school is to turn out children with decent values. Those without respect need to learn it quickly. Those who can't share, who bully their classmates, need to learn social skills. Confidence needs to be fostered, so that all the children feel they have a path they can progress down.

By skills, I mean education has to become more about the different competences and attributes needed to be a good learner throughout life. The emphasis should be on how to learn, not just on what we learn. Secondary moderns in the past, the good ones at least, turned out people who had useful vocational and life skills. For too many children, comprehensives don't do this at all. They focus on the academic pathway for all, with some GNVQs thrown in, so that the vast majority at our school who don't get their five A–Cs have very little to show for eleven years of education. The Tomlinson proposals for proper vocational pathways and a diploma instead of GCSEs and A levels might solve some of these problems.

Students, all students, need to leave school with the basics of reading, writing and maths to a high standard, and they need to be able to make an argument persuasively, talk in proper sentences with coherence and confidence, make a presentation in front of others, be able to touch-type on a computer, know how to use the internet and access information, and be able to handle key software well.

It should not just be Academies that are given the freedom to innovate. It is unfair that a good school in Islington, that has a good head and better results than our school shouldn't have the same freedoms to innovate. We should trust the heads who are not backed by sponsors, as well as those who are.

Alastair arrives in the foyer and the Lib Dem councillors make a bee-line for him. The local press want pictures for their deadlines. I bring over two of my politics students who have won prizes and they are photographed with him. Trevor greets Alastair and they very quickly decide the thing they have in common is that they have both worked next door to someone incredibly messy: me.

It's gone 7 p.m., Alastair Campbell is seated in the front row next to Trevor and Joe Swash is there too. The auditorium is now packed, and I agree with Trevor the show should begin. The lights go down and I go to the wings to stand next to the stage manager, to make sure everything runs smoothly. Paul Blum comes on stage and stands there, as teachers do in Assembly, waiting for silence. I am not sure this is the best strategy in this setting. The power games of assembly, when you can wait for literally ten minutes for silence, will look strange to the VIP guests. The difference here is that Paul has a microphone and if he starts the show, I am sure he will get silence.

He begins by welcoming people and calling Trevor on stage to make a presentation. Trevor is holding his notes. There is chatter as he is about to start: this promises to be a noisy evening. I have suggested to him that he does as much off the cuff as possible – this is when his passion comes through. He begins speaking, but the microphone doesn't work. I hope this is not the first of many glitches. A stage hand rushes on with a hand-held microphone.

Trevor gives what to me is now a familiar speech, what politicians would call their stump speech, the well-rehearsed journey of the school from special measures to an improving school, from more than three hundred excluded, to only one last year. He summarises the highlights of the year, including Shona becoming Prime Minister of Islington and some great sports successes, as well as a lot of rebuilding at the school. He finishes with a personal story:

My daughter goes to a school in rural Essex. It is a converted palace; Henry VIII once lived there. Why should she have a palace and we at Islington Green School not have the same? We are equally deserving of a palace, and my pledge to you is that we will rebuild the school. We will aim high. We have done a lot better in our GCSEs but I want to get up to 50 per cent and then on to 100 per cent in a few years' time.

Trevor has been good to me. He has given me the chance to immerse myself in all aspects of the school. He has given me a real glimpse of what it's like to be a headteacher. It is a great role to have. There isn't a more important or creative job than trying to educate, stimulate, inspire teenagers as they teeter on the tightrope from childhood to adulthood. Winston Churchill once said that: 'Headmasters have powers at their disposal with which Prime Ministers have never yet been invested.' Whether or not he was referring to being caned at school or his inability to whip ministers into line, I don't know, but he was right. The power and responsibility of a headteacher over the 1,000 students in his school seems to me much more immediate than the power of a Prime Minister. If Trevor wants something done, he gets it done. If I have an idea and he likes it, it will suddenly, often to my surprise, be in the staff bulletin and be happening. 'What I don't understand,' says a student in my political class, 'is why the Prime Minister doesn't just say something and it happens. Surely he is the most powerful person in the country.' I try to explain that it isn't quite as simple as that. Parliament has to vote for it. Then it has to be implemented and there are many layers in between government and the school. I look him in the eye and say, 'When Tony promises to deliver on education, what needs to happen is that you pass your exams. How can he guarantee that? You may not even turn up for them.' He looks slightly surprised. For all the talk of Tony being Presidential, the truth, as I saw it at Number 10, was that the Prime Minister's hold over a government is always weaker than people think.

One of the great differences between two strong leaders – Thatcher and Blair – is that Thatcher promised to deliver on things she had power over – tax cuts, privatisation, union legislation, national curriculum, testing; Blair promises to deliver on things he has little direct power over: exam results, crime levels, cancer mortality rates.

The difference between being a number one and a number two is something that people underestimate. Estelle Morris, with undue modesty, made this point when she resigned as Education Secretary. If you are a number two, there is always a part of you that knows the whole show doesn't rely on you. For some that is a great comfort, and for those who then get promoted the pressure is sometimes too much. There is a loneliness in the top job. However much colleagues are consulted, you have to make the final decision – and, as Trevor says, anyone who leads an organisation should have sympathy with the Prime Minister when he sits and makes that call. Everyone outside the room puts their own interpretation on it, but only he takes all the flak. Having seen both Trevor and Tony close up, my conclusion – easy for me to say, incredibly hard to carry through – is that the best you can do is to focus on two or three things and relentlessly drive them forward to conclusion, whatever the distractions. It's easy to become a problem-solver, sucked into the day-to-day, dealing with the urgent rather than the important. However, problem-solving is not the same as agenda-setting. Whether it's dealing with behaviour or literacy at Islington Green or maintaining education as the number one priority in government, focus is the way lasting legacies are created.

Leadership is about taking people on a journey with you;

leaders need followers. The danger for leaders is that after a while they think that 'doing the right thing' is enough, irrespective of who is or isn't persuaded. This leads to isolation and the breakdown of leadership. Tony often looks as if he is running a revolution without many revolutionaries. In government this is the danger for Prime Ministers. At the frontline it is still a danger, but the need for professionals to be carrying out immediate tasks prevents leaders from getting too far out of touch with their troops.

Trevor leaves the stage and some break-dancers appear to giant whoops and monkey noises from the crowd. These noises have been the subject of a heated assembly in which one Head of Year lectured the students on how, in polite company, the monkey noises, which are intended to show support, sound like jeering. I have checked the rap lyrics of the dancers. The consensus amongst the senior management team is that the term 'motherfuckers' is not becoming on a presentation evening. The dancers in jeans and tracksuits, lycra tops and caps, hype the audience up with their pelvic thrusts and hand-stands, their robot impersonations and cartwheels.

Seeing this exuberance, I find the answer to something that has been nagging away at me. There is something missing at the school. It is clearly improving; systems are in place; results are getting better; but the missing ingredient is the sense of joy, and with it a sense of belonging, that I can see fleetingly in the performers. Assemblies tended to be telling-off sessions. Also, there is no point in the year when the whole school comes together as a community for an assembly; there simply isn't the space. One teacher puts her finger on it when she tells me that teachers don't feel confident enough with discipline and order to take risks, to unleash the energy of the kids when most of the time they are trying to contain it. It is this circular argument –

which comes first, the discipline or the creativity? – that has to be broken.

Ten minutes into the break–dancing I realise how difficult it is going to be to get the crowd to simmer down for Alastair's speech. While the first lot of prizes are being handed out he beckons me down to his seat and asks me whether his speech is too long. He too has picked up that this audience will not be on for a long serious speech. We agree a couple of cuts. Though he's used to heckling during his theatre shows, mainly from anti-war protestors, this is going to be a difficult audience just because they are not used to sitting in one place listening for long periods.

It's now time for the two solo singers, one of whom has composed a piece herself. The piano is moved forward. I pace about in the wings, looking at my script making sure everything is in the right place. Then Paul introduces Alastair. He explains that he is a very important man and they might have seen him on television. He then says in his dry way that he has been looking for Burnley, Alastair's football team, in the league tables in the papers and hasn't found them and is wondering whether they are still in the league.

Alastair gets to the podium and starts with some football jokes. There's too much chatter and, although I know he can handle it, I'm a bit embarrassed that the audience aren't quieter for him. He talks about his school days and the potential of all to succeed.

I remember a speech day where the speaker actually said, to a silent groan around the hall, that we would all look back on our school days as the best days of our lives, so I vowed there and then that if I had children myself – and I now have three, aged sixteen, fifteen and ten – I would never tell them that school days were the best days of their life. First, because it is a terrible old cliché. Second, why tell someone with the vast bulk of their life ahead of them that it's downhill all the way from here? And third, and most importantly, it may well not be true.

So, if I have one message for the students today, it is not that school gives you the best days of your life, it is that with a fair wind, and on the basis of your education, your best days are ahead of you. In this room, for all we know, we have the doctors of the future, the head teachers of the future, the inventors of the future, the builders of the future. Though this is less certain, we may have the footballers of the future, the singers and dancers and artists of the future. Perhaps most important of all, we have the parents of the future.

And the likelihood is that the majority of you won't know which way your life will turn. The likelihood is that you will end up doing many different jobs, and in some or all of them, you will draw in some way on what you have learned in this school. But you will all have your own ambitions, maybe now, maybe some time in the near future, and I hope they are high ambitions, and that you strive to meet them.

I had a good schooling I think. Worked hard enough. I got into a few scrapes. Broke several limbs playing sport. Had a long running battle with the head and all the teachers because I was the only Burnley supporter in the school and I refused ever to take my scarf off, and eventually they gave up asking. I imagine most of you are Arsenal supporters. For those of you who have barely heard of Burnley I should tell you that when I first watched football, they were league champions and we did the double over Arsenal that year. So believe me – success doesn't last for ever.

Alastair has shortened the speech drastically and soon finishes to applause. He tells me afterwards that it is weird seeing me in the same suit, with a book under my arm, skulking in the wings as I did for Tony, only now in a completely different setting. It makes me ponder on a question that a friend has asked: what would I do differently if I was joining Number 10 now, having been at the school, instead of the other way round? The answer is: lots.

Perhaps the biggest eye-opener for me on my journey has been how the approach I had been part of creating, to deal with 24-hour media and to demonstrate a decisive government, was entirely the wrong one for convincing frontline professionals, or indeed for ensuring successful delivery. Our approach to political strategy had been based on three things: momentum, conflict and novelty, whereas the frontline requires empowerment, partnership and consistency.

Momentum is essential or politicians are accused of drifting. This meant constantly coming out with initiatives, talking points, speeches, nuggets of policy. What the frontline requires is a policy framework and goals, not hundreds of micro-announcements. I am beginning to see how teachers feel like a circus act having random objects hurled at them by a ringmaster, and being expected to catch them all.

The need to show cutting edge and radicalism means that politicians prefer a conflict model, they relish battles, because it shows that difficult decisions are being taken. What in fact is needed is partnership and support rather than hostility.

Now, looking through the other end of the telescope, I see how unequal is the relationship between politicians and the people, politicians and professionals. Politicians are expected to know everything and often act as if they do. Those at the centre relish ideas and, in the main, are bored by practicalities. Those who suggest better ways of making policy work are too often dismissed as whingers or of obstructing change. Why isn't this more of a partnership? Why can't politicians acknowledge that those on the frontline might know more? Why can't they admit that good policy only works with good practice? I knew that, for my part, I was someone who loved the big vision and the symbolic policy. Now I realise that real 'delivery' is about the grind, not just the grand. It's about the combination of often small things that build over time, through individual relationships and genuine expertise and hard work.

One way of having a better relationship between the two would be for government to have an annual financial and policy statement in each key public service area (for education it should be a few months before the September start of the school year) – very much as the Chancellor does for the economy in his Budget – with no major policy pronouncements in between.

The media requires novelty. The first question a journalist asks about a speech or announcement is, 'What's new?' Novelty is the antithesis of consistency and focus which is what those from the frontline crave from government. The approach to politics necessary in the battle with the media is an approach that makes those who do the hard grind of delivery angry and antagonistic.

Government must take the need to let go more seriously, and to empower the frontline. It must produce a climate where frontline public servants do not become risk-averse. This means less dictating, less putting up pots of money to be bid for – ambitious targets yes, accountability yes, but also back creativity and imagination. The biggest constraints on a school's creativity are the national curriculum and the timetable. The rigidity of both, one serving the other, leads to a school experience that is too formulaic. We want to end one-size-fits-all public services, yet we try to achieve this with one-size-fits-all policy-making – policies suitable for all 4,000 secondary schools when they are all at different stages of reform.

My previous job was all about boiling things down, making them bite-sized and simple, easy to communicate, easy to understand. Simple messages do help, at the school as much as in government, but political communication needs to be about much more. It needs to recognise complexity and diversity. Policy should not be expected to work for the whole country.

For all this to happen, the broken relationship between politicians and the media must be mended. Disillusionment with politics, and the perception that national politics are irrelevant to people's daily lives, are striking in my new world and we should care about it.

What has happened in the last twenty-five years since Thatcher came to power is the redrawing of the 1945 settlement. The Tories began the process by focusing on economic dynamism, curtailing the unions, privatising what would be more effective in the private sector, stimulating entrepreneurship. Labour's great mission is to make the public services dynamic, responsive to new challenges, no longer top-down, but really personal and able to offer opportunity to all. Sometime, I guess in four or five years, when the consensus is that the public services, if not fixed, are on the way to being fixed, the focus will be directed at the third great upheaval that is needed – the remaking of citizenship. Then people will realise that the old monolithic parties, like the old monolithic public services, are ripe for re-invention, that democracy needs to be brought closer to people and that individuals need new ways to take control over their own lives.

My journey has strengthened my belief that New Labour has to move on. The achievement of this Labour government goes beyond individual policies. It is about psychology, replacing the memories of the winter of discontent and economic disaster with fresh images of a competent mainstream government. This is the generation of Labour politicians who have proved that the Tories can be beaten in style, that Labour can dominate the political agenda. But New Labour, at times, feels as if it is in a straitjacket of its own making. Its birth came after 18 years of Opposition. Its architects are scarred by the battles to make Labour electable. Their great achievement is bringing Labour back from the dead. Their great insecurity is that Labour will slip back to its old unelectable ways.

Future generations of Labour leaders will therefore have one great advantage, and a great opportunity too. Their advantage will be that they can draw on the success of New Labour in reshaping politics, of political dominance not retreat. Their great opportunity will be to break free from the Eighties. Future generations will have less fear of the press, of the unions, of our opponents. They will not be required to make changes by stealth. They will be able to reassert Labour's heart and not just rely on its head.

Government will still be a compromise between idealism and realism. It will never cease to be so. The next generation of Labour politicians will all have to be New Labour, whether they say they are or not. They will have to run the economy well, sort out law and order, invest wisely. But they will do so knowing they can win the battle of ideas, that Britain is not intrinsically a conservative country, that the centre of gravity of British politics can move to the left.

The big challenge facing New Labour, indeed any party serious about tackling poverty and inequality, as I found on my journey, is how to make the plight of those at the bottom resonate for the middle-class majority. That is always the test of a progressive party. It is more so today, because the temptation is always to seek out Middle England for sound electoral reasons. But the skill of politics is to use political capital for the more difficult projects. They come no more difficult than finding new ways to help the children I have worked with. I believe more than ever that education can be a liberation, but the odds stacked against some kids are so marked that the liberation must begin early, and be sustained.

Alastair is now handing out prizes, giving books to a hundred students who shuffle on to the stage. He turns each book round so that it's the right way up before giving one to each student.

The performance prizes are awarded by Joe Swash who comes on stage to whoops of delight, the power of celebrity. He means far more to many of the students than Alastair, but then, soaps have a bigger following than political parties by a factor of several thousand.

Afterwards Tessa and Aisha come on stage to make their speeches. They do well and I am proud of them.

Soon it's the moment I have been waiting for with great trepidation: the Year 7 performers. They have been in the audience all evening and are delighted to have their chance to perform. As they appear on stage I have a panic. I have forgotten to tell the stage manager that the piano is needed again. I rush over to her and she radios through to the stage hands who move the grand piano forward for Martin to accompany 'Shout'. To most of the audience the Year 7 students look sweet, almost angelic. To those who have had them for homework club on a wet Thursday evening when they want to be elsewhere, as I have, they are anything but. Martin begins the introduction and there is huge delight from the audience. Looking back, I think this must have put the choir off their stride, for after a dozen notes the song disintegrates. Voices waver, the words are inaudible. There is no catching up. Martin continues, a race-horse galloping for the line, but a new group of Year 7s falls at each successive musical fence until, as Martin crosses the finishing line, there is an empty field behind him. In solidarity the crowd give one final cheer, Paul comes on stage to end the evening, and, before he has finished his final sentence, students are standing up and bolting for the foyer.

The evening has been a great success. I am relieved, though I soon realise that Trevor is disappointed by the amount of noise from the audience. Later we get a complaint from Sadler's Wells that the students have not respected the theatre, in Trevor's view one more indication of just how far the school has to go until its students can be trusted in civilised surroundings.

However, the *Islington Tribune* is just one of the local papers giving the event a resounding thumbs up:

> A private school would have killed for the prize-giving ceremony venue – world famous Sadler's Wells theatre – let alone the star guest Alastair Campbell, the Prime Minister's former media chief.

Another piece of good publicity for the school, another symbol of change.

The theme running through Tony's speeches most is change. I don't know why, but we have never used the quote from Charles Darwin that sums up what he believes: 'It is not the strongest, or the cleverest, of the species that survive but the one most responsive to change.' I have been lucky enough to have been close up to four aspects of change. First was the remarkable transformation of the Labour party from Opposition to power – a small group wresting control of the Labour party and turning it into a hugely successful election-winning machine. Second, I then played a part from the privileged position of Number 10 in our ambitious attempts to change the country: its constitution, its economic management, its public services, its governing ethos. This was change in part by stealth – because we thought the country to be conservative – and in part by persuasion. Third, at Islington Green I was seeing first-hand what it took to turn round a school with a terrible reputation and a history of poor results and bad behaviour. Trevor's preferred method was 'systems plus relentless optimism'. Systems give you the consistency and reliability, the optimism starts to restore confidence. Lastly, I was also part of change at the most micro-level of all, trying to prove that Jimmy was capable of reading after all these years. Here I am attempting to bring about change through emotional connection.

I have learnt a lot from all four aspects of change. The key to change is to make it permanent, or at least long-lasting. The key to that is to change a way of thinking not just to enact a policy. This requires an understanding of motivation and an emotional, not just a rational, connection with an individual or group. In change programmes people often talk about the 'frozen middle' – the large numbers beneath the leadership who don't understand, or don't sympathise with, the leadership. For New Labour to sustain itself, it needs more followers with an emotional commitment to its project as well as a rational one. For lasting change to happen in public services, politicians need to show more humility and bring on board the professionals. For the school, teachers need to be less afraid of trying new things. All depend on self-belief, in having the confidence to shed the baggage of the past, not to be trapped by past failures. But change, I have also seen, takes a very long time. The kids who were five when we came to power in 1997, just starting in primary school, are now just in secondary school. Those who have got the full benefit of the literacy and numeracy strategies haven't even left primary school yet. Turning round Islington Green School is about steady sustained progress, not one-off leaps.

★

I walk out of Sadler's Wells into the crisp night air. A firework is launched by one of the students in an act of mindless euphoria.

I don't know whether I will stay in teaching, because I don't yet know if I've got that ability to control a class, but I do know that it's exhilarating trying to make a connection with an individual or a class. The surprise for me is how much more personally satisfying it is to have made a direct difference to one life than to have helped create a policy that affects millions.

I know too that it's easy to get obsessed with the processes and artifice of politics, and start to forget the reality, the very mundane, muddled, complicated realities of individual lives. I will remember some of the children I have met for the rest of my life. I know in ten years I will wonder what has happened to them, and hope that they are making the most of their talents. Those who think teaching is easy, or that anyone good at public speaking can do it, think again. It is a real craft that has to be learnt, though undoubtedly it comes to some more naturally than others. We should support our teachers, for they have taken on one of the hardest jobs there is: passing on not just knowledge and skills but character and decency. In their hands, and those of parents, will be the kind of people our children become and the type of country we will live in.

I never thought I could be as passionate about anything as much as politics. I have witnessed two landslide victories, cheered Tony Blair into Number 10, met Nelson Mandela, delighted in the introduction of the minimum wage, fought for more money for education. Now, at the sharp end, I have seen the potential and the waste of our young people. I have stood in front of a class and tried to inspire them. I have sat in a library and tried to teach a teenager the joys of reading.

Politicians and teachers are often on different sides of policy arguments, but in the end share the ultimate goal: the success of the next generation. They often seem worlds apart, but in fact their values and their actions make them part of the same tribe: the doers and the believers.

At the start of my journey I was asked by a student, 'Why the hell have you come to a place like this?' I told him I cared about education. But there was more to it than that. I felt it was time to shake-up my well-established assumptions. And in the fragments of life I have shared with Jimmy, my debating students, the exclusion room boys and the teachers, I have done so. I have been touched by raw emotions. Once more I feel – whatever the obstacles – an overwhelming sense of possibility. And I feel, too, a renewed sense of duty to act.